Artwalks In New York

Harry,

Happy Birthday!

Sarah + David

30.9.95.

ARTWALKS
IN NEW YORK

Delightful Discoveries of
Public Art and Gardens
in Manhattan, Brooklyn,
the Bronx, Queens,
and Staten Island

MARINA HARRISON and LUCY D. ROSENFELD

Illustrations by Lucy D. Rosenfeld

Michael Kesend Publishing • New York

Copyright 1994 © by Marina Harrison and Lucy D. Rosenfeld
First Publication 1994

Library of Congress Cataloging-in-Publication Data

Harrison, Marina, 1939-
Artwalks in New York : delightful discoveries of public art and gardens in Manhattan, Brooklyn, the Bronx, Queens, and Staten Island/ Marina Harrison and Lucy D. Rosenfeld : Illustrations by Lucy D. Rosenfeld. — 2nd ed.
  p. cm
  Includes index.
  ISBN 0-935576-47-9
  1. Public art—New York (N.Y.) 2. Gardens—New York (N.Y.)
I. Rosenfeld, Lucy D., 1939—   . II. Title
N8845.N7H3 1994
709'.747'1—dc20   94-23434
                                                            CIP

CONTENTS

CONTENTS

THE BRONX

QUEENS

BROOKLYN

STATEN ISLAND

FOREWORD

This is a book of exploration. We hope that if you have a taste for visual beauty and enjoy walking you will discover many wonderful new sites to pique your fancy in our city. We have brought together twenty-six eclectic outings that will introduce you to the rich and diverse treasures of public art. Although well known as one of the world's greatest cultural capitals, New York has amazed us with its wealth of art and natural beauty—not only in Manhattan, but in the outer boroughs, as well. Parks, lobbies, plazas, gardens, atria, and workshops, as well as the city's great museums, are all home to the visual pleasures of public art.

What do we mean by public art? To us this phrase includes the many forms of the visual arts to be enjoyed with little or no charge in outdoor or indoor public spaces. Our walks include everything from traditional paintings to performance art and auctions, from works in progress to outdoor sculpture, from tapestries to stained glass windows, from W.P.A. murals to contemporary installations. In addition, the natural beauty of New York's wonderful public gardens—such as those with Japanese, Colonial, or Shakespearean themes—add another aesthetic experience to our collection.

Our book includes as large a variety as possible of styles and eras of art. Whether you are a fancier of the latest contemporary works, ethnic artifacts, or arts of the past, we think you will find outings that will inspire you.

In no way can this be a comprehensive guide to all the wonderful works of art in New York. We expect that most of you are already familiar with the great museums of the city (which we only mention in passing). Obviously, the city has hundreds of galleries that sell their work, but we have decided not to include commercial galleries in this book. Nor do we pretend to cover thoroughly every style and era of art gracing our city. There are many books designed for those with specific interests in one period or style. Instead, we hope our walks will arouse your curiosity and lead you to further exploration.

These walks cover diverse neighborhoods and distances, as well as varying kinds of art. All are accessible by public transportation; directions, hours, and occasional fees are listed. You will find that some walks are thematic, while others explore an entire neighborhood. Walks are of varying length and can be combined with museum visits in most areas.

These walks should appeal to anyone with a taste for art, whether connoisseurs or those who simply enjoy visual stimulation while walking. In the back of the book you will find "Choosing an Outing," which will indicate what artwalks might especially interest you. For example, we have included an art treasure hunt for children, a foray into private studios in Soho and Tribeca for those who are attuned to contemporary art, and a biking exploration of outdoor sculpture in Queens.

Bear in mind that our city changes constantly; accordingly works of art come and go regularly. This may be true of material on our artwalks, but we hope that everything mentioned in our book will be there for you to enjoy.

We have had a wonderful time working on this book and are grateful to the following people for their help and encouragement in our efforts to explore New York's art treasures: Anne Davidson, Sally Ann Bailey, Diana Green, Andy Boose, Adrian Benepe, Peggy Hammerle, Peter Rosenfeld, and Heidi Fried.

Lucy D. Rosenfeld
Marina Harrison

MANHATTAN

1

The Tip of Manhattan

*Exploring the Financial District,
Part I*

HOW TO GET THERE
*Subway: #1 train to Cortlandt Street exit, or E train to World
Trade Center, or New Jersey PATH train to World Trade Center
station.*
SUGGESTED TIMES
Avoid rush hours in this area.

This is a walk filled with surprises and contrasts. Dramatic
modern sculptures contrast with the narrow historic streets of
Lower Manhattan, while more traditional art ornaments some
of the sleekest of contemporary corporate headquarters. There
are art deco designs, an unexpected fourteenth-century Italian
triptych, and several plazas of striking sculpture, many by some
of the best known artists of our time. As you make your way
through the winding streets of the Wall Street area and down
to the lovely park at the tip of Manhattan, you are never far
from the sea, despite the crowded sidewalks and closely packed
cityscape. There are many places to stop for a moment on this
route, including two of New York's historic graveyards and
several small parks, in addition to Battery Park. We suggest you
choose a bright day and set out walking from north to south
(beginning at the World Trade Center), so that you can end up
at Battery Park, where several fine sculptures and the view of
New York Harbor will complete your outing.

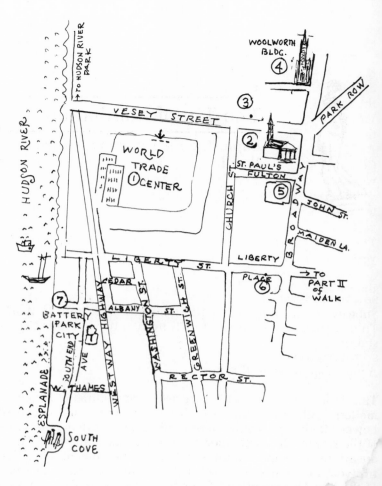

The World Trade Center, known for its sleek 110-story twin towers with their legendary views onto New York Harbor, the Statue of Liberty, and points in every direction, is a good place to begin an artwalk in downtown Manhattan. A first-time visitor will be amazed by the important artworks to be found here, both inside the buildings and within the spacious 5-acre outdoor plaza. Most of this impressive array of art is accessible to anyone who visits. The monumental outdoor sculpture is particularly dramatic in this stark setting of ultramodern skyscrapers.

We suggest you begin your tour at the World Trade Center (1), starting with 7 World Trade Center, a building on Vesey Street directly across from the twin towers, where you will find the first of our recommended artworks. Enter the building on Vesey Street. In the main lobby and to your left on the wall is the first of several works you'll see on this walk by the famed American contemporary sculptor Louise Nevelson. Called *Cloud 1986*, this is an abstract construction of white painted wood consisting of a variety of intricate interconnecting shapes.

Next, go up the escalator to the second floor. As you walk toward the glass doors, you'll see two large contemporary canvases on either side of the long hallway: to your right is *The Third Circle* by the American abstract painter Al Held, and to your left, *Entablature*, by the pop artist Roy Lichtenstein.

Look through the glass to catch your first glimpse of one of the main works at the World Trade Center, the 25-ton, 25-foot-high brilliant red stabile by the American sculptor Alexander Calder. Called *Three Wings*, this surprisingly graceful steel work seems to soar in a lyrical gesture. The three large forms suggest the wings of a giant bird; rivets and ribs brace the steel stabile. The work was installed on the west side of the North Tower, on a sidewalk away from the main plaza, in accordance with Calder's wishes that it be a part of the local street scene rather than an austere monument to be viewed only from afar.

Go through the glass tunnel that connects to the main plaza. (Before you reach the plaza you can walk up to the Calder stabile to get another perspective.) Walk across the plaza and enter the mezzanine lobby of 1 World Trade Center, the twin building on your right, to see another Louise Nevelson work, her imposing black wood relief, *Sky Gate, New York* (1977–78), that hangs on the wall opposite the door. A fascinating composite of abstract shapes, this work actually combines chair slats, parts of a balustrade, barrel staves, newel posts, disks, and other familiar forms into one of Nevelson's largest and most impressive wall pieces. Measuring 17 feet by 32 feet, it is painted uniformly black, representing, as the artist described it, "a night piece." Nevelson's interest in architectonic patterns of lights and darks is reinforced by small disks that create shadows and

5

reflect the light within the overall dark construction. The New York skyline at night was the inspiration for this work.

It is possible to view additional but less accessible interior artworks at 1 World Trade Center—some major paintings and tapestries—if you are willing to make an appointment. Several significant works are displayed in the well-known restaurant Windows on the World on the 107th floor and in nearby rooms used for private gatherings. Among these we recommend *Recollection Pond*, a vivid tapestry of wool and cotton flatweave by the American artist Romare Bearden, measuring 61 inches by 75 inches, and *Le Canapé*, an Aubusson tapestry measuring 87½ inches by 11 feet 8 inches by the Swiss-French multifaceted architect/artist Le Corbusier. To see these and other works, contact Windows on the World at (212) 938-1111, for a short private tour between 3 and 5 P.M. on most days.

Outside of 1 World Trade Center, in the Austin J. Tobin Plaza (the main plaza) you'll find a monumental environmental abstract stainless steel structure of horizontally locked pieces by the American sculptor James Rosati, *Ideogram* (1974), measuring 23 feet 6 inches by 28 feet 6 inches. The tilting, diagonal forms of the sculpture provide framelike views of the World Trade Center, with the angled, geometric lines of stainless steel in contrast with the strong verticals of the skyscrapers. The shining steel beams of *Ideogram* reflect the light on a clear day, making the huge work seem surprisingly light and ephemeral.

Next, enter the lobby of the second twin tower to see the very large *Tapestry* (1974) by the Spanish master Joan Miró. This 20-foot by 35-foot brilliantly vivid tapestry is a colorful blending of roughly woven strands, hemp, and thick pile. The composition is somewhat reminiscent of some of Miró's famous collages. Be sure to view this work from a distance to get the full impact.

Leave the building and walk to the center of the plaza, where you can't miss the 25-foot-high broken-surfaced bronze globe, Fritz Koenig's *Sphere for Plaza Fountain* (1968–71), which forms a large fountain with a basin 90 feet in diameter. The giant globe that is the centerpiece of the plaza is broken by a variety of geometric forms that seem to evolve from the inside of the sphere, suggesting life forces bursting through the sleek brass surface. During the warm season, when the fountain is operating, you can observe the sphere rotating almost imperceptibly—if you have the patience to stand there for some time.

The third sculpture in the plaza—reputed to be the largest freestanding stone carving of modern times and the largest public work in stone outside of Mount Rushmore—is *World Trade Center Plaza Sculpture* (1972) by the Japanese artist Masayuki Nagare. The black granite sculpture—34 feet long, 17 feet wide, and 14 feet high—includes two highly polished asymmetrical parts separated by a rough gully. The surfaces are not uniform; in fact the major parts of the work are highly polished, while the underside and gully are rough. There is a pattern of lines over the surface and occasional indentations, making this a sculpture that invites you to touch it. While it has a certain simplicity of form and balance, the work actually is made up of almost forty separate pieces of granite over a metal frame. Because of its setting in this vast plaza surrounded by gigantic buildings, its own considerable size seems somewhat diminished.

Leave the plaza of the World Trade Center. You are now facing Church Street. Cross over and head one block north, where you'll see the historic cemetery of St. Paul's Chapel (2). Walk into the cemetery, one of the tiny oases in lower Manhattan and one of the oldest graveyards in New York. Many of the tombstones date from the eighteenth century; Revolutionary War heroes are buried here and within the chapel. Although most of the carved designs have long since vanished, this is a good spot to absorb the typical juxtaposition of old and new in this part of Manhattan.

Stand in the cemetery about midway to the back entrance of the church and face Vesey Street, the northern boundary of the plot. Across the street, at 20 Vesey Street (3), you'll see the Garrison Building (1906), home of the *New York Evening Post* between 1907 and 1930. In addition to the charming art nouveau rooftop, note the four unusual statues decorating the front of the building. Known as the *Four Periods of Publicity*, these languid and expressive figures are by Gutzon Borglum, the American artist who created the gigantic Mount Rushmore presidential heads, and Estelle Kohn, the architect's wife. (Another example of Borglum's interest in doing large-scale building sculpture can be seen on the facade of The Cathedral of St.

John the Divine, where he sculpted the Twelve Apostles.) This building and these four rather Gothic sculptures are now preserved by the City Landmarks Commission.

Walk through the back entrance of St. Paul's and directly into the church to see the oldest remaining church building in Manhattan. (Its cornerstone was laid in 1764.) The light, spacious interior with fluted Corinthian columns and barrel vault is airy and delicate; you might find the present color scheme rather saccharine. On the west wall is a bust of John Wells by John Frazee, one of the earliest American sculptors and a tombstone carver. The pew in which George Washington worshiped is marked. Notice also the glory above the altar, which is by Pierre Charles L'Enfant, the French military engineer, architect, and city planner who came to America to fight in the Revolution and stayed on to plan Washington, D.C.

Exiting from the front door of the church onto Broadway, turn left and walk north to 233 Broadway, between Barclay Street and Park Place. This is the Woolworth Building (4), the tallest building in the world (729 feet, 1 inch), when it was finished in 1913. Designed by Cass Gilbert, it is an extraordinary example of Gothic Revival architecture and particularly interior decoration in the age of magnificence. Woolworth's love of display is evident in the brilliant mosaic patterns, the vaulted ceilings, and golden marble (quarried on the isle of Skyros in Greece). The mosaic patterns of birds and flowers recall Italian designs; the brilliance is still dazzling seventy-five years later. Murals by Paul Jennewein representing Commerce and Labor can be viewed on the mezzanine level, or from the center hall downstairs; they are a good example of the stylized academic tradition in American art of the time. Don't miss the grand marble staircase and carved marble balustrade at the end of the entrance corridor. Finally, note the sculpted figures beneath the arches leading to the hallways near the Broadway entrance. Among them is Woolworth himself, clutching a large nickel in his hand. (You can visit Woolworth's office on the 24th floor during business hours to see a collection of memorabilia and furniture relating to Napoleon.)

As you leave the Woolworth Building, turn right and walk down to 195 Broadway, the Kalikow Building (5), formerly the

AT&T Building. In the impressive lobby you'll find yourself surrounded by forty massive columns reminiscent of an Egyptian temple. Against the wall is a bronze sculpture of a winged Mercury with marble figures in relief by the American sculptor Chester Beach. There are also some benches for a moment's rest.

Walk three blocks south on Broadway, passing Fulton, Dey, and Cortlandt streets to 1 Liberty Plaza (6) to Liberty Street. As you cross the bustling square called Liberty Plaza, you will be surrounded by people reading on benches and hurrying across the pavement. Do not miss one of the readers—an inconspicuous bronze, life-sized statue on one of the benches, who not only is dressed exactly like his real-life counterparts in this financial district, but whose open briefcase contains such sculpted amenities as a calculator, tape recorder, pencils, and whatever else passersby donate. This piece is called *Double Check* (1982) by J. Seward Johnson, Jr., a sculptor noted for his lifelike all-American figures.

A detour of the new Battery Park City (7) to see some of New York's newest and most interesting outdoor art sights is well worth taking if you have the time and energy. Going due west from Liberty Plaza, you can walk several blocks and cross the Westway highway (either by overhead walkway or by street level at the traffic light) to reach the far side of the World Trade Center complex. Turn south and walk on South End Avenue to Albany Street, where you turn once again west, toward the Hudson River. Battery Park City is a planned community of high-rise apartments and parks that face the Hudson River. The designing of artworks to enhance the site has been a part of the project from the beginning, and works by Mary Miss, Ned Smyth, R. M. Fischer, Richard Artschwager, and Scott Burton (among others) are very much in evidence. The Battery Park City Fine Arts Program has become a sort of test laboratory for the combining of architecture, city planning and art at a spectacular site; it is fascinating to view this contemporary version of an ancient idea

At the north end of Battery Park City, you'll find the stunning Winter Garden, a large, interesting, airy indoor space with shops, restaurants, and a particularly attractive open area.

9

While there are occasional art exhibits among the palm trees of this neo-Edwardian atrium with vaulted glass roof, it is mostly used for concerts and other public functions. But on the balcony level there are regular art shows; a recent exhibit was called "Masks of Mexico." Outdoors there is a plaza which is in itself an environmental work of art. Designed by Cesar Pelli, M. Paul Friedberg, Siah Armajani, and Scott Burton, this grand space includes granite benches and chairs (by Burton) that are an integral part of the design.

Across the way you will see what appears to be an Egyptian temple set before you. *The Upper Room* (1984–87), a large work by Ned Smyth, is one of the more intriguing outdoor sculpture complexes to have been placed in the city's open spaces in years. Made of a pinkish combination of stone, mosaic, cut glass, and cast concrete, its forms are definitely ancient, somewhat Egyptian, a touch classical Roman, with here and there a Renaissance arch. The spacing and design of the series of columns, seating areas (there are even inlaid chess boards), a kind of altar, an arcade, and the varied textures of the stone are fanciful and appealing. The view of the promenade along the river and the far shore adds to the tranquillity of the spot. Smyth tried to create what he called a "space of respect"; he also wanted his work to relate well to the architectural complex of the new community being constructed around it. Gestures of postmodernism in the buildings are echoed in his arches and details, while the pinkish color of the sculpture picks up the warm brick tones of the architecture. It's a nice place to interrupt your walk for a few moments and to imagine yourself surrounded by ancient (but crisply new) ruins.

Walk along the shoreline to the northern edge of Battery Park City for a must-see stop at the brand new Hudson River Park. These 8.2 greenacres include a playing meadow and children's playground complete with carousel, child-size bridges, climbing nets, slides, games, swings, and animal sculptures. But of particular interest is "The Real World," an enclosed paved terrace featuring some fifty whimsical bronze sculptures by Tom Otterness. Conceived as a playground to stimulate the curiosity

of children, it is an unusual collection of odd objects and creatures—animal, human, imaginary, real, giant, and lilliput-
tian—in the most imaginative and unlikely combinations. Children and adults alike will delight in these sometimes surreal,
always clever vignettes: a cat dressed in a bowler hat plays
chess at a picnic table; Humpty Dumpty fiddles away, while a
creature looking like a vacuum cleaner/dinosaur is about to
attack; a dog carefully observes a cat stalking a bird about to
catch a worm; a frog atop a lamppost looks down on the pro-
ceedings, while a fierce-looking dog is tightly chained to a water
fountain. Footprint and penny motifs (in apparent acknowledg-
ment of nearby Wall Street) can be found throughout, in the
most unexpected spots. Overscaled bronze pennies and child-
size footprints are interspersed in a winding stone path and
an island made entirely of pennies is surrounded by a moat.
Children will enjoy discovering and identifying these and the
other items that are sometimes cleverly disguised by Otterness's intricate designs.

Battery Park City has other sites to visit as well. Walk south
along the windy landscaped promenade, one of the city's nicer
amenities. En route you'll find Rector Park, an unusually
charming spot with wrought-iron fence and elegant plantings.
Don't miss Rector Gate, an airy steel construction that faces the
park. Created by R. M. Fischer in the late 1980s, it consists of
various circular shapes—globes, open spheres, cones, and a
lacy cupola—in an imaginative arrangement. Just beyond, at
the end of Thames Street, is "Sitting/Stance," Richard Artschwager's rather obscure park furniture sculpture garden.

All of the art at Battery Park City was commissioned by the
city and was chosen expressly to enhance the new site. One
of the most important and successful of these commissions is
environmental artist Mary Miss's design for the esplanade at
its south end. Her proposal for the shoreline included a lookout,
pilings that rise and fall with the river tide, wooden wisteria-
covered archways, boardwalks lighted with blue lanterns, and
Japanese-style rock gardens. The architect, Stanton Eckstut, and
a landscape architect, Susan Child, helped execute her design.
While the site-art is surely a form of gentrification of the natural
shoreline (you can see what the banks originally looked like,

just over the fence at the edge), it is a major attempt to balance the sophisticated urban setting on the shore with the Hudson's rather wild and somber coastline. From the top of the curving steel staircase, you can enjoy an extraordinary view of the shapes and patterns of Mary Miss's design, as well as of the city, the river, and New Jersey.

From here you can wend your way back to the crossover at the World Trade Center.

... And in Addition

- Appointments to see art in the Windows on the World restaurant at the top of the World Trade Center can be made by telephone in advance: 938-1111; tour hours are between 3 and 5 P.M.
- South Street Seaport Museum is a short walk from this area; see listing in back.

2

The Tip of Manhattan

*Exploring the Financial District,
Part II*

HOW TO GET THERE
Subway: #2, 3, 4, or 5 train to Wall Street or Broadway/Nassau
Street stop on the A train. Walk north on Nassau Street to
Liberty Street.
SUGGESTED TIMES
Avoid rush hours in this area. Plan to reach 33 Maiden Lane
between 11 A.M. and 4 P.M. (perhaps avoiding its most crowded
time—lunch hour).

Find your way to the plaza of the Marine Midland Building
(1) on Liberty Street, to view one of the best known outdoor
sculptures in all of New York City, the famous orange-red cube
by Isamu Noguchi (1967). This fascinating structure, with its
hole through the center, balances amazingly on one corner,
looking as though it might topple at any moment. The Red Cube
is really a rhombohedron, a six-sided figure whose opposite
sides are parallel at oblique angles; this distortion creates the
illusion of dramatic force, as well as contrast with the bland
glass facade of the tower behind it. Noguchi commented that a
cube on its point was like chance "or the rolling of the dice."

From the cube it's a very short walk to 33 Maiden Lane (2),
also called 1 Federal Reserve Plaza, where a whimsical tapestry,
The Circus (1954), by the important French cubist Fernand

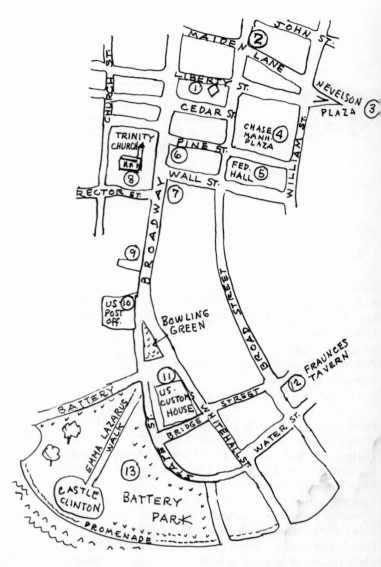

Leger hangs in the main lobby. This tapestry adds warmth and interest to the large impersonal public area.

Leaving 33 Maiden Lane, continue east on Maiden Lane to Louise Nevelson Plaza (3), on the corner of William and Liberty streets. This small triangular plot set in the midst of a busy downtown area of intermingling winding streets contains seven black steel sculptures of varying sizes and shapes called *Shadows and Flags* (1978) that form a cohesive outdoor environment. Although each sculpture could be regarded as a separate entity able to stand on its own as a work of art, the group was conceived as a harmonious whole. When commissioned to design sculpture for the plaza (created when streets were widened), Nevelson said she wanted to place the sculptures on poles so they might appear to "float like flags." Always concerned with the interaction of lights and darks and the relationship of art to the total environment surrounding it, Nevelson constructed these 40-foot-high pieces in black, geometric shapes that echo modern city forms. Squares, cylinders, angled bars, and jagged planes intersect one another high above eye level, forcing the visitor to view from below. The small park in the plaza also has seating benches where you can enjoy your surroundings in comfort.

From the plaza cross William Street and enter the Chase Manhattan building (4) at its lower-level entrance. Here you'll find an assortment of art on different levels. In this giant lower-level lobby you'll see a glass partition and beyond it a sunken Japanese garden designed by Noguchi. Elegantly composed of black basalt rocks, lily pads, trickling water, and an unerring sense of design, this garden can be viewed from the lower level or from above—two entirely different perspectives. Noguchi wanted to show how art and nature could be successfully integrated into an urban setting. The floor of the area is contoured with patterns that suggest waves (much like traditional Japanese raked gardens), and the rocks (brought from Kyoto) are set in a design that relates them to the uneven ground surface. When the fountain is in operation, the rocks seem to be rising out of the water; Noguchi describes them as bursting forth, "seeming to levitate out of the ground." (But when it is dry, the garden is rather bland.) Although you cannot enter this garden, the varying views of it can suggest any number of landscapes to you, from seaside to moonscape, from traditional Japanese sunken garden to desolate winter scenery.

Walk to the end of the lobby and note the large stainless steel

15

sculpture decorating the far wall. This car-fender sculpture, by Jason Seeley, a contemporary sculptor, is called *Triptych* (1969). Its setting against the Chase Manhattan's red mosaic wall creates a dramatic effect in the immense lobby. Take the escalator up one floor and walk left toward the outdoor plaza. Outside the bank of doors you'll find one of downtown's masterpieces: Jean Dubuffet's giant sculpture, *Group of Four Trees* installed in 1972. This 43-foot, 25-ton sculpture is supported by a steel skeleton and made of aluminum, fiberglass, and plastic resin covered with polyurethane paint. Perhaps the sculpture looks more like enormous mushrooms than trees, but its overall appearance is fanciful and bright, and the visitor can walk through and around it to view it from many different angles. Dubuffet called it an *hourloupe*, meaning "some wonderful or grotesque object . . . something rumbling and threatening with tragic overtones." Dubuffet did not characterize his works as painted sculpture; he called them "unleashed graphisms" or "drawings which extend and expand in space." Dubuffet's *Group of Four Trees* (1972) dominates Chase Manhattan's plaza and provides a striking contrast to the tall and sleek buildings of corporate New York. The curious placing of the work of one of the art world's most antiestablishment artists as a centerpiece of one of America's most hallowed capitalist symbols adds to the fascination. Here also you can view Noguchi's sunken garden from above; the design of rocks from this vantage point seems quite different from the view below.

From here walk south a couple of blocks on historic Nassau Street to Federal Hall National Memorial (5), on the corner of Pine and Nassau. This site is filled with historic significance: here Washington took his oath of office; Congress enacted laws to create the departments of State, Treasury, and War, and the federal courts system; and here, too, the Bill of Rights was enacted. The present building, dating from 1842, is in the Greek Revival style, inspired by the Parthenon. It is operated by the National Parks Service as a museum of American history. Inside you can wander around a gallery of historic prints, a fine library of Americana (with a diorama showing the Washington inaugural), and a beautiful central hall with Corinthian columns.

Leave Federal Hall, turning left on Pine Street. Your next

stop will be the Bank of Tokyo (6), on the corner of Pine and Broadway, at 100 Broadway. The work of art we recommend you see within this columned building is a brushed aluminum sculpture by Noguchi suspended within four huge interior Corinthian columns.

Walk around the Bank of Tokyo to Wall Street, cross over Wall, and enter the side doors of the Irving Trust Company Building (7). The lobby on this side of the otherwise new and nondescript corporate-style building is a lasting reminder of the kind of artistic taste that New York enjoyed in the art deco period. The rich gold and crimson mosaic interior is a memento of a bygone era. Note the leaded windows with their exotic shapes reflecting the pattern of the wall mosaics.

Directly across Broadway is Trinity Church (8), one of the most beloved of New York landmarks. This church, the third on the site, was built in 1839. Explore the graveyard either before or after seeing the interior; here are the graves of Alexander Hamilton, Francis Lewis, and Robert Fulton, among many other notable Americans. Inside the building you'll find a number of artistic gems. On the north wall of this lovely Gothic Revival building designed by Richard Upjohn, note the baptistry triptych. With the traditional gold background and the unmistakable colors and style of the early Renaissance, this is indeed a "find." Also of note within Trinity Church are three sets of bronze doors that resemble Ghiberti's doors to the Florentine baptistry; note particularly the pair on the west portal by Karl Bitter, a well-known carver of architectural details in many historical modes. The large stained glass window above the altar was completed in 1846 and is strikingly beautiful on a clear day; the designer was the architect Richard Upjohn, one of the leading designers of Gothic ecclesiastical buildings in America. For more information on Trinity Church, visit the church's small museum, which offers an interpretive slide program as well as a history of the building and its many well-known parishioners.

From Trinity Church walk south to 45 Broadway (9). Inside this very modern building we discovered a pleasant atrium filled with a wide variety of exotic and decorative plants, a welcome respite for the urban tourist.

Proceed on Broadway to number 25, the Old Cunard Building (1921) (10), now housing the Post Office. As you enter, look up to the ceiling. A relatively modestly decorated entrance hall leads to an overwhelmingly ornate Great Hall, which is said to have been inspired by Raphael's style. The main dome, 65 feet high and rising majestically above the octagonal hall, is aglow with impressive frescoes by the American mural painter Ezra Winter representing various shipping scenes: the Viking vessel of Leif Erikson, Columbus' galleon, the crossings of Sir Francis Drake, and John Cabot amid turbulent seas. The interior of this building is one more example of the exuberance of 1920s design in New York.

As you leave this building, we suggest you walk across Broadway to see the giant bronze bull recently placed in front of 26 Broadway. It is by Arturo Di Modica (see page 116), whose sculpture studio is one of those we invite you to visit on your walk through Soho and Tribeca. This realistic, massive bull, of course, is a symbol of good times in the financial district.

You will now find yourself at tiny Bowling Green Park. Here you can sit on a park bench and get a good view of the U.S. Customs House (11), which directly faces you. This imposing 1907 Beaux Arts–style granite palace (soon to house the National Museum of the American Indian of the Smithsonian Institution) is said to stand on the site where the first European settlers in New York built their crude shelters in 1624. It is graced with an impressive flight of steps, forty-four Corinthian columns, a fine arched entrance, but, most especially, with one of the city's most impressive works of sculpture. A group of four monumental statues by the American sculptor Daniel Chester French adorns the front of the building and represents the four continents. Each statue consists of a seated female figure surrounded by other symbolic attributes. America's attitudes and impressions of the rest of the world at the turn of the century are clearly defined by these allegorical ladies. Placed prominently and significantly nearer or farther from the center of the building, each bears small symbols to suggest her continent's character. To our twentieth-century eyes, they are predictably biased historical curiosities. The four figures are all seated, but differ in subtle ways and you'll enjoy "reading" their allegorical messages.

America and Europe are in the center, to the left of the doorway sits America, the most idealistic and fervent, as she holds the torch of prosperity, her left arm sheltering a strong crouching man who turns the wheels of labor. She stares dramatically into the future, prepared to inspire and lead. On the other side of the doorway we find Europe, representative of the past, but nonetheless regal in a Grecian gown, surrounded by symbols of knowledge and ancient glory. She wears a crown, signifying royalty, and her arm rests both on a book and a globe. But, unlike America with her steady gaze into the future, she stares straight ahead, arms and legs equally balanced, the representative of solid, classical values. On the outer edges, Africa and Asia are less able to deal with the modern world. On the far right, Africa is portrayed in a state of slumber, leaning against an Egyptian sphinx and a lion from the jungle. The nearly naked figure holds no other symbols of past or present; she is the personification of the dark and sleeping continent. Asia, on the far left, is the most formal of the group. She holds a small Buddhist figure and the lotus flower; she is the mother of religion and mysticism. But surrounding her meditating figure are emaciated and prostrate bodies, and her foot rests on human skulls. Asia is unable to care for her masses, this sculpture tells us, and the figure turns away in its meditative trance.

In addition to these impressive symbolic works in front of the Customs House, be sure not to miss the cornice sculptures at the roof's edge. Made in 1907, there are twelve statues that symbolize both ancient and modern nations engaged in sea trade. Each figure wears a much-embellished national costume and gazes rather severely down at us. In keeping with the building's Beaux Arts style of elegant sculptural ornamentation, the statues were made by leading artists of the time: Holland and Portugal by Augustus Saint-Gaudens, France and England by Charles Grafly, Greece and Rome by Frank Edwin Elwell, Phoenicia by Frederick Wellington Ruckstull, Genoa by Augustus Lukeman, Venice and Spain by Mary Lawrence Tonetti, Denmark by Johannes Gelert, and Belgium by Albert Jaegers.

The Customs House is the new site of the National Museum

of the American Indian (which is moving here from Audubon Terrace). This extraordinary museum, part of the vast Smithsonian Institution, was founded in 1916 by George C. Heye. It is the largest Indian museum anywhere and is devoted to the collection, preservation, and exhibition of all things having to do with the Native Americans in North, Central, and South America—from the Arctic to Tierra del Fuego. This ambitious collection is varied and motley. You can see such items as Huron moosehair embroidery, Pomo feather baskets, two-thousand-year-old duck decoys, Sitting Bull's war club, Crazy Horse's feather headdress, and Apache playing cards. You can also enjoy ancient Pueblo pottery, Iroquois silver jewelry and beadwork, archaeological textiles from Peru, Northwest Coast masks, and animal figurines from Central America. The exhibitions are colorful and varied; they will also interest children who are intrigued by American native cultures. When moved to the U.S. Customs House, more of the collection, now housed in galleries on three floors in this building, will be on permanent display. Telephone: (212) 283-2420. You may wish to go directly to Battery Park from here; or, if you're still feeling energetic, make a two-block detour to see Fraunces Tavern (12).

If you walk around the Customs House Building you'll find yourself at the corner of State and Bridge streets. Two blocks east on Bridge Street will bring you to Broad Street, and here on the opposite corner you'll find New York's famous Fraunces Tavern, on the corner of Broad and Pearl. Built about 1719 for a merchant named Stephen Delaney, it was converted by Samuel Fraunces to a tavern in 1762. Its long and illustrious history including visits by Washington and other notables, is well preserved and commemorated. But today's Fraunces Tavern is mostly a reconstruction. Downstairs there is still a pretty eating place; upstairs houses the museum with a number of prints and dioramas that relate to Old New York. The museum, which is quite small, presents a series of exhibitions and other events, and there is a fee for entry. While the building itself is a charming reminder of the past, it is not only dwarfed by its surroundings but seems somewhat touristy, and the art inside is generally of a minor nature.

To enter Battery Park (13), the very tip of Manhattan directly from the Customs House, simply cross State Street to the entranceway and head down the path, Emma Lazarus Way, to the water ahead. The first major sculpture you will encounter is called *The Immigrants*, by Luis Sanguino. Created in 1981, it is a strong and impressive near-naturalistic work depicting America's immigrants who came across by the thousands from Ellis Island to this very point, once the Immigrant Landing Depot, now Castle Clinton. Sanguino's sculpture shows a variety of ethnic figures, including a freed African, an Eastern European immigrant, a priest, a mother and child, all seeking a better life. Within its rough-hewn style and social message, this work is in a distinctly different mode from the other outdoor sculptures one sees in public parks. Instead of conquering heroes in smooth marble, or the sleek modern designs of abstract sculpture, Sanguino has attempted a synthesis of naturalism and historical interpretation.

At the end of the short walkway (well lined with benches), you'll find a small museum of immigration and reconstructed fortress. Walk through to the promenade along the water and turn left. Following this waterside walkway you will come to several notable sculptures: among the most interesting artistically is the great bronze eagle made in 1961 by Albino Manca. This work, called *The East Coast Memorial*, is simple and very strong; the eagle seems to stare out to sea as it guards the eight marble pylons that bear the names of 4,596 Americans lost in the Atlantic in World War II. The combination of simple vertical forms with the names carved into them, and the large bold eagle is a powerful one. The great eagle symbolically places on a wave of the ocean a wreath that is made from the arrows and branches of the Great Seal of the United States, signifying an official act of mourning.

Other park sculptures that you can see as you wander in the area are a bronze statue (1909) by Ettore Ximenes of Giovanni da Verrazano, the first European to sail into New York Harbor; the *U.S. Coast Guard Memorial* (1947) by Norman M. Thomas, depicting two guardsmen supporting an injured man; and several changing modern works exhibited in the grassy areas at various times.

21

. . . And in Addition

The latest addition to New York's museums is New York Un
earthed (17 State Street at Pearl Street). This glass-enclose(
museum is actually an underground laboratory displaying ma
terial from the South Street Seaport Museum and archaeologi
cal finds from Lower Manhattan, which are being worked o
as you watch. Telephone: (212) 363-9372.

- The South Street Seaport (see page 70).
- The Continental Insurance Building at 180 Maiden Lane i
  whose elegant, contemporary lobby you'll find a branc
  (with changing exhibits) of the International Center of Pho
  tography (see page 139).
- 127 John Street, corner of Water Street: an office buildin
  whose playful environment includes a neon and corrugate(
  steel tunnel designed by Rudolph de Harak, a scrap meta
  bike sculpture by Albert Wilson, and large painted plasti(
  dolls à la Alice in Wonderland by Mary Lomprey. Don't mis
  the giant digital clock outside.
- In front of 88 Pine Street, an intriguing two-piece, interre
  lated stainless steel sculpture by Yu Yu Yang, a Taiwanes(
  artist. The four thousand pound disc appears to fit withi
  the large square.
- In the lobby of 199 Water Street (Seaport Plaza) you'll fin(
  three large colorful, striped Frank Stella works.

3

Around the World in Twenty Blocks

International Art Centers

HOW TO GET THERE
Subway: #6 train to 68th Street station.
Bus: Fifth (downtown) or Madison (uptown) Avenue M1, 2, 3,
4; Lexington (downtown) or Third (uptown) Avenue M101, 102.
SUGGESTED TIMES
We recommend weekdays for this walk, after 10 A.M. and pref-
erably not in late July or August, when many of these places
are closed. Saturday is possible in most cases; see individual
listings for hours.

New York, the "capital" of the art world, is also one of the world's most international cities. In about twenty blocks you can enjoy a round-the-world artwalk that combines the polyglot, multiethnic nature of the city with some very fine art. No, you will not have to wander from foreign neighborhood to foreign neighborhood; instead we recommend a stretch of East Side Manhattan that will transport you (artistically speaking) quite easily around the world. In fact, a visit to the embassies, regional centers, and galleries of this area will acquaint you with some of the newest art being done abroad, as well as with the antiquities and native art that you might usually only see in museums. And, because these exhibitions change periodically,

23

you can do this walk every few months for a new artistic ad venture!

Begin by taking the subway to Lexington Avenue and 68th Street (or the bus to 65th). Walk across 65th Street (heading west) to 165 East 65th, where you will find the first stop on your hopscotch around the world: China House. China House Gallery sponsors a series of exhibitions, symposiums, video tape programs, and gallery talks. It specializes in introducing Chinese art to Westerners, and its recent shows have included modern Chinese painters, Chinese antiquities, Ming land scapes—in fact, a wonderful array of Eastern art can be seen here. The discussions that accompany these exhibitions go on for days at a time, bringing scholars of Chinese art to speak and offering to the public unusually interesting commentary. The gallery itself is open Monday–Friday, 10–5; Saturday, 11–5 Sunday, 2–5. (It occasionally closes for reinstallations.) To find out what is showing when, call (212) 744-8181.

Having immersed yourself in Chinese art, walk over to Park Avenue and turn north. Go up to Park and 68th Street, where you will find several stops bunched together. First, at the Americas Society at 680 Park is a fine gallery devoted to art from Latin America, the Caribbean, and Canada. This is a must-see stop, with three or four changing exhibitions per year. The elegant landmark 1912 townhouse is a gracious home for the most varied and interesting of art shows. A recent exhibit, for example, contained altar decorations and wood carvings from South American Guarani Indians who had adopted a "baroque" Christian style. Other recent exhibitions in the large ground floor rooms have included Venezuelan landscapes, Realism in Ecuadorean art, and the paintings of Fernando Botero and Diego Rivera. Other activities at Americas Society include concerts, stage readings, workshops, publications, and an active outreach program for schools and the Hispanic community. For information, call (212) 744-6650. The Society is open daily from noon to 6 P.M.

Having jumped from Asia to the Americas in only a few blocks, you'll find yourself "in Europe" next door at the Spanish Institute at 684 Park. Like its neighbor, the Spanish Institute is housed in an imposing building, and its galleries are on the ground floor. Often combining literature and art, their exhibitions include a variety of unusual subjects: a recent show was called "Po(e)(li)tical Object: Visual Poetry from Spain." They have also exhibited Spanish paintings, manuscripts, and sculpture; occasionally you will have the opportunity to see new Spanish art, just as if you were wandering among the galleries of Madrid and Barcelona. An array of Spanish cultural events and courses in art history is also available. The Spanish Institute is open Monday–Sunday, 11–6. The telephone is (212) 628-0420.

Walk next door to 686 Park, where you will see the imposing entrance of the Italian Consulate. Here you will find a small display board listing exhibitions and events, and most likely you will find a show of Italian art in its upstairs gallery. The elegant surroundings, the polished wood, and architectural details of the Consulate building are well worth a visit in any case, but, if you're lucky, there will also be a show to see. The Italian Cultural Institute is open Monday–Friday, 9–12:30, 1:30–4:30. Their telephone is (212) 879-4242.

Think of yourself as leaving Europe for the moment, to return again to the Far East; for, only two blocks north, at 725 Park (70th Street), you'll come to the well-known Asia Society. This elegant building (designed by Edward Larrabee Barnes and dedicated in 1981) houses a true museum collection of Asian art, from stone Buddhas to Chinese ink paintings, from Japanese ceramics to Nepalese statuary. This is a rare collection in which you can spend a long or short time, as you wish. (If your interests lie in Asian art, you might want to save this visit for a single day, but we enjoyed juxtaposing it with the others on the artwalk.) Asia Society sponsors a vast collection of cultural and educational events. The Society is open Tuesday–Saturday, from 10 to 5; Thursday until 8:30; and Sunday from 12 to 5. Its telephone is (212) 288-6400.

Continue north up Park Avenue and make a quick detour to the east at 73rd Street. Before you reach Lexington you'll find 123 East 73rd, the American-Scandinavian Foundation. This small center presents a series of shows of Scandinavian arts, including painting, design, furniture, and—at this writing—four young Icelandic artists' works. Their exhibitions have

25

been particularly noteworthy in the field of design, and you might enjoy their offerings. They can be reached at (212) 879 9779; hours are Monday–Friday, 10–5.

Retrace your steps to Park Avenue and walk north one block to 74th Street. Now head east toward Madison Avenue. At 31 East 74th you'll find the little Gallery of Eskimo Art. Here the carved bone figures and curious shapes of Eskimo art are dis played. Although this is a commercial gallery, they don't object to browsers. The gallery is open Tuesday–Saturday, 11–6.

By now you are probably ready for a rest. Cross Madison Avenue and walk over to Fifth Avenue, where you'll see Central Park before you. You can enter the park at 76th Street to find a quiet spot of grass or sit down on a bench along the avenue to think over the art you've seen so far. (You are only part of the way around your world art voyage!)

Your energy revived, cross back over Fifth Avenue and walk north to 78th Street, to the glorious 1902 building at 972 Fifth Avenue, the French Consulate. About six times a year French artwork (frequently photography shows by the French or on French themes) is exhibited in the beautifully columned circu lar entranceway. Information on other sites for French exhibi tions, including the French Institute Building (the Alliance Française) on East 60th Street, is also available. Hours are 10–5 Monday–Friday; telephone: (212) 606-3600.

Next, walk around the corner to 2 East 79th Street, the en trance of the Ukrainian Institute of America. This imposing building with iron gates was designed to resemble a French chateau, but inside you will be transported to a world of Ukrai nian folk art, paintings, and posters. Among the works are per manent displays of art by notable Ukrainians, including Alex ander Archipenko and Alexis Gritchenko. There is an exhibition hall on the ground floor, and paintings literally cover the walls as you climb the great staircase to the upper stories. Upstairs you'll find traditional decorated Easter eggs, costumes, textiles, and folk decorations. When we were there recently we found political posters and an exhibition celebrating a millen- nium of Christianity in the region. There is a general air of another time and place here, and a definite political overtone o much of the art shown. The Ukrainian Institute is open Tuesday–Friday, 2–6, and weekends by appointment. You can call the Institute at (212) 288-8660.

Back on Fifth Avenue, walk north for several blocks to one of our favorite spots, the busy Goethe House, at 1014 Fifth Avenue (at 83rd Street). In a newly renovated Beaux Arts townhouse opposite the Metropolitan Museum, Goethe House is devoted to German art and cultural activities. There are exhibitions (in addition to every sort of cultural event), as well as some permanent paintings to see. Goethe House is nothing if not eclectic; a recent show featured the history of German rock and roll, and other exhibitions have included works by German painters and art from German museums. Goethe House is open on Saturday, from noon to 5; Wednesday and Friday, from 9–5; and Tuesday and Thursday from 9–7. The telephone number is (212) 439-8700.

YIVO Institute for Jewish Research has moved to temporary quarters 555 West 57 St (corner of 11th Avenue). Covering the years since the mid-1800s to the present, YIVO has a vast collection of art and publications—from religious to agitprop, from literary to photographic documentation of the history of Eastern European Jewish life. Exhibitions change frequently. Recently they showed photographs of life in prewar Eastern Europe, an exhibition of rather primitive paintings of Jewish life in Romania, and artwork by concentration camp inmates. Needless to say, the most gripping and poignant material on display are photos and pictures from the Holocaust. Be sure to note the permanent display in the far corner of the lobby: a curious collection of tiny little character study masks made for I. J. Singer's play *Yoshe Kalb*. YIVO has a large collection (over 8,000 art items, 100,000 photographs, and 300,000 books) that can be seen on request—a treasure trove of Jewish history. YIVO will move to new space downtown near Union Square, at 15 West 16th Street within the next few years. Its replacement in its grand Fifth Avenue mansion will be an exciting new addition to the art institutions of the city: a museum founded by the Serge Subarsky Foundation to be devoted to Austrian and German expressionist painting. YIVO's hours are Monday,

27

Tuesday, Thursday, and Friday, 9:30–5:30, closed on bot American and Jewish holidays. Call them at (212) 535-6700.

Before turning to Madison Avenue, we should note that yo are in the vicinity of New York's most famous "Museum Mile (see Artwalk 6). Included in this neighborhood are the Met, c course, the Jewish Museum, and several other notable collec tions—among them, the Frick. (Although you might wish t combine this artwalk with visits to these famous collectior while you are in the neighborhood, we think they deserve sep; rate trips at another time, and therefore we are purposefull turning east to the galleries on Madison Avenue.) Here, betwee 80th Street and 68th Street, you will find an astonishing arra of international art. This section of Madison is one of the thre major art gallery areas in Manhattan (visit Soho and the 57t Street area for the others). As you walk down the avenue er joying the generally posh and artistic stores, you will find (bot upstairs and at street level) perhaps two dozen interesting a: galleries. Among them are several devoted to Asian antiquitie one showing large contemporary Soviet art, a charming shop gallery featuring primitive objects carved in Oceania, Sout America, and elsewhere, several showing American primitive two devoted to African carvings, and of course many exhibitin contemporary European painters and sculptors. We recon mend that you pick up "Gallery Guide" in any one of thes galleries for particular information on current shows in th neighborhood, or, if you prefer, duck in and out of whicheve galleries you find of interest. (Remember that New York dealer welcome browsers; you don't have to pretend you are a pro spective purchaser.)

If you are still feeling energetic, we can suggest an additiona leg to your artwalk, which will take you downtown as far a 57th Street. The remaining three stops on our walk will intro duce you to French, Korean, and Russian art. If you wish t continue (and here you can take another brief respite in th park), head back to Fifth Avenue and walk down to 59th Stree At 781 Fifth Avenue you'll find the elegant shop/gallery/mu seum called A la Vieille Russie. This is a New York landmar of sorts, featuring pre-Soviet Russian antiquities, jewels, anc of special interest, wonderful icons. Upstairs on the mezzanin

s a truly extraordinary collection of these icons from medieval
o nineteenth-century Russia. Some have been lent for exhibi-
ions, others are for sale. When seen together they are a vivid
epresentation of Russia's past. A la Vieille Russie is open Mon-
lay–Friday, from 10 to 5; the telephone number is (212) 752-
1727.

Just around the corner at 22 East 60th Street (between Fifth
ind Madison) you'll enjoy the French Institute or Alliance
'rançaise. This branch of the French cultural offices has a nice
exhibition space that houses amusing and sometimes very fine
exhibitions in addition to every sort of French cultural event,
ilm, and concert. We saw a show featuring art and cookies that
vas sponsored by a baking company who commissioned artists
o create works inspired by the cookies! You can phone the
Alliance at (212) 355-6100 for general information or 355-6160
or box office information. The hours are Monday–Thursday,
10–8, and Friday, 10–6.

Finally, at the corner of Park Avenue and 57th Street (460
'ark), you'll find the Korean Cultural Service Gallery. In this
nodern building you must take the elevator up to the 6th floor
o the elegantly appointed gallery to see a stunning series of
Korean exhibitions. Korean art is not as well known as Chinese
or Japanese art in this country, but judging by the exhibitions
"5,000 Years of Korean Art" at the Met recently and the con-
emporary Korean drawings at the Brooklyn Museum), there is
nuch to appreciate. The center can be reached at (212) 759-
1550; hours are Monday–Friday, 9–6.

. . And in Addition

t should be added that this tour of New York's ethnic collec-
ions is not all inclusive. We hope you will also visit—if not
oy foot on this outing, then another way on another day—the
following collections: The National Museum of the American
Indian, at Broadway and 155th Street, (212) 283-2420 and new
location downtown; the Hispanic Society at Broadway and
155th Street, (212) 690-0743; the Chinatown History Museum
at 70 Mulberry Street, (212) 619-4785; the Caribbean Cultural
Center at 408 West 58th Street (212) 307-7420; the Museo del
Barrio at Fifth Avenue and 106th Street, (212) 831-7272; Swiss

Institute at 35 West 67th Street, (212) 496-1759; the Ukrainia
Museum, at 203 Second Avenue and 12th Street, (212) 228
0110; Japan House Gallery, 2nd floor at 333 East 47th Stree
(212) 832-1155; and Galeria Venezuela, on the ground floor c
the consulate general of Venezuela, at 7 East 51st Street, (212
826-1660. India House at 3 East 64th Street has very occasiona
shows. You can call them at (212) 879-7800. Intar Lati
America, 420 West 42nd Street, 2nd floor, is a gallery specializ
ing in art from the Americas, particularly contemporary works
Telephone: (212) 695-6134.

On Staten Island you'll find the Jacques Marchais Center fo
Tibetan Art at 338 Lighthouse Avenue, Richmond. Telephone
(718) 987-3478.

Almost every one of these institutions has extensive series o
lectures, concerts, symposiums, films, language classes, art dis
cussions, and so on. Telephone numbers are listed for each stop
or pick up flyers and listings when you visit. This area also in
cludes many major museums; see Artwalk 6 for hours and ad
dresses.

4

The Unexpected Art Treasures of Audubon Terrace

National Museum of the American Indian, Hispanic Society of America, and the Numismatic Society

HOW TO GET THERE

Subway: #1 (local, marked "242nd Street") train to 157th Street station and walk two blocks south.

Bus: Madison Avenue (uptown) M4 or M5 to 155th Street.

SUGGESTED TIMES

Museum hours are as follows: Museum of the American Indian: Tuesday–Saturday, 10–5; Sunday, 1–5. The Hispanic Society of America: Tuesday–Saturday, 10–4:30; Sunday 1–4. American Numismatic Society: Tuesday–Saturday, 9–4:30; Sunday, 1–4.

Nestled in a partially enclosed block on Broadway, between 155th and 156th streets, the Audubon Terrace Historic District is a welcome respite from its lackluster and drab surroundings. For here, amid an otherwise unattractive section of Upper Manhattan—noisy, congested, commercial, and shabby—lies an unexpected pleasure: a group of three museum/art societies containing rich collections of art and historic treasures that can

easily be seen on one visit. And at the center of this symmetrica
cluster of neoclassical buildings is a grand courtyard domi
nated by a group of dramatic statues by Anna Vaughn Hyat
Huntington. The National Museum of the American India
(moving to a more spacious downtown location), the Hispani
Society of America, and the American Numismatic Society ar
located literally next door to one another, in Beaux Arts contig
uous buildings that were once part of the estate of John Jame
Audubon—hence, the name Audubon Terrace. Archer Milto
Huntington (son of the railroad magnate Collis P. Huntington
founded and financed much of this complex and commissione
his wife's dazzling sculptures. On this Audubon Terrace mu
seum visit, you can literally walk out of one museum door int
the next, until you reach the end of the plaza. There you'll fin
yet another august institution, the American Academy of Art
and Letters, which has occasional exhibits of interest to th
general public, although on a sporadic basis.

Begin your walk at the National Museum of the America
Indian, just at the left as you enter the imposing front gates o
Broadway, if it is still operating at this location. It is schedule
to move a portion of the collection soon to new quarters in th
old U.S. Customs House in lower Manhattan (see page 18 fo
a description).

Your next stop is literally next door, at the Hispanic Societ

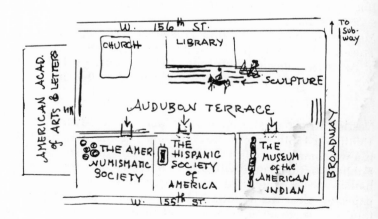

of America. This surprisingly rich collection was created through the efforts of Archer M. Huntington who, from an early age, was fascinated by Iberian culture. He traveled throughout Spain and Portugal, collecting manuscripts, paintings, and decorative artifacts from prehistoric times through the Moorish period, to the present. The results can be enjoyed both in this impressive structure and in the facing building, which houses an extensive reference library (over 100,000 volumes and manuscripts having to do with Spanish and Portuguese history, literature, and art). In 1904 Huntington founded the Hispanic Society of America to promote Spanish culture and arts; the museum was opened in 1908, and the library in 1930.

From the moment you enter the building you feel as though you are in an authentic Renaissance-style Spanish mansion. A gracious central two-story atrium (the main exhibition room) with skylights above is surrounded with smaller, more intimate galleries and niches. Carved woodwork on the walls and staircase, deep-red terra-cotta archways, rustic tile floors, and decorative, brightly colored wall tiles make the interior especially lovely. The rooms are filled with art treasures—a surprising number of fine paintings, drawings, sculpture, as well as decorative arts (rugs, furniture, ceramics, textiles, etc.). The paintings—from the earliest, intensely religious fourteenth-century works of the Catalan, Aragonese, Valencian, and Castillian schools to modern works—include an exceptionally rich collection of masterworks by El Greco, Zurbaran, Velazquez, Ribera, Morales, and Goya. El Greco's early Toledan period is represented in his *Pietà* and *Holy Family*, both deeply spiritual works, as well as in his mystical *St. Jerome*, showing the mesmerized figure with a long, white beard, gazing intently upon Jesus on the Cross. The two fine José de Riberas, *Ecstasy of St. Mary Magdalen* and *St. Paul*, embody the baroque ideals of volume and light. Velazquez, the great master of portrait painting in the court of Philip IV, is represented in several fine works at the Society; in particular his *Little Girl* is certainly one of his best portraits. The Society has several splendid Goyas (five paintings and ten drawings). In the central gallery you'll find the very large painting *Duchess of Alba* (1797), an enigmatic

33

work that has left art historians wondering about her relationship with the painter. Her expression is defiant, and she i flaunting two rings on her fingers, one inscribed with "Goya" and the other with "Alba."

A more recent Spanish artist, Joaquin Sorolla y Bastida, a great friend of Huntington's, is especially well represented. Hi magnificent series of murals called *The Provinces of Spain* (1911)—fourteen canvases colorfully illustrating Spanish life and culture—take up a full room. In addition, the collection owns at least another one hundred works of his (not in view however). Telephone: (212) 690-0743.

And, finally, you come to the American Numismatic Society which contains one of the world's largest coin collections, a well as the premier numismatic library (over 70,000 items). Even though coins are not technically "fine art," they are arti facts of interest to anyone concerned with visual arts and his tory. The 800,000 or so pieces that form this extensive collec tion include everything from Greek, Roman, Byzantine, and Renaissance coins to those of the modern era. Here you can also see metals and decorations from the Middle Ages to the present and an interesting display of money in early America Admission is free, but you must ring the bell for admittance Telephone: (212) 234-3130.

As you walk from one museum to the next, you can't fail to see the dramatic grouping of sculptures in the central courtyard. These impressive works are by Anna Vaughn Hyatt Huntington, especially known for her equestrian statues and animal pieces. In the middle, in heroic stance, is *El Cid Campeador* (1927), a vivid representation of the eleventh-century Spanish knight who valiantly (and successfully) fought the Moors. He is shown on his equally heroic horse, proudly holding a pennant, a strong and victorious expression on his face. (It may amuse our readers to know that according to common lore, the position of horses' hooves in equestrian statues reflects the way in which the rider died. If all four hooves are on the ground, the rider died a natural death. If one hoof is raised, the rider died of his wounds. If two hooves are in the air, the rider was killed in battle.) The four warriors surrounding him in a symmetrical design at the base of the statue's pedestal symbol-ize Spain's Order of Chivalry. Alongside this group are two very interesting high reliefs in the limestone wall, both depicting characters of major importance in Spanish culture: *Don Qui-xote* (1942) and *Boabdil* (1943), the last Moorish king of Gra-nada. Don't miss the wondrous collection of marble and bronze animals in the courtyard as well; they are all animals that are found in Spain: a bronze stag (1929), a doe and fawn (1934), and on a fiercer note, vultures, wild boars, jaguars, and bears (1936). Anna Huntington was clearly drawn to Spanish culture, as was her husband, and she claimed that his interest in all things Spanish "gave me the wish to supplement his work by my sculpture." The concept is grand and the result stunning.

. . . And in Addition
Check with each of the three museums for special events, lec-tures, and demonstrations.
- The National Museum of the American Indian has work-shops and demonstrations featuring such items as bas-ketmaking, story-telling, and featherwork, in addition to per-formances of dance and music.
- The American Academy of Arts and Letters contains a won-derful library that includes first editions, musical scores, and memorabilia of its famous past and present members. (Visits possible by appointment.) You might also check on their annual art exhibition. Telephone: (212) 368-5900. Hours: Tuesday–Sunday, 1–4.
- Trinity Cemetery and Church of the Intercession (a.k.a. Graveyard of American Revolutionary Heroes) at West 153rd to 155th streets, between Amsterdam Avenue and Riverside Drive, open 9–4:30 daily. This landmark cemetery, the largest in Manhattan, dates from 1846 and is the burial site of such prominent people as John James Audubon, John Jacob Astor, Madame Jumel (of Jumel Mansion fame), members of the family of Charles Dickens, and Clement Clark Moore, author of *'Twas the Night Before Christmas*. A quiet, shady, and hilly spot, surrounded by an ornamental iron gate, it is reminiscent of old New York with its rural ambience and unleveled topography. Attached to it is the Church of the

Intercession, a neo-Gothic complex including bell tower, cloister, parish house, and vicarage. Inside the church you'll find a fine wooden ceiling, wood carvings, and an altar decorated with many stones collected from early Christian shrines.

- American Indian Community House Gallery, 708 Broadway, 2nd floor. This gallery exhibits Indian art, with emphasis on contemporary native American works. Recent shows included group exhibits by various tribal artists and the work of a contemporary Iroquois artist. Telephone: (212) 598-0100.

5

Art in the Lincoln Center Area

Music for the Eyes

HOW TO GET THERE
Subway: #1 train to 66th Street and Broadway.
Bus: M5 via Broadway and Riverside Drive, M7 via Broadway and Amsterdam Avenue, M11 via Amsterdam Avenue.
SUGGESTED TIMES
Some of the sites are always accessible; others can only be seen during performance times (with ticket). Tours are held daily from 10 A.M. to 5 P.M. at Lincoln Center.

No art tour of New York can claim to be complete without a visit to the famed Lincoln Center, on the Upper West Side of Manhattan. This magnificent cultural center not only celebrates the performing arts—music, theater, and dance—but the visual arts, too. For within these few blocks of modern buildings and connecting expansive plazas that make up the Lincoln Center complex, you will find—both inside and out—a surprising number of art treasures, from the splendid Chagall murals that can be admired through the arched glass facade of the Metropolitan Opera (as well as up close) to dramatic sculptures, constructions, and mobiles in plazas and interior lobbies. Although most of the works are contemporary in style—in keeping with the modern architecture by such masters as Philip Johnson and

Eero Saarinen—some are more traditional, such as the statue of Dante Alighieri located in the small park in front of Lincoln Center.

And this profusion of art doesn't stop at Lincoln Center. Literally next door, at Fordham University's Columbus Avenue campus, you'll find a variety of outdoor sculptures that can be enjoyed by any passerby. Finally, to end your walk, we'll take you one block south to the Church of St. Paul the Apostle for a change of pace, where you can admire the lovely LaFarge stained glass windows.

While you can see the outdoor sculptures in this artwalk at any time, you'll have to do a bit more planning to see the interior art. Your options are to take a guided tour (Lincoln Center sponsors them daily, 10–5, on a continuing, regular basis; call (212) 875-5350 for information), or to attend a perfor-

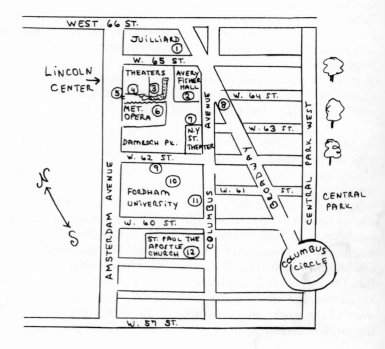

mance of the ballet, opera, or Philharmonic where you will have time during intermission (or before and after the performance) to go from one art piece to the next. Occasionally, one can also peek in on a quiet day, if the security guards don't mind. You'll be walking only about five blocks—from 65th Street and Broadway to 60th—but in those concentrated blocks there is a great deal to see, so allow plenty of time.

Begin your walk at the Juilliard School (1), at Broadway and 65th Street. Outside the building and facing Broadway stands *Three Times Three Interplay* (1971), a 32-foot-high stainless steel sculpture by Yaacov Agam. The three tall zigzag columns of this kinetic work are movable, "a constant becoming," rather than a set statement—perhaps appropriate in front of a school. Inside the building are two works of art worth seeing: Louise Nevelson's wood construction, *Nightsphere-Light* (1969), in the Juilliard Theater lobby, and Antoine Bourdelle's bronze work, *Beethoven à la Colonne* (1901), in the foyer of Alice Tully Hall, around the corner on Broadway.

Cross 65th Street and walk one block south on Columbus until you come to the dramatic main plaza of Lincoln Center, dominated by the three largest halls of the complex: the Metropolitan Opera House in front of you, Avery Fisher Hall on your right, and the New York State Theater on your left. In the center of the vast space is a fountain by Philip Johnson where, on a warm day or evening, you might well see crowds of New Yorkers sitting casually on the edge of the fountain wall and enjoying the passing scene.

Avery Fisher Hall (2), built in 1962, contains a number of impressive sculptures. Looking in through the huge windows from the outside you can already catch a glimpse of Richard Lippold's giant hanging mobile, *Orpheus and Apollo*, which stretches across the entire main foyer. This decorative work is made of 190 strips of shiny metal suspended from the ceiling by steel wires. Apparently (according to a knowledgeable security guard), the sculpture will move slightly in air currents, which adds to its shimmering presence. As you enter the building you'll find two main works in the entrance foyer, both large bronze sculptures—and not well identified, unfortunately. Tucked away on the left is an abstract piece by Dimitri Hadzi called K.458—The Hunt, inspired by a Mozart string quartet; on the right, behind a small café is Seymour Lipton's Archangel (1964), also an interesting abstract composition. On the Grand Promenade level are Antoine Bourdelle's Tragic Mask of Beethoven (also in bronze) and Auguste Rodin's head of Gustav Mahler (1901).

Walk toward the Vivian Beaumont Theater, just behind Avery Fisher Hall, where you'll see the stunning Lincoln Center Reclining Figure (3), by Henry Moore. This massive bronze piece sits in splendor in a large reflecting pool, which is, unfortunately, kept empty most of the time because of a leak. Henry Moore hoped this work would create a welcome contrast to the stark geometric architecture in the background. The rough texture and strong lines are reminiscent of primitive pre-Columbian figures, like many other such reclining figures by Moore. You can sit here and enjoy the work in a tranquil atmosphere. Inside the front lobby of the Beaumont, by the way, is David Smith's Zig IV (1961), an abstract bronze work that can also be seen from the outside through the large windows, if you cannot enter the lobby.

Near the entrance to the New York Public Library at Lincoln Center and adjacent to the Beaumont, is a wonderful Alexander Calder work made in 1965. Called Le Guichet (4), this 14-foot-high painted black steel stabile is like a giant tentacled creature branching out across the plaza. (Calder thought it was too large for this space and had not intended for it to be placed here.) Its name means "ticket window" in French, appropriate enough in an area of performing arts. Enter the Performing Arts Library (5) and take the elevator to the lowest floor. Here you'll find a series of exhibits relating to music, musicians, productions, and artistic subjects.

Return to the street level plaza and walk to the Metropolitan Opera House (6), the centerpiece of Lincoln Center. This impressive building of travertine arches and columns is the best known part of Lincoln Center. It is particularly dramatic when lighted up at night, and the two striking Marc Chagall murals impose themselves even more boldly on the facade of the building. (Note that on sunny mornings the murals are covered with curtains to protect them from excessive light, and thus you will not be able to see them.) If you choose to attend a performance or take a tour, you will have the opportunity to enter the building for a better view of the Chagall works. You can walk up the sweeping staircase to the mezzanine level. On the south wall is *Le Triomphe de la Musique*, a predominantly red mural depicting thirteen different themes in typical Chagall fashion: many figures (singers, ballerinas, musicians) are seen moving, flying overhead, celebrating the joys of music amid scenes from opera, jazz, and folk music. Chagall himself and his wife appear, as does former Metropolitan Opera manager, Rudolph Bing, playfully (and somewhat incongruously) dressed in gypsy garb. The other mural, on the north wall, *Le Sources de la Musique*, is predominantly in yellow tones. Here—if you know your composers—you'll recognize Beethoven, Bach, Wagner, Verdi, as well as such personages as Orpheus and King David. Several operas are depicted and the tree of life is seen floating down the river. These masterpieces are mesmerizing and always fresh; and even if you've seen them many times, you can discover new things in them at each viewing. Among other works to note within the grand opera house are three by the great French sculptor Aristide Maillol: two figures, *Summer* (1910) and *Venus Without Arms* (1920) on the Grand Tier, and one on the level above, *Kneeling Woman: Monument to Debussy* (1931). And you should not miss the amusing gallery on the ground floor (below the main foyer), where you'll see paintings of opera composers and the most famous opera stars who have sung at the Met. If you're an opera buff, you'll recognize such famous singers as Enrico Caruso, Chaliapin, Maria Callas, or Lily Pons, all in costume and in appropriate dramatic pose.

There are many interesting artworks to see in the last of the three main Lincoln Center buildings, the New York State Theater (7). If you're lucky (and not on an official tour), you might find the same cooperative security guard who was so helpful in telling us about the artworks here and letting us see them by day. Otherwise, you can view the following by attending a performance or by taking a tour. One of the first works to see (on the right as you walk in) is Lee Bontecou's *Untitled Relief* (1964), a canvaslike wall construction reminiscent of Native

American designs. On the left side is a gray painting by Jasper Johns, appropriately called *Numbers* (1964), as a series of digits appear in various configurations. On both left and right stair cases are companion pieces by Kobashi—*Dance* on the left and *Ancient Song* on the right. These abstract wall pieces are made of gold leaf on fiberglass. Reuben Nakian's *Leda and the Swan* and Jacques Lipchitz's *Birth of the Muses* (1949) and Francesco Somaini's *Grande Martirion Sanquinante*—all bronze abstractions—are scattered about by the orchestra level. One floor up on the promenade level, are a pair of massive sculptures dominating either end of the hall. Both by Elie Nadelman, *Two Nudes* (1930) and *Two Circus Women* (1931) are of chalklike white Carrara marble, and have become well-known landmarks of New York's sculpture scene.

Now you've seen the major works in the Lincoln Center complex. But our artwalk is not finished. If you walk to the small triangular park (8) at the intersection of Broadway and Columbus (at 63rd Street), you'll find Dante Park and, not surprisingly Dante Alighieri himself on a tall granite pedestal overlooking—perhaps disdainfully—the modern world. Created by Ettore Ximenes in 1921, this work was a commemoration of the six hundredth anniversary of the poet's death, although it's not clear why it was placed in this particular spot. Dante is shown in the typical stance of the poet, with laurel wreath, stern and strong expression, holding a copy of *The Divine Comedy*. In the same triangle is a more modern limestone work by Mark Rabinowitz called "Pygmalion's Dilemma."

From here it's a very short walk to the Lincoln Center campus of Fordham University, which occupies the two blocks between 62nd and 63rd streets and Columbus and Amsterdam avenues. Two large buildings form this complex, with a newly landscaped plaza between them. In front of the Leon Lowenstein Center (9) at 62nd Street, is a gangly, 28-foot-high bronze statue of St. Peter, called *Peter, the Fisherman* (10) (1965), by Frederick Shrady. This emaciated, almost Giacometti-like figure dramatically casts a 14-foot net over a fountain pool. The sculptor felt that this symbolism could also represent the function of the university as an agent of influence in the community, "casting its lines of influence, knowledge, and concern over the metropolis."

Walk up the steps to the refurbished plaza between Lowenstein and Fordham Law School (11). This 2.2 acre space has lately become an inviting location for sculpture. Actually a roof-garden over the library and computer center, it includes contemporary art works, a mini-amphitheater, and wisteria arbors. Fordham has another area of well-kept gardens and sculpture. Walk back down the steps out onto Columbus Avenue and south. On this busy block—where pedestrians rush by, perhaps unaware of the artworks they are passing—you'll walk past a surprising number of contemporary sculptures, all set within the enclosed Fordham Garden (12), amid well-maintained lawns and shrubs—quite a contrast to the plaza above. The sculptures are all well marked and can be easily identified and seen from the sidewalk. *Circle World #2* (1969) by Masami Kodama is reminiscent of work by Noguchi in its simplicity of line and use of material. Made of pink and black granite, the geometric sculpture consists of two halves of a circle that, significantly, do not meet. *City Spirit* (1978) by Lila Katzen is a large stainless steel work that, with its fluid curls and loops, represents the "interlocking of all the elements of the city"—a noble theme in front of an institution of learning. Others include *Peace* (c. 1985) by Leonardo Nieman, which reminded us of a huge bronze flame; *Moses* by Larry Mohr, another geometric bronze abstraction; and *Simple Justice* by Vivienne Thaul Wechter, a mainly stainless steel and brass tripodlike form with a circle on top. The only figurative work is *Mother Playing* (1961) by Chaim Gross. This bronze statue depicts a reclining mother with her small daughter precariously perched on her knees in a sort of balancing act. Gross was intrigued by figures in action, such as acrobats and dancers, as well as the mother-daughter theme.

At the end of the block, on Columbus and 60th, is the imposing Church of St. Paul the Apostle. The massive basilica, late Gothic in style, was built in 1885 by the architect James O'Rourke and has recently undergone a wonderful restoration. The talents and energies of some of the eminent artists and architects of the day were used, such as John LaFarge, Augustus Saint-Gaudens, and Stanford White. Their legacies are still in evidence today, and the church is full of wonderful surprises.

43

As you walk in, notice the unusual mosaic-like pattern on the floor at the entrance. Made of different types and colors of marble, it represents the buildings of the Acropolis, which the Apostle Paul saw before him from the Hill of Mars. The ceiling, a deep blue, is an artistic interpretation of the constellation on the very day the church was dedicated. (It was researched methodically and precisely by the Paulist Father George M. Searle, who was also a competent astronomer.) As you walk around the church you'll see several murals—some unfortunately very dark—including the one that is high on the south wall of the sanctuary. Called *The Angel of the Moon*, it is by John LaFarge, who also designed the columns and the narthex. The altar at the far end of the south side is by Philip Martiny. But the stained glass windows are especially worthy of your attention. The blue windows on the end behind the altar, by LaFarge, are remarkable in their brightness and luminosity. And one of our favorites is another LaFarge creation, the great East Window over the main entrance. We recommend you pick up the small free pamphlet guide inside the book shop at the entrance, which will point out every art piece in the church, since nothing is marked on site.

... And in Addition

Just beyond Lincoln Center at 66th Street and Amsterdam Avenue you'll find the Sculpture Memorial to Martin Luther King, Jr. (1973), by William Tarr. This massive cube resembles a giant printer's block bearing numbers and letters relating to King's life.

6

New York's Magnificent Museum Mile

HOW TO GET THERE
Subway: #4, 5, or 6 train to 86th Street and Lexington Avenue; walk west to Fifth Avenue and south to 84th Street.
Bus: Fifth or Madison Avenue M1, 2, 3, or 4.
SUGGESTED TIMES
Avoid Mondays (when most museums are closed); free access to most museums on Tuesday evenings, but often crowded then. Some museums not open Saturday or Sunday mornings, so check each individual listing.

Needless to say, any New York art lover—or visitor to the city—won't want to miss the Museum Mile. Here on upper Fifth Avenue are some of the world's greatest museums, all within walking distance of one another. And though we doubt anyone would want to include so much art on one walk, the following is a listing of the offerings. (Don't forget that each of these museums has changing exhibitions in addition to their permanent collections.) Our suggestion on how best to enjoy this embarrassment of riches is to plan a single day or two at the Metropolitan (if you see all of it, you'll be covering a good mile indoors). Depending on your particular interests, you might want to spend longer at various of the collections listed here, but if you are a marathon museumgoer, you could conceivably take all of them in. You will have the pleasures of

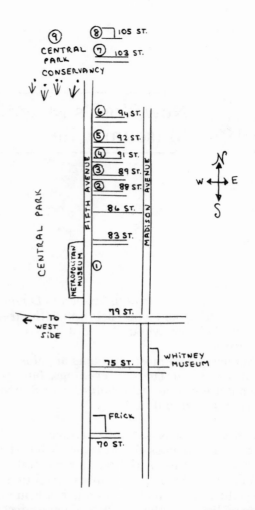

Central Park available to you all along your artwalk, both for tired feet and a respite from looking at everything from medieval icons to modern photography.

Begin your walk at 81st Street and Fifth Avenue, where you'll find one of the world's most illustrious museums of art: the Metropolitan (1). But before you enter, note an outdoor artistic addition to the museum at Fifth Avenue and 80th Street. Isamu Noguchi's creative presence can be seen throughout the city;

here you'll see his 1979 *Unidentified Object*, an abstract basalt form set on a pedestal among the trees.

The giant and comprehensive museum includes one of the great collections of European paintings (some two thousand), contemporary art, furniture, musical instruments, medieval manuscripts and statuary, costumes, Asian art, African sculpture, Egyptian art including the well-known Temple of Dendur, drawings, American paintings, Roman and Greek statuary and vases, medieval and Renaissance armor, and much, much more. There are always several shows, either visiting from abroad or drawn from the thousands of items that even the colossal museum cannot show regularly. Don't miss the lovely roof garden with its large outdoor sculptures and the Charles Engelhard Court, which also contains sculpture. You'll find many different types of guidebooks to the collections, as well as docents available, and, if you prefer, guided tours with earphones. The Museum has lectures and a wide variety of educational events, including many for children. The Met asks for a contribution. Hours: Tuesday 10–8:45; Wednesday–Saturday, 10–4:45; Sunday 11–6. Telephone: (212) 879-5500.

Our next stop is at 88th Street and Fifth Avenue, Frank Lloyd Wright's extraordinary circular building housing the Solomon R. Guggenheim Museum (2). Guggenheim, a great industrialist and philanthropist, began collecting paintings before World War I. In addition to buying old masters, he had a fine eye for early modern art. He commissioned Wright to build a museum to display his collection; the fascinating Wright museum building opened in 1959. Its cylindrical form is in six stories, and you'll walk up (or down, if you prefer to take the elevator to the top) a gentle ramp round and round the interior. The circular exhibition space is now—since its recent renovation—used for changing shows of contemporary art, while their new gallery space adjacent to the ramp on each floor houses some of their amazing collection of Kandinskys (there are about 180 in the collection), Mondrians, Mirós, Braques, and many of the other giants of modern art. The Guggenheim's exhibitions are almost always top quality, and the experience of walking through Wright's building is not to be missed. (Even the curving lunch counter is a Wright design.) The Guggenheim has also opened

47

a new branch in Soho, which is described in Walk 13. Hours at the main branch: Sunday–Wednesday, 10–6; Friday and Saturday, 10–8; closed Thursday. Telephone: (212) 423-3500.

The National Academy of Design (3) is just north of the Guggenheim, at 1083 Fifth Avenue at 89th Street. While not strictly speaking a museum, it does have a series of exhibitions. Founded in 1825 for the purpose of showing American art, the Academy has both juried shows and a permanent collection. While the taste in painting may be considered conservative, we have particularly enjoyed their watercolor shows. The emphasis is on figure drawing here, and on architecture and representational painting. Art classes are offered as well. The Academy is open Wednesday–Sunday, 12–5; free Friday, 5–8. Telephone: (212) 369-4880.

From here walk north to 91st Street, where you'll find the entrance to the Cooper-Hewitt Museum (4) just around the corner at 2 East 91st Street. This is the National Museum of Design of the Smithsonian Institution. It exhibits an eclectic collection of items. It's great fun to wander through the rooms of the former Andrew Carnegie mansion and examine such things as advertising art of the nineteenth century, glass and ceramic figurines, textiles, salad bowls, architectural drawings—or whatever objects the curatorial staff has decided would make a historically and artistically interesting exhibition. Recent shows have included nineteenth-century jewelry and watercolors from the Vatican collection. One of our favorites was a show of Victorian wallpapers. The Cooper-Hewitt also has a full agenda of lectures and other programs. You'll find the museum open Tuesday, 10–9; Wednesday–Saturday, 10–5; Sunday, noon–5. There is a fee except on Tuesday after 5. Telephone: (212) 860-6868.

Only one block north is the newly and magnificently renovated Jewish Museum (5) between 92nd and 93rd streets on Fifth Avenue. This museum, which is devoted to Jewish art and history from ancient to modern times, also presents some of the city's best and most timely changing exhibitions. The permanent collection features hundreds of ceremonial items, decorative arts, photographs, paintings, prints, and manuscript illuminations from medieval Jewish communities. Major exhibitions of contemporary artists, as well as historical shows—an especially interesting one was devoted to the Dreyfus case—make this a must-see museum. The admission fee entitles you to attend films, lectures, and classes. Tuesdays from 5 to 8 are free. The museum hours are Sunday, Monday, Wednesday, Thursday, 11–5:45; Tuesday, 11–8 (free 5–8). Closed Saturday. Telephone: (212) 423-3200.

The old Willard Straight House at the corner of Fifth Avenue and 94th Street is the new home of the International Center of Photography (6). This major research source for the history of photography was founded by Cornell Capa as an archive and exhibition space. Changing shows are accompanied by a terrific series of lectures, classes, seminars, and other events relating to the history and practice of photography. (Do you realize that photography more or less as we know it is only about 140 years old?) Recent exhibitions have included "I Dream a World: Portraits of Black Women Who Changed America" by Brian Lanker and "The Naked Nude: An Installation by Dorit Cypsis." The hours are Wednesday–Sunday, 11–6; Tuesday, 11–8. Telephone: (212) 860-1777.

A brisk walk north to 103rd Street will bring you to the Museum of the City of New York (7). This collection is a must with children, who will find all kinds of things to love, from antique fire engines to doll houses that can only be described as sensational. There are also many fine paintings, including portraits of important New Yorkers, dioramas of the early days of the city, wonderful costumes of "olde New Yorke," memorabilia of all kinds, toys, theater programs, prints, and—in general—a retrospective look at the city as it was long ago. There are occasional events such as puppet shows. The museum has the kind of collection that makes you go back time and again, with or without your children. The hours are Wednesday–Saturday, 10–5, and Sunday, 1–5. They are always free. Telephone: (212) 534-1672.

Our final museum stop is the inviting building at 1230 Fifth Avenue, at 105th Street: El Museo del Barrio (8). The fine brick building houses a collection devoted to Hispanic culture. Here you'll find an extensive collection of prints, paintings, and arti-facts of Puerto Rico and Latin America. There are exciting things to see, including works by contemporary Latin American painters and sculptors. At the southern end of the building you'll find the Taller Galeria Boricua, or Puerto Rican Work-shop. This is the neighborhood's artists' workshop, an exhibi-tion space for the community's creative artists. Since 1970 the Taller space has provided studios and an exhibition gallery for a number of artists; the Hispanic community is well repre-sented in the shows held here. The Museo also holds a series of lectures and other cultural events relating to Hispanic art and music that are of interest to the general public. Hours are Tuesday–Friday, 10:30–4:30, and Saturday and Sunday, 11–4. There is a fee. Telephone: (212) 831-7272.

Your last stop is not a museum in the traditional sense, but it, too, will provide you with color and form. Cross the street and enter the *Central Park Conservancy* (9) between 104th and 105th streets, where you will find yourself in a garden of great elegance and beauty; it was a gift from the Vanderbilt family a century ago. Classically styled with columns, walkways, areas of lawn, flowerbeds, two fountains, and stairways, this per-fectly maintained garden is a delight. You can stroll through its elegant paths, rest among the vine-colored trellises, admire the changing flower garden. Truly an oasis in the bustle and cement of the city, the Conservancy is a rare, beautifully kept spot to end your Museum Mile walk.

One of the city's favorite fountains, the *Untermeyer Fountain* with its three dancing maidens, is a centerpiece of the Conser-vatory Garden to the north. Made some time before 1910, the fountain has three whimsical bronze figures dancing around its single jet of water. It was made by Walter Schott, a German sculptor and portraitist. Its light, airy design is a charming addi-tion to the harmonious spaces and bright colors of the garden. Also in the Conservatory Garden to the south is a memorial to the author of *The Secret Garden* and *Little Lord Fauntleroy*, the *Francis Hodgson Burnett Memorial Fountain*. The sculpture surrounding the fountain consists of a small boy playing the flute while a young girl holding a seashell listens. A birdbath at her feet spills into a small pool. The fountain was created by Bessie Potter Vonnoh between 1926 and 1937 when it was given to the Garden. Hours are daily before dusk. Admission is free. Central Park is not recommended after 5 P.M., but don't miss this garden during the day.

. . And in Addition

The Frick Museum, 1 East 70th Street and Fifth Avenue. Once the grand home of Henry Clay Frick, today it houses a fabulous collection of European art from the fourteenth through the nineteenth centuries set in exquisite surroundings. Fee. Open Tuesday through Saturday, 10–6, and Sunday, 1–6. Telephone: (212) 288-0700.

The Whitney Museum of American Art, Madison at 75th Street. Contains one of the largest collections of contemporary American art in the world. Changing exhibits including the latest in avant-garde film, video, and installations. Fee. Open Wednesday, Friday, Saturday, 11–6; Thursday, 1–8, free from 6–8; and Sunday, 11–6. Telephone: (212) 570-3676.

And while you are in the neighborhood, Louise Nevelson's *Night Presence IV*, made in 1972, is one of the artist's earliest outdoor metal works. You'll find its complex collection of knobs, bird shapes, ribbon forms, and other abstract designs in the center median of Park Avenue at 92nd Street.

51

7

Lower Fifth Avenue and Washington Square Area Walk

HOW TO GET THERE
Subway: A, B, D, E, or F trains to West 4th Street, or RR trai.
to 8th Street and Broadway.
Bus: Fifth Avenue bus downtown (M1, M2).
SUGGESTED TIMES
We recommend weekdays after 10 A.M., when galleries, muse
ums, and art schools are more likely to be open; check individ
ual listings.

This is a walk that encompasses lower Fifth Avenue and th
Washington Square area, a historic district with several univer
sity campuses, as well as a smaller art school, that provid
unusual settings for artworks of major importance. A significan
private collection, two off-beat galleries, and two histori
churches add to the interest of this walk. Sculpture lovers
particularly, will find much to excite them, as will those wh
especially admire the most contemporary art. But on this tou
you'll find everything from nineteenth-century stained glas
windows to the famed, fabulously decorated Fabergé Easte
eggs.
   Our first stop is the Grey Gallery (1), 33 Washington Squar
East, New York University's fairly recent, and very elegant

rofessional gallery. A series of exhibitions—most with un-
sual and original themes—is open to the public (small dona-
ion requested, but not required). The modern, well-designed
allery makes you wish more museums and art spaces had its
imensions, lighting, and size, for it is not too large, and each
tem is well documented. The unusual themes of recent shows
ncluded handwritten and illustrated letters by famous persons,
etrospectives by Sonia Delaunay and David Hockney, contem-

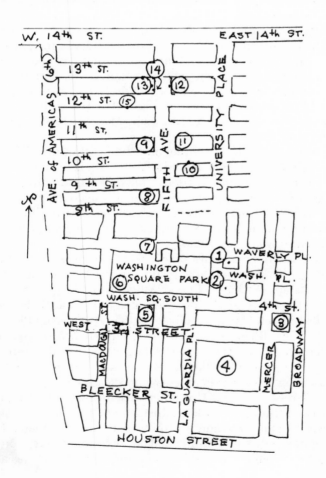

porary Indian art, and caricatures from the French Revolution One of their five or so exhibitions per year is devoted to work from their own collection, which includes more than four thou sand items. Incidentally, don't miss the display windows which present art in a striking, nontraditional way. For further information, call (212) 998-6780.

Walk next door to 80 Washington Square East Galleries (2 another NYU gallery open to the public. On either side of the outside front door you'll find two charming terra-cotta medal lions representing the *Muses of Art and Music*. As the plaque beneath them indicate, they are late nineteenth-century anony mous works donated to the university. Inside, in the attractive well-lighted rooms, you will more often than not see works by students (mostly graduate) or faculty, although there is a well regarded annual "small works" exhibit that attracts partici pants from all over the world. Note that the gallery is ope Tuesday–Saturday, after 11 A.M. Call (212) 998-5747 for further information.

Continue south to 4th Street and the heart of the NYU cam pus. At Gould Plaza, just outside Tisch Hall, is Jean Arp's stain less steel construction called *Threshold Configuration* (3 Twenty-nine years ago it was given to the Metropolitan Mu seum, which loaned it recently to NYU. The statue, a large and rather ambiguous form, is reminiscent of the shapes found in Arp's paintings of the 1950s.

You'll find the most stunning of NYU's artworks behind these buildings, in the open space surrounded by the university' housing: Pablo Picasso's *Bust of Sylvette* (4). To get there, wal through the university's courtyard area to LaGuardia Place and West 3rd Street. One more block south on LaGuardia Place wil bring you to Bleecker Street. On your left before you reach Bleecker you'll see the high-rise buildings of NYU's housing and in the center court the massive Picasso sculpture. Sylvett was a young French woman of whom Picasso made some eigh teen different portraits. This colossal sculpture, a reproduction of Picasso's 2-foot-high 1954 cubistic work, combines a simulta neously frontal view and a profile of a young woman's head neck, pony tail, and shoulders. The monumental version wa executed in 1967 by a Norwegian artist named Carl Nesjar; it

60 tons are sandblasted concrete and black basalt. In conjunction with I. M. Pei, the architect, Nesjar and Picasso worked together to make this giant artistic landmark a centerpiece of NYU's campus, though it stands in what seems to be somewhat isolated splendor in a big, empty space.

Walk north on LaGuardia Place to Washington Square South and walk to your left one block. Facing the park is Judson Memorial Church (5), an amber-colored Italian Romanesque-style building with a square bell tower. This turn-of-the-century landmark building was designed by Stanford White (like so many others in New York) and features symmetrical rows of rounded arches and graceful mouldings. Inside, in the auditorium, past bulletin boards filled with information of social concerns and upcoming events, you'll find an imposing John La-Farge creation, a large stained glass window, that is obviously best seen on a sunny day. LaFarge's stained glass, for which he used his knowledge of the techniques of the Renaissance tradition, was influential in bringing a revival of this art to America. He was also noted as a painter and muralist: later in this walk you will see one of his murals. While in the church also note the marble relief on the south wall, based on designs by the famous American sculptor, Augustus Saint-Gaudens.

As you leave Judson Memorial Church, cross over to Washington Square Park (6), the historic and beautiful (if frequently very crowded) oasis of downtown New York. Enter the Square just opposite and turn around. Behind you on the outside (north) front of Loeb Student Center (one of NYU's buildings facing the park), you'll see an aluminum sculpture by Reuben Nakian, which was made in 1959–60. NYU's first contemporary commission, Nakian's work is a collection of aluminum shapes in three groups set against the building's brick facade. Although generally abstract, these forms suggest flying objects or birds; Nakian is said to have remarked that they were a metaphor for the "University and the freeing of the spirit."

If you next turn slightly to your left, you'll see a large and very strange tree, now carved by unknown artists into a somewhat grotesque totem pole. This was once "the Hanging Tree," from which unfortunate New Yorkers ended their days.

On the eastern side of the Square and in a completely different mood stands the peculiar statue of Giuseppe Garibaldi
sword in hand. Made by Giovanni Turini in 1888, it purport-
edly took only three weeks to sculpt. It is indeed an awkward
curiously unheroic figure for its time and its most romantic
subject—the great revolutionary Italian general of the Risorgi-
mento.

There is one other statue in the park, an elaborately mounted
bust by John Quincy Adams Ward of Alexander Holley, ar
engineer of Bessemer steel fame.

But the park itself deserves to be admired as a work of art ir
its own right, with its geometric patterned paths, its circular
sunken sitting areas, its fine trees and shrubbery. And on week
ends and nice days you'll find frequent art shows and performances; occasionally you might see an artist or film maker a
work.

Of course Washington Square Arch (7) is the central landmark of Washington Square. Walk under it, and then stand
back to admire it. While the Square may be the heart and sou
of Greenwich Village, the Arch is its gateway and symbol.

The Arch was the inspiration of Stanford White, who de
signed it in 1892; it also represents the works of several notable
sculptors. The winged figures above the circular interior arch
are by Frederick MacMonnies. On the right side of the Arch
you'll find George Washington in front of two figures represent
ing "Wisdom" and "Justice"; this work is by A. Stirling Calder
(mobile maker Alexander's father and a noted artist). On the lef
column you'll find Hermon MacNeil's sculpture of Washington
this time dressed as the General. The other parts of the Arch
bear traditional designs suitable to its grand proportion and
imposing setting at the entrance to the Square.

Walk north up Fifth Avenue to 8th Street and turn left to 8
West 8th Street. One of the joys of wandering around in this
part of Manhattan is discovering relatively little known art gal
leries, artists' studios, or art centers. In our meanderings we
visited The New York Studio School of Drawing, Painting, and
Sculpture (8). This landmark building has quite an intriguing
history. Originally a stable, it was remodeled by the sculptor
art lover and patron Gertrude Vanderbilt Whitney to become

her personal studio and gallery. It then evolved into The Studio Club, a place where she arranged for artists to meet and exhibit their works. From 1931 to 1949 the building housed the collection of the Whitney Museum of American Art before it was permanently moved to its present uptown location. Finally, in 1964 the building became the home of The Studio School.

The school calls itself "an alternative to the prevailing trend in American art schools" and, as such, is appealingly uncommercial. The atmosphere is serious, industrious, vibrant, yet unpretentious and friendly. The pleasant smell of fresh paint is noticeable as you wander through, as are other signs of works in progress. Although visitors don't normally have access to the working studios, they are invited to stroll through the attractive, airy galleries where one-person or group shows are regularly on display. These often (but not always) feature works by faculty and students. We liked the intimacy and charm of the school and recommend it as a different place in which to view sculpture, painting, or drawing in a creative environment. Telephone: (212) 673-6466.

Return to Fifth Avenue and walk to the corner of 10th Street. You are now standing in front of the Church of the Ascension (9) a Gothic Revival Episcopal church and the oldest on Fifth Avenue (1840). The church has surprisingly short visiting hours (noon–2 P.M. and 5–7 P.M. daily), so plan your time accordingly. Designed by Richard Upjohn and later redecorated from plans drawn up by Stanford White, it contains two artworks certainly worth seeing: a large, dark, muted mural, *The Ascension*, by John LaFarge, and two facing sculptured angels over the main altar, by Louis Saint-Gaudens, or his more famous brother, Augustus. (The church isn't sure which.) We were shown around by the enthusiastic and obliging rector, who invited us to hear in rehearsal the fine organ and to admire the acoustics. (The church sponsors many fine concerts.)

Cross Fifth Avenue and walk to the attractive brownstone at 16 East 10th Street, home of The Pen and Brush (10). This active organization for women artists and writers regularly sponsors painting and sculpture exhibits. The shows, which are judged by a jury of prominent artists, include member artists as well as men and women artists from the outside. You'll enjoy ambling

57

through the high-ceilinged Victorian rooms; the atmosphere i
friendly and comfortable, almost like being in someone's home
There is no entrance fee and gallery hours are 1–6 daily excep
Monday. Call (212) 475-3669 for further information.

Go around the corner to another nice brownstone at 47 Fift
Avenue, occupied by the Salmagundi Club (11), the oldest pri
vate club for artists in the nation. It has been at this locatio
since 1917, and the interior has the ambience of old-time club
biness (with the resident art much the same). The bottom two
floors are open free to the public daily including Sundays
when you can view the dimly lit living room, dining room, an
hall with its unidentified portraits and landscapes, and the two
imposing exhibition galleries. The latter house a series of larg
group exhibitions. While the Salmagundi Club was once hom
to many of America's most distinguished artists, its rosters now
include amateurs as well as professionals; the club sponsors
number of activities for art lovers, including lectures, demon
strations, and auctions, which might be considered somewha
conservative by today's tastes or standards. It is a nice stop o
your artwalk for a brief reminder of another time and taste.

Two blocks north, at 65 Fifth Avenue between 12th and 13t
streets, is one of the two buildings of The New School for Socia
Research (12). Since its founding, this innovative urban institu
tion has primarily fostered the social sciences, but has als
been a center for the arts. This bustling building houses a mu
seum's worth of contemporary art (as does its other building
which we will visit later on), some of it unidentified. As yo
walk through the front doors along with the rushing student
and faculty, you have only steps to go before you see som
striking modern constructions and paintings. Don't miss work
in the main lobby, including two figures by Chaim Gross;
work by Christian Eckhart consisting of laminated plasti
pieces arranged randomly; a steel hippo by J. Kearney; *Mutc
tion*, made of chromium and steel by Joseph Kurhajec; an
Robert Anderson's *Big Sam*, a large wood construction, amon
others. In the reading room, also open to the public, is a Marc
Gastini work made of bits of glass, as well as a number of print
by Roy Lichtenstein and Jack Youngerman. Around the corne
from the library entrance (still within the lobby) you'll fin

Mark Stahl's *All That Heaven Allows*, a construction made of rock and toothbrushes. If you take the escalator upstairs to the 2nd floor lobby, and walk around the hallway, you'll find a variety of other very miscellaneous artworks, some permanent, others on loan, and few identified. Among the works there when we visited were a major construction of a farm combine with real corn by Will Mentor, a wax beehive construction by Garnett Puett, some nice old-fashioned photos by Berenice Abbott, and, believe it or not, among this contemporary miscellany, a late Renaissance painting of St. Andrew praying, attributed to Carlo Dolci, properly installed but dimly lit along a hallway wall. A visit to this building of The New School will certainly interest you in one way or another, though the lack of identification—of even the artists' names—can be frustrating. But don't give up. If you really want to identify a particular work, you can contact the art office of the school at (212) 229-5600, and they might be able to help, if you describe the work to them.

Cross Fifth Avenue (again!) at 13th Street and walk to 2 West 13th, the rather modest entrance to the Exhibition Center of the Parsons School of Design (13), now a division of The New School. The monthly shows in this bright, elegant, and spacious gallery display works by the most promising students and alumni. Around the corner, at 66 Fifth Avenue, is the other attractive gallery operated by Parsons. Walk through the doors of the school's main entrance to the space directly in front of you. The quality of exhibits in this more intimate place is of particularly high caliber, featuring shows by faculty members as well as others within the Parsons community. There is no entrance fee at either gallery, and hours are 9–6, Monday–Saturday, and 9–9 Wednesday. Call (212) 229-8900 for information on shows.

Walk next door to 62 Fifth Avenue, the stately home of the Forbes Magazine Galleries (14). This unusual museum, which exhibits the private collection of late publisher Malcolm Forbes, is much more vast and varied than you might imagine. Forbes's eclectic tastes are revealed in this amazing potpourri of objects: from ship models, to trophies, to toy soldiers, to presidential papers, to fine works of art, and finally to the famed

Fabergé Collection. Visiting the galleries requires some plan
ning. They are open Tuesday–Saturday from 10–4 (except lega
holidays), but Thursdays are reserved for group tours, and entr
is limited to 900 persons a day on a first-come, first-serve
basis. These limitations make viewing the collections un
crowded and pleasant. There is no admission fee. Telephone
(212) 206-5548.

The first gallery features quite a collection of ship model
(including reproductions of yachts owned by the Forbes fam
ily), from pleasure crafts to military vessels of the 1870s to th
1950s. Nostalgia buffs might enjoy seeing the panels on displa
from the ocean liner Normandie. In the "On Parade" gallery
which comes next, hundreds of toy soldiers are exhibited i
dioramas of various periods. The Trophies room is just tha
almost 200 of them, in all sizes and shapes—not necessaril
"art," but certainly a curiosity. In the next gallery you can se
some of the literally thousands of American historical docu
ments that are part of this vast collection. One of the mo
engaging displays to us was that of the four miniature roo
constructions taken from late eighteenth- and early nineteenth
century American history: Washington's headquarters in Vi
ginia, John Adams' law offices, Jefferson's bedroom, and Grant
dining room. Note the incredible detail in these rooms—fro
the flowered chintz curtains, to the moldings on the walls, t
the faithful rendition of furniture styles.

But most visitors are especially thrilled with the unique Fab
ergé Collection: particularly the twelve imperial Easter egg
made by the House of Fabergé for the last two czars of Russi
These precious eggs, which were presented by the czar to mem
bers of his family on various Easter occasions, are full of fu
and surprises: a mechanical bird leaps out flapping its wing
an egg yolk is removed to reveal a hen, a replica of the coron
tion coach suddenly appears, or family portraits rise up whe
a mechanical device is activated. The collection also include
the extraordinarily luxurious objects Forbes was able
gather—from the whimsical music boxes to the most elabora
of jewels and decorated objects in unusual shapes and configu
rations. All of these intricate objects are more than dazzling 1
our modern eye.

Finally, you can wander into the picture gallery, where a miscellany of American paintings and photographs is exhibited on a rotating basis. Here you have the opportunity to experience the entire gamut of American art (or one family's views as to what is representative of American art). You might see such masters as Thomas Hart Benton, Milton Avery, Thomas Eakins, Gilbert Stuart, John Singer Sargent, and Reginald Marsh, to name a few. Contemporary works include those of Andy Warhol, Jack Nelson, Loren Munk, and an interesting construction by Nancy Grossman.

Around the corner, at 66 West 12th Street (between Fifth and Sixth avenues), is the main building of The New School (15). Its somewhat unprepossessing 1930s modern facade belies the surprising wealth of artistic works inside, unbeknown to many a passing New Yorker.

The most impressive of these is surely the spectacular five-wall fresco by the Mexican master muralist, José Clemente Orozco, which he painted in the 1930s. Newly restored after years of neglect, these brilliantly bold images depict the broad themes of revolution, oppression, and freedom. You can distinguish the faces of Gandhi, Lenin, and Stalin amid enthusiastic crowds of workers, soldiers, and rallying citizens. The idealistic values represented in these panels reflected Orozco's sympathetic feelings for Leftist politics and for the New School, which was at that time a haven for intellectuals fleeing Nazi Germany. The work was commissioned by Alma Reed, partly as a tribute to her fiancé who was assassinated during the Mexican revolution.) The panels incorporate the richness of Mexican folk art with their bright colors and geometric shapes, as well as the simplicity and starkness of Italian Renaissance art (which Orozco had also studied).

Amazingly, this 300-square-foot work is more or less hidden away in an upstairs classroom—room 712—on the 7th floor (once the cafeteria). To view the panels you must first inquire in the lobby at the entrance of the building, or check the nearby bulletin board to find out whether a class is in session or whether the room is free.

After seeing the murals, you might wish to make several stops on your way back down to the main floor, to see assorted works of art displayed on walls outside of classrooms or in hallways (Note that many of these works are moved around periodically which makes it more interesting for the students and faculty who pass by them regularly.) On the 5th floor down some steps from the elevator you'll see a number of current works that The New School has either purchased or received as gifts. These are mostly hanging on corridor walls outside the classrooms where the light is not always the best, but at least they are displayed. On the fourth floor are a series of lithographs by James Rosenquist. You'll also see a glass-enclosed bridge connecting two sections of the building; it provides a choice space for smaller visiting exhibitions. From this passageway you have a fine view of the sculpture garden on the ground floor below as well as adjacent rooftops. Take the elevator to the third floor On the wall facing you are three aquatints by Sol Lewitt, *Untitled* (1987). Beneath them is a wonderfully shaped bronze sculpture by Isamu Noguchi, *Jocasta's Throne* (1945). This whimsical abstraction of a Shaker rocking chair was used in Martha Graham's first production of *Appalachian Spring*. To the right of these works is another interesting wall piece, Carol Hepper's *Comet* (1988). This large, basketlike sculpture is made of wood, wire, and nails.

On the ground floor of The New School are several works of art worth seeing. Before you go through the glass doors to the sculpture garden, look around you in the lobby. Nearest the doors hangs a bold, vertical sculpture by Petah Coyne, *Untitled* (1987–88). Made of wood, barbed wire, hay, mud, rope, and cotton cloth, it is a sober yet striking work. On the wall next to it, you'll see an ocher and brown aquatint, *Untitled*, by Julian Schnabel. And on the wall facing the glass doors is a large striking geometric mosaic mural also called *Untitled*, by Gonzalo Gonseca.

Walk through the glass doors to the sculpture garden in the courtyard. Immediately on your left is an abstract wall piece in stainless steel, *Untitled* (1977), by Guy Miller. Unfortunately the remaining sculptures in the garden are not identified. In front of you, somewhat to the right is Noguchi's *Garden Elements*, two medium-sized granite structures punctuated by geometric holes. To your right is Chaim Gross's *Acrobats—Family of* Five, a vertical bronze column made up of intertwined human figures. One of our favorite sculptures is *The Little Dinner* (1968) by William King. This delightful rendition of two couples seated at the dinner table is made of cast aluminum.

As you leave The New School building via the regular doors (not the revolving doors) note on your left a curious, somewhat mysterious enshrouded figure. This is Muriel Castanis's fiberglass *Clothed Figure*. It is easily overlooked if you don't know it is there. The New School is open daily Monday–Saturday, from 8:30 A.M. to 10 P.M. Except for the Orozco murals, all other works of art can be seen during school hours. For art information telephone (212) 741-5955.

. . . And in Addition

- New School for Social Research: lectures, special events. Telephone: (212) 229-5600.
- Grey Art Gallery and Study Center: lectures, symposia, seminars, and other special events in connection with each show. Telephone: (212) 998-6780.
- Salmagundi Club: auctions, demonstrations, and lectures. Telephone: (212) 255-7740.
- New York Studio School: art lectures, usually on Wednesday evenings. Telephone: (212) 673-6466.
- A George Segal sculpture has been placed in Christopher Park at Seventh Avenue South and Christopher Street. It depicts, in Segal's ultra realistic style, two couples—one male, one female.

8

Americana

Historic Houses, Gardens,
and Collections Around the City

HOW TO GET THERE
Subway: To Museum of City of New York, #6 train to 103rd
Street and Lexington Avenue; walk three blocks west. To Mor-
ris-Jumel Mansion, B train to 163rd Street and Amsterdam Ave-
nue; walk two blocks south on Amsterdam and turn left. To
Abigail Adams Smith Museum, Q train to Lexington Avenue
and 63rd Street. For New-York Historical Society, C train to
81st Street and Central Park West; walk south on Central Park
West.
Bus: To Museum of City of New York, take 1, 2, 3, or 4. To
Morris-Jumel Mansion, take bus #2. To Abigail Adams Smith
Museum, take bus #5 or crosstown #66. To New-York Histori-
cal Society take #10 bus on Central Park West.
SUGGESTED TIMES
See individual listings for hours.

New York is such a changing and up-to-date city that it is easy
to forget that some corners here and there have been preserved
from earlier times. Recent aggressive landmarking of buildings
and entire neighborhoods is helping in the effort to protect
some of the city's architectural past. And there are many worthwhile collections, historic houses, and even reconstructed old-
fashioned gardens that will give you a taste of the old days in

the city. While you can't walk quickly from one of these spots to the next, each is well worth visiting for a composite portrait of pre-twentieth-century New York. If you're a history buff and enjoy Colonial and Federal period art and artifacts or the creations of America's folk artists, be sure to visit the sites specializing in Americana and New York's history that are listed in the pages that follow. (There are many other historic houses in the five boroughs, but we have chosen these as among the most interesting to garden and fine arts enthusiasts.)

If you wish to be authentically historical in your hop, skip, and jump through New York's history, you should begin with the National Museum of the American Indian on Upper Broadway at Audubon Terrace and 155th Street or at its new building downtown. (See Artwalk 2 for a description of the museum.)

Perhaps for an overview of the city's history (through art, costumes, and numerous other objects of interest), you will next want to visit the wonderful Museum of the City of New York on Fifth Avenue at 103rd Street. Here you'll take a quick time-trip through the early days of Old Amsterdam, the Colonial period, the Federal era of growing importance in the city, midcentury's mores, and the gay nineties. Portraits, costumed figures, landscapes, and numerous examples of art and artifacts make this a wonderfully appealing and attractive collection. (Children will love this museum, with its outstanding examples of toys, fire engines, and doll houses.) In addition to its permanent collection, the museum features a variety of shows relating to the city's early life. The museum is open Tuesday through Saturday, 10–5, and Sunday, 1–5. Admission is free. Telephone (212) 534-1672 for current exhibitions.

Your next detour—and not one to be missed by the Americana enthusiast and history buff—is the Morris-Jumel Mansion, at 160th Street and Edgecombe Avenue, in upper Manhattan. The borough's oldest private dwelling (1765), it is its only surviving pre-Revolutionary house, and an important New York landmark and museum. Once a grand mansion within 130 acres stretching from one river to the other, its territory has inevitably been reduced to a small park, surrounded by apartment houses, as well as a charming street of well-preserved historic townhouses. The lovely colonial house (now in need of some exterior restoration) has undergone many incarnations through the years, the evidence of which can be seen inside. Originally the summer house of a British colonel (Roger Morris) and his American wife, in 1776 it became the temporary headquarters of George Washington, and then a popular tavern. In 1810 a wealthy French merchant named Stephen Jumel bought the house and, with the help of his ambitious and scandal-plagued wife Eliza, refurbished it. After his death, the eccentric Mme. Jumel married (very briefly) Aaron Burr. She remained in the house until her death (at age 91). After more ups and downs (including a short time when the house became an exhibition space for the newly invented motion picture process), the Morris-Jumel Mansion was transformed into a museum dedicated to America's past.

You'll enjoy wandering through the lovely old house, whose interior has been restored with great care and concern. The nine restored rooms, two halls, and a Colonial kitchen include many original Jumel pieces—furniture and artifacts—wallpapers (note especially the handpainted Chinese wallpaper in the octagonal drawing room), paintings, and lithographs. We especially liked a grand painting by Alcide Ercole of Eliza Jumel and her grandchildren, as well as handsome portraits in a bedroom of George Washington and (in the dining room) the hero of the Battle of Bunker Hill, Colonel John Chester, shown with his wife. You can take a group tour or go from room to room on your own.

You should not miss a walk through the small Colonial-style garden, which has great charm. Herbs and flowers are mixed in together, unlike American gardens of later times. Herbs were central to Colonial life; they were used not only for cooking, but also for dyes, medicines, teas, and fragrances. You'll see quite an assortment of herbs that were common then, including mint, sage, bee balm, comfrey, rosemary, catnip, and lemon balm (which, apparently, George Washington added to his sherry). These are informally arranged with hollyhocks (from Thomas Jefferson's garden), loose strife, and a collection of different types of roses. When we last visited, the garden was still not completed, but promised to be a bright spot in our overcrowded city. The Morris-Jumel Mansion is open Tuesday–Sunday, from 10–4. There is a small entrance fee. Telephone: (212) 923-8008.

Further downtown, also on the East Side, at 421 East 61st Street, is the Abigail Adams Smith Museum and its eighteenth-century garden. Here, in the somewhat formal atmosphere of the "historic house type" of museum, you can see one of only eight surviving eighteenth-century buildings in Manhattan. Abigail Adams Smith was a daughter of John Adams, the second president. This house—which has had a typically checkered career similar to the Jumel Mansion—was purchased by the Colonial Dames of America in 1924 and resurrected as a historic museum, after many years as a hotel, a gas company headquarters, and an antique shop.

Of particular interest, besides the handsome stone building and its period furnishings, is the eighteenth-century garden (which surrounds the house and can be walked through without entering the front door). Planted in characteristic eighteenth-century way, this quaint garden is a charming example of America's most decorative style. Influenced by the Dutch idea of patterned gardens surrounded by colonial board fences, the flowering area is delightful. We recommend a visit in springtime, when tulips, crocus, and hyacinth interspersed with patterns of brickwork and English ivy make this a bright and charming place to visit. (It is particularly astonishing because it is in the middle of a nondescript block of East Side Manhattan, and invisible from the street.) A brick terrace with old-fashioned benches sits above the flower area. On this level is an herb garden. There are trees and shrubs—many of the flowering varieties, whose best blossoms can be seen in May—including mock orange, viburnum, and flowering quince. Under these trees you'll find a profusion of violets and other bright flowers. But all is orderly in the garden, as recommended by early American (and European) gardeners. This is a well-kept garden, despite the harsh environment of the city. And also a well-kept secret, even among natives of the city. A garden map is available at the desk. Hours: 10–4, Monday–Friday; 1–5, Sunday (September–May); and 5:30–8, Tuesday evenings in June and July. The museum is closed in August. There is a small admission charge to see the house; none for the garden. Telephone: (212) 838-6878.

Although folk arts and crafts were long neglected in the world of fine art, they are nowadays often described as the most indigenous of America's early art. In fact, early primitive art in the United States has become somewhat of a fashion in the collecting world. Art historians no longer regard these types of Americana as mere oddities, but as fine examples of a national art unhampered by European influences and academic styles. You'll find a museum devoted to this subject at 2 Lincoln Square, opposite Lincoln Center. (The Museum of American Folk Art/Eva and Morris Feld Gallery is presently housed at this location; it plans to move near the Museum of Modern Art in the future.) This museum is one of the country's leading centers of research and exhibition of folk art. Included in the collection are examples dating from mid-eighteenth century to the present, encompassing everything from quilts to weathervanes, paintings to furniture, carved wooden sculpture to pottery and tinwork. Although the present site is cramped, it is still worth a visit, and we've heard that the new site will be quite magnificent. Needless to say, you won't be able to view the entire collection at any given time, but you should enjoy examples of their permanent collection and their exhibitions, which range from "The Needlework of American Schoolgirls, 1740–1840" to "The Language of Wood" to "African-American Quiltmaking." Hours are daily, 9 to 9, and admission is free. Telephone: (212) 595-9533 or (212) 977-7298.

Your last stop of this New York/Americana odyssey is the New-York Historical Society at 170 Central Park West (between 76th and 77th streets). Currently undergoing administrative upheaval, the Society expects to reopen soon. You will be fascinated by this very rich and comprehensive collection (more than two million works of art) ranging from first-rate American paintings, furniture, and period rooms to antique silver, craftwares, early American toys, prints, and photographs. Here you will find 435 of James Audubon's famous original illustrations for Birds of America (two are missing), as well as important American paintings by such masters as Rembrandt Peale, Thomas Cole, John Durand, Gilbert Stuart, and Thomas Eakins. There are four floors of exhibition space, which may be more than you can take in on one visit (especially after having already seen many things), but the museum is rarely crowded, and you can take your time as you wander from one gallery to the next. One of the most impressive exhibits is a veritable "who's who" gallery of famous Americans, such as George Washington (painted by Gilbert Stuart and Rembrandt Peale), Thomas Jefferson (Peale), James Madison, James Monroe, John Quincy Adams, Andrew Jackson (Asher Brown Durand), as well as wonderful portraits by John Singleton Copley, Ezra Ames, and Abraham Tuthill. A landscape gallery features paintings by the Hudson River artists—many of these works have recently been restored—including pictures by Durand, Samuel F. B. Morse, and Albert Bierstadt. The New-York Historical Society organizes interesting changing exhibitions that, usually, deal with some aspect of New York history, although recently they have gone further afield, with such exhibitions as "Paris 1889: American Artists at the Universal Exposition." Their recent efforts of refurbishing the museum have included arranging displays to focus more on New York's cultural and ethnic diversity: paintings depicting blacks and Native Americans and a first translation of the Bible into a Native American dialect. Hours: Tuesday–Friday, 11–5; Saturday, 10–5; Sunday, 1–5. Suggested voluntary contribution. Telephone: (212) 873-3400.

... And in Addition

If these listings of Americana have intrigued you, perhaps the following suggestions will also be of interest:

- The Bartow-Pell Mansion in Pelham Bay Park in the Bronx has extensive formal gardens and a number of paintings worth seeing. The mansion, dating to 1842, is a grand mid-century house with period furnishings, a fountain, and a carriage house and stable. The gardens have been carefully maintained by the International Garden Club since 1914. Hours: Wednesday and Sunday, noon–4. Closed in August. Telephone: (718) 885-1461.

- The Van Cortlandt Mansion, also in the Bronx (at Broadway and 242nd Street), is a stone house of Georgian design constructed in about 1748. It has a flower garden and an herb garden, as well as some paintings and period furnishings.

Hours: Wednesday–Saturday, 10–4:30; Sunday, noon–4:30. Telephone: (718) 543-3344.

- Gracie Mansion, the mayor's residence, is also open in part to the public. The house at 89th Street and East End Avenue, overlooking Hell's Gate, a stretch of water where the Harlem and East Rivers meet, is a grand building dating to 1799, with a later addition. Of particular interest in the formally furnished historic home are the art and antiques, almost all of which were created by New York's own artists and craftspersons. Hours: By appointment, Monday–Thursday. Telephone: (212) 570-4751.
- The Alice Austen House Museum and Park on Staten Island is described in Artwalk 26. Hours: Thursday–Sunday, noon–5 (May–November).
- The Conference House, also on Staten Island, at 7455 Hylan Boulevard, is wonderfully situated overlooking the harbor. A seventeenth-century stone manor house, it has some formal gardens (as well as a great rolling hillside down to the water) and a number of historic paintings. Hours: Wednesday–Sunday, 1–4. Closed January and February. Telephone: (718) 984-2086.
- The Conservatory Garden in Central Park in nineteenth-century style (see Artwalk 6).
- Fraunces Tavern Museum, at 54 Pearl Street in Lower Manhattan: this continuously active tavern/restaurant and upstairs museum has been operating in the same building since the eighteenth century. For information, call (212) 425-1778.
- The South Street Seaport Museum, at 207 Front Street: presents a series of exhibitions devoted to New York's maritime history. Telephone: (212) 669-9424.

9

The Heart of Downtown

The City Hall Area

HOW TO GET THERE
Subway: #2 or #3 train to Park Place, #4 or #5 train to Fulton Street, or A train to Broadway/Nassau Street.
SUGGESTED TIMES
We recommend weekdays between 10 A.M. and 3 P.M. (government buildings are closed on the weekend).

A lot of people, including New York's legion of municipal employees, are unaware of the wealth of art that is collected in the concentrated downtown City Hall region. Much of it is "official art" commissioned by the city beginning in the late eighteenth century, and a great deal of it is architecturally related. There are wonderful paintings in City Hall (open to the public), numerous allegorical sculptures gracing the city's official buildings, statues everywhere, and an occasional contemporary work. Traditionalists and history buffs will particularly enjoy this outing. (This is not a region known for its avant-garde art.) Wherever you turn you'll see examples of art demonstrating nineteenth- and twentieth-century exuberance and civic pride.

Your first stop is the Woolworth Building (1), at 233 Broadway, a testament of the very spirit of American optimism and pride. This dramatic structure, which soars over 700 feet, was the highest building in New York when it was completed in

1913. Designed by Cass Gilbert, it embodies the spirit of F. W. Woolworth, in its unabashed grandiosity and its display of luxury. But Woolworth believed wholeheartedly in the work ethic to attain these riches: on the outside of the building above the arched doorway to the entrance are carved figures of industrious men and women (possibly working so they could earn enough to shop at his stores!). Above these you'll see allegorical representations of the four continents—Europe, Africa, Asia and America—and, if you continue to look upward, you'll also see curious animal gargoyles. This Gothic Revival building is especially grand inside. Note the brilliant mosaic patterns on the vaulted ceilings, representing birds and flowers in the Italian tradition, and the golden-toned marble (from Greece) on the walls. On the mezzanine level are murals by Paul Jennewein symbolizing "Commerce" and "Labor" in the stylized mode of American art of the time. The resplendent marble staircase with its carved marble balustrade is at the end of the entrance corridor. Finally, note the humorous group of sculpted figures beneath the arches leading to the hallways near Broadway. Among them is Woolworth himself, clutching a large nickel! (He was considered a penny pincher.)

As you leave the building, cross Broadway to the small triangular park called City Hall Park (2). Much like a town common, it has been used in many different ways through the years: as a burial ground for paupers, a site for public executions, and the setting for ceremonies (and riots). Today it is a place filled with the bustle of city life, including occasional demonstrations. Of primary interest to us are their outside art shows.

Across Park Row you will see Pace University and a statue of a much-loved American, *Benjamin Franklin* (3). (You might want to cross the street to get a better view.) Sculpted in 1872 by Ernst Plassman, a German who had settled in New York, this representation of the statesman, inventor, diplomat, and printer stands, appropriately, on a spot known as Printing House Square. The original buildings of three New York newspapers used to be near this site, and Franklin is shown here in his guise as printer, holding in his hand a copy of the newspaper *The Pennsylvania Gazette*. The bronze figure was a gift to the press and printers of New York City. Its unveiling was a major event, at which Horace Greeley, editor of the *Tribune* (see #6 of this walk), made the principal address and Samuel F. B. Morse swept off the "star-spangled" covering of the statue. The statue is set up high above eye level, which is just as well for the viewer, as this is a corner of great activity and many pedestrians.

Pace University's (4) new building (1970) is right behind the statue. It is not a must-see stop on this artwalk, but the thorough explorer will want to note several pieces of art belonging to the

73

university. On the front facade is *The Brotherhood of Man*, a welded metal work by Henri Azaz. It consists of a series of metal strips with varied surfaces. If you walk down the block alongside the Pace Building at Spruce Street, you'll see a gated sculpture garden that includes some nice pieces. To get into the garden you can no longer enter from the street, but it is open to the public nonetheless. (Go in the main doors on Park Row, follow directions of the guards to the elevators, go to the basement, where you can walk in and examine the mostly bronze abstract works in the gardens close-up.) Unfortunately, nothing is identified, nor does there seem to be a list available. However, the viewer has the opportunity to admire works without a thought to any context whether of history, artist's fame, or subject matter, which can also be fun!

Returning to City Hall Park, walk toward City Hall (5), itself a jewel of a palace on a small, intimate scale. It stands serenely within an urban landscape as a reminder of a more gracious era. Although it seems almost dwarfed by its giant neighbors, it is one of the loveliest buildings in the city. This refined Georgian Renaissance–style edifice, built between 1803 and 1811, is rich with artistic and architectural interest, both inside and out.

As you walk toward the building, be sure to notice the figure at the very top of the cupola. It is a statue of "Justice," the third such statue to occupy the site. The first, made of wood, burned in 1858 after a rooftop fireworks display; the second, also of wood, rotted by 1878; and the current statue of white-painted copper has been at its present location high above the park for more than 100 years (since 1878). Its designer is unknown; it comes from a commercial producer of public statuary (The William H. Mullins Company of Ohio), but it serves its purpose well. This stately representation of justice resembles white stone and is a graceful addition to this beautiful building. The figure of "Justice" holds one arm aloft (not unlike the Statue of Liberty). In her hand is a scale, at her side, a sword. Like so much of our nineteenth-century public sculpture, this symbolic figure is vaguely ancient-looking, from her drapery to the classical face and traditional pose.

Pause for a moment on the front steps of this handsome building, where you can enjoy especially nice views of the Brooklyn
Bridge and the Woolworth Building. As you enter the building
through the imposing portico, you are, first, struck by the grand
central hall, its sweeping double staircase with elegant
wrought-iron railings, and the huge columned rotunda above.
You'll enjoy walking around, envisioning all the famous events
that have taken place here. (One of the most impressive was
when the body of Abraham Lincoln lay in state at the top of
the grand staircase in April 1865, as 120,000 New Yorkers lined
the stairs and poured onto the streets.) This building is still
open to the public, free of charge, Monday–Friday, 10–3.

City Hall is justly famous for its important collection of works
by American painters; it reads like a "who's who" of late eigh-
teenth- and nineteenth-century portraitists. From 1790 (when
New York was for a brief moment the nation's capital), city
legislators commissioned the great artists of the day to paint
New York politicians, war heroes, generals, and other notables.
Today you can see this rich collection of paintings (and a few
busts here and there) throughout chambers and hallways of
City Hall, and especially in three rooms: the Governor's Room,
the Board of Estimate Room, and the Council Chambers.

Particularly impressive is the elegant Governor's Room (on
the gallery level at the head of the stairs), which was used from
1814–1820 as an office by New York governors visiting the city.
Here you can see twelve paintings by the well-known American
master and patriotic artist John Trumbull, who painted portraits, scenes from the American Revolution and other historic
themes. Note in particular his portraits of George Washington
in New York (with Bowling Green behind him), George Clinton
(with the Hudson River as a background), Governor John Jay,
and Secretary of the Treasury Alexander Hamilton.

Most of the other works on view at City Hall are rotated
periodically from one room or hallway to the next. You will
see pictures by such prominent American artists as John Wesley
Jarvis; the dashing portraitist Thomas Sully; John Vanderlyn;
John Trumbull; George Catlin; and Rembrandt Peale, the Phila-
delphia "renaissance man." We especially liked the portrait of
De Witt Clinton, mayor of New York, by George Catlin, the

great painter and champion of the American Indians; and the dignified portrait of the Marquis de Lafayette, the French revolutionary leader, by Samuel F. B. Morse (who later invented the telegraph). On a more contemporary note are four abstract "fabric glass" paintings by Susan Mohl Powers on display on the sixth floor.

As you leave City Hall, turn to your left and walk north toward the back of the building. In this northern section of City Hall Park, you'll find a bronze of another giant of nineteenth-century America, the editor of The New York Tribune, Horace Greeley (6). Sculpted by John Quincy Adams Ward, this statue captures Greeley's appearance, his rumpled clothing, distinctive chin whiskers, and relaxed seated position with newspaper resting on his lap. Greeley's statue was made in 1890, and the sculptor revealed that he had used a death mask of the famous man's wide face to capture the peculiarly shaped dimensions of the head. The statue even looks at us somewhat sideways, a typical gesture of Greeley's. It was considered by those who knew him to have been an excellent likeness. Ward, the grandson of President John Quincy Adams, was one of the first well-known American sculptors to study at home rather than in Europe.

To the left of the statue and just behind City Hall stands the so-called "Tweed" Courthouse, formerly the New York City Courthouse—and today known as the Criminal Court Building (7). The scandal surrounding the construction of this building, which was completed in 1872 after more than ten years of controversy and $14 million in costs, eventually caused the demise of the infamous William M. "Boss" Tweed, who, with his cronies, was charged with inflating construction costs some three-and-a-half-fold. Today it is no longer a courthouse, but a dilapidated city government office building. Its once fine Anglo-Italianate exterior has been allowed to deteriorate, and its grand staircase and front entrance are now gone. Fortunately, recent renovation efforts have paid off, especially in the newly restored, resplendent rotunda. And, in connection with some interior renovation, a lovely round art gallery has been created on the main floor, directly below the rotunda. It's a challenge to find the entrance to this somewhat unfriendly looking building, but, once you've entered through the grimy basement doors (directly opposite the back of City Hall) and are safely inside, you will be glad you made the effort. Sign in with the guard at the front desk (there is no entrance fee) and walk directly to the gallery in front of you. The exhibition space is at once intimate and grand: intimate because of its actual size, but grand because of its dramatic location in the center of the building, directly below the tall glass rotunda and a series of richly decorated arched passageways. You are also standing on a fine marble floor whose quality is rarely matched in newer buildings. The intimacy of this gallery makes it ideal for shows on a smaller scale. The frequent exhibits concern a variety of themes not necessarily related to the city. (On one occasion we saw striking dance photographs and on another, an exhibition of art from WPA times.) The gallery is open weekdays from 9 A.M. to 5 P.M.

Cross Chambers Street behind this building, and, at 31 Chambers Street, you'll find Surrogate Court, also known as the Hall of Records (8). This building has lavish sculptural ornamentation in keeping with its era, and its function as a government building meant to inspire civic pride. The sculptures that decorate its facade profusely are thus both symbolic and elaborate in design and number; in fact there are forty-two of them. The main ones dating from 1903–8 are all by Philip Martiny, a Frenchman who settled in New York and worked in the studio of Saint-Gaudens. He was apparently a very busy man; both the major groupings are his, as well as twenty-four figures on this building and you'll see two other allegorical works of his in Foley Square where you'll find both "Justice" and "Authority." The two major groups by Martiny on this Surrogate Court building flank the entrance. On the right is a group with a woman clutching books and wearing a headdress of feathers. She represents New York in its infancy. To the left of the doorway is another group with a female figure holding both globe and torch and wearing a helmet. She is New York in Revolutionary times. All are made of granite. The twenty-four cornice figures high up on the building are either portraits or allegories. Such notable New Yorkers as Peter Stuyvesant, De Witt Clinton, and a number of the city's mayors (whose names are familiar from the street names of downtown New York) appear on the

Chambers Street facade. On the Centre Street side are eight female figures representing such subjects as "Medicine," "Commerce," and "Industry"; while, on the Reade Street side, you'll find figures representing either virtues such as "Justice" and "Tradition," or symbolic figures of "Electricity," "Printing," "Painting," "Sculpture," and "Force." (This interesting amalgam certainly suggests some national preoccupations of America's early twentieth century!) Other decorations high on the building are the work of Henry Kirk Bush-Brown, and they represent the "Four Seasons," as well as such traditional subjects as "Philosophy," "Poetry," and "Maternity." We know of almost no other building in the city so lavishly decorated with sculpture on the exterior. It is interesting to keep in mind that the American emphasis on growth and grandeur included public art for all to enjoy; unlike the Woolworth (see #1), this building was not designed to celebrate one man's empire, but to inspire and please the public at large. However, this lavish Beaux Arts building was constructed during the same exuberant era as the Woolworth, as well as the U.S. Customs House on Bowling Green (see artwalks 1 and 2). Originally intended to serve as a storage place for municipal records, over the years it has recently functioned as a court dealing with guardianships and trusts.

The inside of this elegant building is as spectacular and ornate as the outside. You walk into a marble foyer with sculptured reliefs above the doors by Albert Weinert, depicting scenes from the early period of New York City. Note the unusual windows laced with wrought-iron designs. On the ceiling you'll see a wonderful mosaic in deep, rich shades by the muralist William de Lefwich Dodge, showing Greek and Egyptian allegorical beings representing "Justice," "Sorrow," "Labor," and "Retribution." But the most spectacular architectural elements within are the grand marble Piranesi-like staircase dominating the central lobby and the impressive colonnaded rotunda above. Upstairs are several chambers (you might be able to peek inside a few), some elaborately decorated, others simple and functional.

From the Surrogate Court you'll see the giant Municipal Building (9) directly across the street. This mammoth structure has numerous exterior sculptures, including *Civic Fame* (1913–14) by Adolph Alexander Weinman. A gold-leaf copper statue sits atop the tower of the building, and, surprisingly, is the largest statue in Manhattan. (No, the Statue of Liberty is not in Manhattan.) *Civic Fame* is a graceful and unusually charming sculpture in the allegorical "shield" and "laurel branch" style of municipal building decorations. She balances delicately on a globe and holds a crown aloft that has five turrets to symbolize the city's five boroughs. Best seen from a distance, you might want to back up into the park for a better view or use binoculars for a detailed look.

Civic Fame is 582 feet above the street. Made of about 500 pieces of hammered copper over a steel frame, the statue was installed in 1914. But this is not Weinman's only contribution to the decoration of the building, which bears many other sculptural ornaments, including a series of medallions, leaf patterns, coats-of-arms, and several major groups of figures. You guessed it: there are figures representing such virtues as "Civic Pride," "Progress," "Guidance" (left of the entrance), "Executive Power" (right of the entrance), and "Prudence." And on the 2nd-story level, you'll find bronze relief panels showing "Water Supply," "Building Inspection," "Records and Accounts," and a number of additional municipal functions. Most of these allegorical and illustrative works date to the first part of this century. This building is another example of that period's use of architectural sculpture for the "edification" of the public.

For a jolt from all the virtuous "Justice" and "Authority" statuary of this part of town, walk through the Municipal Building (take the pedestrian walkway that is to the right of the entrance), and you'll find yourself in Police Plaza (10), a rather new-looking brick-faced area. Here you can't miss Tony Rosenthal's *Five in One*, a 30-foot-high, 75-ton steel sculpture consisting of five large abstract intersecting disks. Made of Cor-Ten steel in 1974, it sits in an area that is supposed to be improved with artistic brickwork and other amenities, but at this time we found it harboring an immense amount of junk and trash in and around its forms, as well as a goodly amount of graffiti. You are welcome to walk into the Police Headquarters (11) to

79

see a brick wall construction by Josef Twirbutt on the left back wall of the lobby. This abstract design is made of various colored bricks arranged in somewhat geometric patterns. This and the Rosenthal are both recent additions to the new Police Plaza area, and are among the only contemporary artworks on this walk.

Leave Police Plaza and walk to Pearl Street and then to Foley Square. The New York County Courthouse (12) is on your right. Elegant columns and stone steps lead up to its entrance, where two large granite statues sit on either side of the doors. Like many sculptures at the Surrogate's Court Building (8), they are by Philip Martiny, the French-American sculptor of so many allegorical figures. Here we find "Authority" and "Justice." On the right is "Justice," a seated female once again holding shield and scroll. On the left is "Authority," who holds a scroll and the Roman fasces, the emblem of official power. Curiously, these seated figures have a sort of modern simplicity of shape, despite the traditional symbolism; their stoic expressions and large forms bring to mind more contemporary sculpture (these were made in 1906). Inside the Court House are several cycles of murals painted for the W.P.A. in the '30s. On the main floor (adorning the vestibule and dome of the central rotunda) are murals depicting "Law through the Ages," "Truth," "Security," and other glowing allegorical conceptions painted in rich tones and grand courthouse style by Attilio Pusterla.

Upstairs on the fourth floor, adjoining jurors' rooms numbers 448 and 452, are a series of murals by Robert K. Ryland and Pusterla, among others. These paintings depict the history of New York and vast panoramas of the city from earliest times to 1938.

Walk up Centre Street from Foley Square to the Civil and Municipal Court Building (13) where, on the Centre Street side, you'll find "Law," a sculpted relief by the twentieth-century artist William Zorach. Appropriately, it depicts a family surrounding the central figure of a judge. The relief is in the style for which Zorach was well known, with its large, rather primitive, stylized groups of figures reminiscent of murals and reliefs of the 1930s. Though Zorach began as a modernist painter, he soon turned to sculpture and to more representational works.

A traditionalist in method, Zorach insisted on using a chisel and working from a solid mass to create his monumental bas reliefs. This granite work, made in 1960, graces a large, dull wall of the Court building—Zorach's was an optimistic view of the law's ability to aid the ordinary people entering this hall of justice.

Walk south through the small park connected to this building to see the corresponding bas relief on the Lafayette Street side. You might want to take a moment to rest your feet in this vest-pocket park. The Zorach sculpture's counterpart on the Lafayette Street facade is "Justice," made in 1960 by Joseph Kiselewski. Like the Zorach, it is a bas relief set into the bland wall of the building. Kiselewski's work is a more allegorical scene than Zorach's, but both bear the distinctively stylized look of public murals and reliefs of the prewar era. "Justice" is a less tightly knit composition than is "Law"; in it a "floating" female figure bearing scales hovers above a baby and a snake, perhaps protecting the innocent from harm.

If, after this outing you crave some of the latest trends in contemporary art and you still have the energy, walk west a few blocks on Franklin Stree to Tribeca. A description of Tribeca's art sites appears in Artwalk 13.

To go back uptown, walk north to subways at Canal Street and Broadway.

... And in Addition

- Pace University: lectures on a variety of art-related topics.
- City Hall park: outdoor art shows in season.
- In the Governor Smith Houses in New York, Chinatown (at 21 St. James Place and Madison Street): an environmental work by the sculptor Hera is a recent addition. Called *Orbital Connector*, the work celebrates the tenants' multiethnic roots. It consists of a great map with an orbit connecting China, the Caribbean, and the United States.
- Criminal Court Building at 100 Centre Street houses three of the city's oldest surviving murals. By Edward Emerson Simmons, they represent "Justice," "The Rights of Man," and "The Fates" in American Renaissance allegorical style.

10

Restaurant Hopping

*Surprising Art Collections
in Manhattan's Eateries*

HOW TO GET THERE
*Because most of these restaurants are in Midtown Manhattan,
they are easily accessible by public transportation.*
SUGGESTED TIMES
*If you're going to see the works of art (and not to eat), visit in
the morning between 11 A.M. and noon or in the afternoon
between 3 and 5 P.M., or phone each restaurant for the best
time to visit.*

There are many reasons to visit restaurants in New York besides
the obvious one of being hungry. Among them, as any New
Yorker can tell you, is the atmosphere, whom you'll be likely
to see there, the music, the location, the cost, and whether it's
where everyone is going. You might add to that list by noting
the following midtown restaurants that display art worth seeing
on their walls.

Not all art, as we've discovered, is in galleries and museums.
In fact, restaurants are a good place to see unusual art you won't
see elsewhere: personal collections, odd finds, original works
given by the artists to the restaurants, or works on loan. Our
wanderings took us in and out of dozens of restaurants and
eateries, sometimes just to look, sometimes for a meal, too.

Which brings us to the best way or method to see the art

mentioned in this outing. If you visit these spots at off-hours (11 A.M. or 4 P.M., for example), you are most likely to be invited in courteously to look around. You can also, of course, go and eat or have a drink during regular hours, although it may be more difficult to view the artworks during busy lunches or dinners.

Most restaurants are proud of their art and like to show it, so don't be embarrassed to ask. You can phone ahead to find out a good time for visiting. All of the following eateries were hospitable—with or without food. So we leave to you the best method for seeing the "finds" on these restaurant walls. You might wish to see them over a leisurely dinner or, if you just want to pop in and out, go right ahead. Needless to say, the life of restaurants is often uncertain in our trendy city. As of this writing, all of the following were alive and well.

Trattoria dell'Arte

You might think that dining in a room filled with body parts might sound odd, if not downright macabre, but it is anything but that at Trattoria dell'Arte. Located on 7th Avenue and 57th Street, directly across the street from Carnegie Hall, this stylish Italian bistro was designed with flair and wit by Milton Glaser. His off-beat decor features Milton Steckel's grand anatomical sculptures—classical in style and of heroic proportions—which are prominently displayed on the walls. You might well find yourself seated below a giant plaster ear or torso or nose. Indeed, the emphasis here is definitely on noses, of which there are many in all shapes, sizes, and configurations.

The upstairs dining room sets the scene for a whimsical collection of pictures by well-known illustrators depicting famous noses throughout the ages. This amusingly incongruous grouping includes, among others, Caesar, Lorenzo de Medici, Verdi, and Jimmy Durante.

In the downstairs dining area you can also enjoy some tasteful prints scattered about in nooks and crannies. The imaginative art, helpful staff, and savory Italian food will all put you in good spirits. Telephone: (212) 245-9800.

Café Des Artistes

Café des Artistes, located in a historic turn-of-the-century building at 1 West 67th Street, has to be one of New York's most romantic and gracious restaurants. Its dark wood walls, lead-paneled windows, and sparkling tables create an ambience of old world charm and sophistication. But what makes the decor special are the lush, wall-to-wall bucolic murals by the American painter and illustrator Howard Chandler Christy installed when the café opened in 1917. Fetching sylvan nymphs frolic and dance playfully within woodlands and glades. The overall romantic effect of these saucy yet innocent nudes is somewhat reminiscent of eighteenth-century French painting, particularly Francois Bouchet, who often depicted elegant pastoral scenes with lovers dallying in rustic landscapes. Many of these idealized figures resemble the so-called "Christy Girl," whom the painter made famous in the pages of *Harper's* and *Scribner's* magazines.

If you plan to visit the restaurant just to see the murals, a good time is either late morning or between 3 and 5. (Because the restaurant is close to Lincoln Center, many pre-theater diners arrive early.) If you eat here, you'll discover that the menu—a very ambitious one, indeed—is a combination of French bistro fare and nouvelle cuisine. Telephone: (212) 877-3500.

San Domenico

San Domenico, at 240 Central Park South, is one of New York's most notable Italian restaurants. And it comes as a wonderful surprise to discover that it also contains an impressive art collection—in fact, all twentieth-century works, with the exception of one painting by the nineteenth-century Italian, Massimiliano Lodi. On the walls of this sophisticated, refined ristorante—where the simplicity of the decor sets off its artworks—you will find a remarkable number of prints by the Greek-born Italian surrealist painter, Giorgio de Chirico—perhaps more works by this artist than you will see anywhere else. The compelling metaphysical landscapes with figures, antique statuary, and plunging lines of perspective are unmistakably de Chirico. Don't miss additional de Chiricos in a downstairs lining area. This collection is truly a "find" for enthusiasts of his modern master.

You will also notice four intriguing circular Venetian glass sculptures tastefully displayed so as to add just a bit of shimmer to the decor. These abstract translucent glass and stainless steel works by the contemporary Venetian artist Livio Seguso were created on the famous island of Murano, where glass has been handblown for centuries.

San Domenico features specialties from Bologna, one of Italy's most famous gastronomic regions. On the menu you are likely to find original dishes you may not have sampled before. Telephone: (212) 265-5959.

The Rainbow Room

The Rainbow Room, 30 Rockefeller Plaza (at Rockefeller Center) is a sumptuous sky-high restaurant with a collection of contemporary art and an unusual collection of hand crafts. If you visit in the late afternoon (through the dinner hour), you can see this fine selection of art throughout the restaurant, offset by spectacular views of the New York skyline. Among the interesting pieces of art visible to the art lover (a brochure describing each piece is also available) are a distinctive contemporary sculpted Athena by a French artist named Arman; an exotic Nancy Graves construction made up of welded materials; a 1930s style painting of the very view before you by Stefan Hirsch; works in glass by Dale Chihuly, Howard Ben Tré, and William Morris; an heroic sculpture by Paul Manship (whose art is so much a part of Rockefeller Center); several woven bark works by John McQueen; and unusual woodcraft by Ed Moulthrop.

For those with an interest in the history of design, there are several examples of seminal American industrial designs including early radios, a futuristic boat model by Norman Bel Geddes (he was instrumental in designing the Coke bottle, among other lasting American idioms), and some startling lighting fixtures by various artists.

The Rainbow Art Program is not confined to the restaurant. There are changing exhibitions in a small gallery at Club Central in Rockefeller Center, and a continuing project of collecting

and exhibiting art that they claim reflects—or is in the spiri
of—Rockefeller Center's history. Telephone: (212) 632-5100.

Hotel Carlyle
Two side-by-side cafés in the well known Carlyle Hotel at Mad
ison and 76th Street house murals that many New Yorker
know and love. To the left of the entrance you'll find the Bemel
mans Bar. Ludwig Bemelmans (of *Madeleine* fame) was an ac
complished artist and writer of note, as well as the classic chil
dren's story creator. He was invited to spend some time livin
in the hotel and giving free rein to his imagination on the wall
of the bar. What the hotel got from Bemelmans is a charmin
panorama of imaginary figures in Central Park (people in cages
animals running free), among the many, whimsical, cartoonlik
designs. The overall scene is reminiscent of children's book
in the days before Action Jackson or Ninja Turtles. You migh
call and ask if you can bring your children (off-hours) for
quick look at this world of long-necked, well-dressed giraffes
pastel trees, and odd creatures cavorting in beautiful sunli
greenery. You can have a pleasant grown-up style drink her
among Bemelmans' designs, but you might find them dis
turbing after a few drinks!

Across the hall is a companion bar, the Café Carlyle, anothe
distinctively decorated café, where the walls were painted by
the French artist Vertes. Delicate and soft, Vertes's style make
you think of 1920s Paris, its young, poetic women smellin
roses and dreaming in their pastel surroundings. Jean Coctea
described Vertes's women as "pretty, gracious, charming, ador
able, soft, tender, graceful . . ." words that should give you ar
idea of Vertes's style of painting. Both bars serve drinks anc
snacks. Telephone: (212) 744-1600.

Twenty-One
A curious setting for Wild West art, but Twenty-One, the posl
nightspot at 21 West 52nd Street, happens to own one of the
city's largest collections of Frederick Remington works. Rem
ington, probably the best known artist of cowboys and the ro
mantic "old" West that this country has produced, specializec
in dynamic action scenes of Indians, cowhands, rodeos, anc

war. Remington was actually an Easterner who went west to ride through Indian territory. His drawings, paintings, and sculptures brought him acclaim back East. It is one of those odd quirks of the art world that the great outdoor artist who adored the wide open spaces should be so memorialized in a quintessential New York restaurant/club. Actually, the collection is to be found in the comfortable living room on the ground floor of Twenty-One, and you can just walk in and enjoy the more than thirty paintings and drawings, which have titles such as *Turn 'im Loose, Bill,* and *Pony Tracks.* Telephone (212) 582-7200.

Windows on the World
Windows on the World, the restaurant at the top of the World Trade Center, has an impressive collection of art, as noted in Artwalk 1. Under renovation. Telephone (212) 938-1111.

Arcadia
Arcadia, at 21 East 62nd Street, is a serene, elegant restaurant whose decor is dominated by a large 70-foot seasonal mural enveloping the entire dining room. Painted in brilliant colors by the poster artist Paul Davis, it depicts in a folk mode an idyllic landscape reminiscent of the mythical Arcadia of ancient Greece. In creating this work, Davis found inspiration in the Hudson River School and its dramatic landscape. In addition to the bucolic scenery harmoniously set in this sophisticated ambience, you will enjoy the innovative menu, which also celebrates the seasons. Telephone: (212) 223-2900.

Aquavit
Aquavit, an unusual Swedish restaurant at 13 West 54th Street, is decorated in a most artistic way. The many-storied main dining room makes dramatic use of paintings, pennants, a colorful mobile, and a fountain. Many of the paintings and the mobile are by Swedish artists, among them Peter Aström and Peter Dahl, who made the bright, colorful paintings at the bar upstairs. You can visit Aquavit during off-hours, if you prefer, but the Swedish food and the pleasant ambience and the friendly staff make this a good place for lunch or dinner. Telephone: (212) 307-7311.

87

The Four Seasons

The Four Seasons, at 99 East 52nd Street, is a legendary restaurant in the Seagram Building. It has several art treasures of note. The interior, designed by architects Philip Johnson and William Pahlmann, is noted as one of the first landmark modern restaurants in the city. The Four Seasons Bar Room Grill, with its deep-toned brownish color and woody textures is a perfect setting for a Richard Lippold sculpture. Made of glittering brass rods dipped in gold, this large work is suspended above the bar, catching flickering light on its hundreds of thin, shining forms—like some sort of celestial body descending from the sky.

And in the outer room, between bar and restaurant, is another surprise: a very large tapestry by Picasso. A 1919 stage backdrop for a ballet called *Le Tricorne*, it is a striking and recognizable Picasso. On the floor below (use the staircase) are more tapestries—some decorative contemporary works by Monika Correa representing, aptly, the four seasons. They are nice examples of the present-day art of weaving/tapestry making. Eating at the Four Seasons is notoriously expensive, though you can get a drink at the Bar Room Grill under the Lippold, or go in just to look. The staff doesn't seem to mind visitors with only art in mind. Telephone: (212) 754-9494.

Eight and a Half

Eight and a Half, at 208 East 52nd Street, is an Italian restaurant that boasts a series of paintings with a distinctive flavor. Reminiscent of Fernando Botero's large nudes, these are also Colombian in origin. The artist is Leandro Velasco, and he has supplied the restaurant with quite a few voluptuous figure paintings that combine a kind of folk art innocence with a sardonic touch. Not to everyone's taste while eating, they nonetheless provide the restaurant with unusual ambience. Telephone: (212) 759-7373.

La Grenouille

A favorite culinary/art shop of ours is La Grenouille, located in an elegant townhouse at 3 East 52nd Street. This famous restaurant has long (since 1962) been known for its stylish French cuisine and its beautifully decorated dining room filled with exquisite and lavish bouquets. It also happens to have—upstairs on the second floor—an enchanting private dining room filled with works of art. For this was once the studio of French painter/illustrator Bernard Lamotte, who lived and worked here during the 1940s. When we visited we were given a private tour by Charles Masson, who owns the restaurant with his mother, and who remembers the artist well. (As a boy, Masson studied painting with Lamotte and became a good friend.) Lamotte, a native of Paris, had come to New York to pursue his career. His studio became a cultural salon for artists, actors, musicians, and writers—indeed it was a favorite meeting place for Antoine de Saint Exupery (who wrote his masterpiece, *The Little Prince*, in this very room), Salvador Dali, Charles Boyer, and Greta Garbo, among other habitués. Lamotte called his studio "Le Bocal," or "the fishbowl," for its lively ambience. In 1987, twenty-five years after the Massons had created La Grenouille, the studio was finally converted into a special dining room for private parties. Today this handsome room is filled with Lamotte's elegant impressionistic-style paintings that evoke life in Paris, tastefully displayed on whitewashed brick walls. As you walk around the room, you feel you're viewing a private collection in the intimacy of someone's small, private French chateau. The atmosphere is warm, inviting, and comfortable. At the back is a tiny room full of sketches, brushes, and other art accoutrements left virtually intact.

If your visit to La Grenouille is to be art oriented rather than culinary, we recommend you come between 11 and noon in the morning, or between 3 and 5 in the afternoon. If you're lucky, Charles Masson himself might be available to show you the upstairs room and tell you about Bernard Lamotte and his life in New York back in the old days. Telephone: (212) 752-1495.

Union Square Café
The Union Square Café at 21 East 16th Street (off Fifth Avenue) is a bustling, bi-level restaurant well known for its excellent food and a large and eclectic collection of contemporary art on

its walls. Small works by such artists as Richard Polsky, Frank
Stella, and Claes Oldenburg are among many hung throughout
the restaurant; a big, splashy mural by Judy Rifka is over the
bar. There are painted sculptures (Gail Starr), collage (Robert
Kushner), photographs, silk screens, and prints. You are wel
come to walk around and see the art in this relaxed but crowded
and popular place, but be careful not to bump into the waiters
dashing about. You may borrow a list of all the art if you ask
Telephone: (212) 243-4020.

Michael's

Michael's Restaurant at 24 West 55th Street is—with or without
the food—one of the best settings for recent art in the city. The
light is terrific, the spaces well designed for pictures, and the
informality of the place makes walking around and looking no
only possible but actually encouraged. With a helpful guide
(the maître d' who knew all about them) you can see a variety
of art mostly from the recent past. Included are a number of
Richard Diebenkorn lithographs from the Ocean Park series
two bright-colored David Hockney prints from the Acatlan se
ries; a collection of odd sculptures by Robert Graham—both
nudes (along the wall) and a construction set in front of the
windows; a charming Marcel Duchamp; seven tiny and fasci
nating pictures by the composer John Cage; two life-size con
crete and bronze sheep by Jean Francois Lalande; and a nice
Helen Frankenthaler work. Quite a few Jasper Johns works are
among the prize acquisitions of the owner, Michael McCarthy
who is said to have the other half of his collection in his West
Coast restaurant. The food, by the way, is California style and
moderately expensive. If you go for a late lunch, you can stay
after most of the diners have left and take your time looking at
the pictures. If you just want to visit, go between 11 A.M. and
noon or 4 and 5 P.M. Telephone: (212) 767-0555.

Palio

At the small, circular bar at Palio, at the Equitable Center, 151
West 51st Street, you'll find a brilliant four-walled mural
painted in 1985 by the Italian artist, Sandro Chia. Its bright
colors are mostly reds and oranges; its theme, centaurs, horses

nd Picassoesque figures, all evoking the Palio, the famous me-
lieval horserace held twice a year during the summer in Siena,
taly. The painting makes an extraordinarily strong and colorful
statement in this bar, and we particularly liked the futuristic
lesign. By all means, stop and have a drink here. Telephone:
212) 245-4850.

O'Neal's
A visit to O'Neal's at 49 West 64th Street is like walking into
a cozy and comfortable dining room in an art lover's old house.
There is lots of art on the walls, and it is an eclectic mixture
of oils, posters, drawings, prints, and collages. The informal
atmosphere makes it possible to look around and enjoy such
works as a nice still life by Robert Crowl, an early *Saturday
Evening Post* cover, some artist's proofs for Lincoln Center by
Larry Rivers, Robert Indiana, and Marc Chagall (who used to
have lunch at this site when he was painting the murals at
the Metropolitan Opera), a David Hockney design for Amnesty
International, a charming French-style gouache depicting a dining scene (by Christopher Wood), and many other various and
sundry works, including several by the co-owner, Chris O'Neal.
The upstairs dining room features a series of plastic figures by
Mimi Gross-Grooms taken from New York characters in the
1970s. And in the center of the restaurant is a large mural
depicting the New York City Ballet corps in the late '60s (its
present director, Peter Martins, can be seen on the right). This
collection and its setting are refreshingly unpretentious.
O'Neal's is a pleasant place to eat, with moderate prices. You
can also sit at the bar, if you don't want a meal, or during off-
hours, simply walk in and ask to look around. Telephone (212)
787-4663.

La Côte Basque
You could combine a visit to La Côte Basque (at 5 East 55th
Street) with La Grenouille, for here, too, the lovely and luminous works of the French artist Bernard Lamotte help to create
the special atmosphere of this elegant restaurant. But here, unlike at La Grenouille, the Lamotte works—all murals the artist
painted in the 1950s—are in the main dining area, rather than

upstairs in a private room. These enchanting and bright impre
sionistic murals depict scenes of Saint-Jean-de-Luz (a Basqu
town near Biarrritz) and are, like the name of the town, full c
light and joy. As you sit and feast on classic French fare (som
of New York's finest, and priced accordingly), you feel a
though the town is just outside your window. The clever ligh
ing and the way the murals were painted help to create th
illusion. For some of the murals have trompe l'oeil shutte
framing them, as if you were observing the scene from a wii
dow; others have balconies in the foreground, as if you migl
step out to admire the view. At every turn you are seduced b
the charms of southwestern coastal France, with its softly co
ored houses, delightful open squares filled with flowers, an
the blue sea, a constant presence. For any lover of French pain
ing, scenery, or cuisine, this restaurant stop is a treat. Tel
phone: (212) 688-6525.

Café Loup
This cozy French bistro at 105 West 13th Street at 6th Avenu
has a number of small works of art scattered about in virtuall
every possible wall space. Here you'll find an impressive serie
of art photographs by Berenice Abbott, Henri Cartier-Bresso
Brassai, Irving Penn, and Joel Meyerowitz. There are also litho
graphs by Adolph Gottlieb, Dorothy Dehner and George Tooke
A major wall is devoted to a large collage by Nancy Grossma
The atmosphere in Café Loup is very friendly, and the restat
rant is pleased to let you wander about to look at the art in the
collection. They will show you a list of the works displaye
Telephone: (212) 255-4746.

. . . And in Addition
- In the heart of Soho's art district at 103 Greene Street, you'
  find the *Soho Kitchen and Bar,* which displays an interestin
  collection of contemporary art. Telephone: (212) 925-1866
- *The Russian Tea Room Restaurant* at 150 West 57th Stree
  has a remarkable collection of Russian art, but you must e
  there to view it. Telephone: (212) 265-0947.
- *An American Place* at 2 Park Avenue (at 32nd Street) is
  spacious ocher-walled dining room with stunning geometri

art deco lighting fixtures and a small collection of abstract American art. There are three Frank Stellas, including a large white on black calligraphic work, and two in brighter colors; a giant multicolored abstraction by Gary Bandy; and three small, delicate nonobjective works by Fred Cray. (Dining is moderately expensive.) Telephone: (212) 684-2122.

● At *Les Celebrités*, a very elegant restaurant located in the Essex House at 160 Central Park South, you will discover that some of Hollywood's favorite stars and other well-known figures have been artists on the side. Decorating the walls of these choice dining rooms, you'll find paintings (some quite good) by such an unlikely combination of celebrities as James Dean, Elke Sommer, Gene Hackman, and e.e. cummings. The restaurant is only open for an expensive dinner, but you can stop in to see the art works in the late afternoon. (There is a list of the paintings on display and we found the staff to be courteous and helpful.) Telephone: (212) 247-0300.

Garden Café at the Museum of Modern Art, 11 West 53rd Street, provides food in the presence of great works of art. You can eat here (by entering the museum first). On Friday nights you can pay what you wish to visit the museum. Telephone: (212) 708-9719.

In a lighter vein, we suggest three original and highly amusing restaurant decors:

● *Tatou*, at 151 East 50th Street (between Lexington and Third avenues), is a former intimate opera house surprisingly located in this rather nonartsy neighborhood. In the 1930s when it ceased being an opera house, it became "The Versailles," the setting for memorable evenings with entertainment by Edith Piaf and Judy Garland. Several incarnations later it is now a charmingly decorated restaurant and boîte. The pseudo-mid-nineteenth-century ambience is created by statuary, satyr-lamps, brocaded upholstery, and a variety of whimsical artifacts. The staff is happy to let you look around. Telephone: (212) 753-1144.

Also in a whimsical vein is *Gonzalez y Gonzalez*, a Mexican eatery at 625 Broadway (between Houston and Bleecker streets). Its raucous decor includes oversized papier-mâché

figures, carvings, southwestern skulls, brilliant colors, piña
talike structures, a giant fake cactus, and carved unicorns o
the bar. Attractive painted chairs and a general good-humore
aura make this a fun place to visit. Telephone: (212) 473-8787

One of the city's newest restaurants featuring decor-cum-ar
is *Iridium* at 63rd Street and Columbus Avenue. The colorfu
topsy-turvy, hallucinatory interior was designed with a package
of "Chuckles" in mind.

11

Black New York

The African, Caribbean, and American Heritage

HOW TO GET THERE
Subway: To the Museum for African Art, E train to Spring Street, or N or R train to Prince Street or #6 train to Spring Street. To the Studio Museum of Harlem and Adam Clayton Powell State Office Building, #2 or 3 train to 135th Street; walk west. To the Schomburg Center, #2 train to 135th Street and Lenox Avenue. To Harlem School of the Arts, A or D train to 145th Street; walk south one block.
Bus: To reach the Harlem sites mentioned, take 1, 101, or 102.
SUGGESTED TIMES
Call the various organizations listed in this walk for times.

From its African origins to Caribbean and American contemporary art, black art is enjoying a cultural boom. New York has major exhibition spaces that focus on a variety of aspects of black art—from African tribal masks and three-dimensional sculptures, to the most modern of abstract paintings, to the exquisite craftsmanship of black folk arts. Following is a hop-skip-jump type of outing that will introduce you to the black diaspora—the extraordinarily widespread branching out of black culture.

Begin your walk with African art in its purest form, at the

Museum for African Art, recently moved to beautiful new quar ters designed by architect-sculptor Maya Lin, at 593 Broadwa in Soho. This center of African sculpture is both a gallery and museum. This is a good place to begin your outing if you wan to "see" black art in terms of a visual diaspora. Here are mag nificent masks, figure sculptures, and other arts of various triba origins. You will find many visual references to these shape and styles as you journey into contemporary black art. The museum has changing exhibitions as well as a permanent col lection. Recent shows included "Face of the Gods: Art and Altars of Africa and the African Americas" and "Fusion: Wes African Artists at the Venice Biennale"; another show con cerned architectural sculpture by contemporary African artists Hours: Tuesday–Friday, 10:30–5:30; Saturday, noon–8; and Sundays, noon–6. Telephone: (212) 966-1313.

From here go uptown to New York's main black cultural center: Harlem. The major exhibition space for black art in New York is surely the Studio Museum of Harlem (2). This facility at 144 West 125th Street, is a lively place with frequently changing exhibitions. Some shows are coordinated with other museums—for example, their recent exhibition called "The De cade Show," which was mounted in conjunction with the Mu seum of Contemporary Hispanic Art and the New Museum of Contemporary Art (see page 114). Other exhibitions at the Stu dio Museum include works from their permanent collection (black art by sculptors, painters, and craftspersons)—mostly by living artists. Occasionally they have major retrospective exhibits by a great black artist such as Romare Bearden. Other recent exhibits include works by contemporary black photogra phers and works by the museum's own artists in residence, one of the most interesting aspects of the Studio Museum. In the same building as the exhibition space are studios where artists can work and then have their output exhibited. This supportive setup encourages a number of black visual artists to work within their community. Among the many other activities of the museum are seminars and classes, both in art itself and in collecting, art history, and other aspects of the field. The mu seum sponsors tours and workshops. Hours: Wednesday–Fri day, 10–5; Saturday and Sunday, 1–6. Small entrance fee. Tele phone: (212) 864-4500.

Directly across the street is the Adam Clayton Powell State Office Building (3), at 163 West 125th Street. This large modern building contains several works of art worth seeing, both in the lobby and in the upstairs art gallery. The gallery is an exhibition space not only for community arts, but also for emerging regional and national artists. A student show is held annually: when we were there, paintings, sculpture, and prints by students from ten public schools in the Harlem community were being exhibited. Usually about five shows a year are put on display, sometimes as a cooperative venture with the Studio Museum. (For information on current exhibits, phone the Studio Museum.) The gallery is open Monday–Friday, 12–3.

In the street-level lobby you'll find two large sculptures. (We were told that other sculptures might be added or substituted at a later date.) Both are bold works that add interest to an otherwise anonymous office building lobby. One, *The Family* (1975) by Rodner Wright, is a stylized sculpture of African figures in burnt sienna steel. The other, *Black Dream Column* (1976), by Barbara Chase Riboud, is a strong, symbolic work depicting ropes and chains.

From here it's only a short hop to the Schomburg Center for Research in Black culture (4), at 515 Lenox Avenue at 135th Street. The Center has every sort of material relating to black life and culture, including many kinds of art. Among its major assets are a research library, Swahili recordings, and an important collection of books on African and black history. Special exhibits by black artists are ongoing. And there is also a permanent collection of African metalwork and carvings. You will receive a listing of their changing exhibitions schedule by phoning them at (212) 491-2200.

Also on 135th Street at the Harlem Y.M.C.A. (180 West 135th Street) you'll find a W.P.A. mural by the well-known Harlem Renaissance artist Aaron Douglas. This lively scene of outdoor dancers can be found in the lobby. (Other murals in the building from the same period have been painted over; restoration is a goal for the future.)

Nearby, on 137th Street between Fifth and Lenox Avenues, in a foyer of Harlem Hospital are two murals by Charles Alston, an artist well known for his use of African symbols in his paintings of the black experience. The subject of these newly restored murals is medicine—both ritualistic and modern.

At 144th Street you'll find the famous Harlem School of the Arts (5), at 645 St. Nicholas Avenue. This institution is not only known for teaching the performing and visual arts, but also for sponsoring a number of art exhibits a year—both by its students and outside professional artists. This is a good place to discover up-and-coming young artists in an atmosphere of great enthusiasm. Phone them before you go: (212) 926-4100.

If you're interested in seeing more black art throughout the five boroughs, don't neglect to visit the following:

- Caribbean Center (408 West 58th Street): stop by this center to find out about the latest exhibitions of black art throughout the city. Telephone: (212) 307-7420.
- Bronx Museum (see listings in the back): the museum has occasional exhibitions relating to black culture.
- Brooklyn Museum (see listings in the back): one of the city's best collections of African art is on permanent display here.
- Metropolitan Museum (see page 46): the African art collection of the Metropolitan is one of the greatest in the world, as it encompasses the collection once housed in New York's Museum of Primitive Art, as well as a magnificent, recently donated, private collection.
- Brasserie Creole (227-02 Linden Boulevard in Queens): this restaurant mounts about five exhibitions of Haitian art a year. You can combine your art appreciation with a nice Caribbean meal, or just come to look at the Haitian art by contemporary artists. Telephone first: (718) 291-4354.

... And in Addition

Major programs in black art and culture can be seen at the Studio Museum of Harlem, which provides everything from workshops to concerts to studio space.

- Genesis II Museum of International Black Culture has a yearly festival of the arts. For information call, (212) 666-7222.

- Jamaica Art Center (Queens) has a variety of programs. Telephone: (718) 658-7400.
- Two experts on Haitian art and culture that you might wish to consult are: Jeff Joseph: (718) 953-5230, or Henry Frank: (212) 297-0325 or 697-9767.
- Mythic Arts Africa, 594 Broadway, 3rd floor, is a gallery devoted to traditional African arts and artifacts, including sculpture and textiles. Telephone: (212) 941-5968.
- Graven Images, Ltd., 476 Broome Street, 6B, is another gallery specializing in African (and Oceanic) artifacts—masks in particular. Telephone: (212) 226-2550.

12

Crisscrossing
Forty-Second

Gardens, Architecture,
Art Deco, and Modern Art

HOW TO GET THERE
Subway: #4, 5, 6, or 7 to 42nd Street and Grand Central Station
and walk east to First Avenue.
Bus: 42nd Street (M42) crosstown bus; Second (downtown) or
(uptown) Third Avenue (M15).
SUGGESTED TIMES
Preferably during the week and during business hours, since
some of the lobbies are closed to the public during the weekend.
Note that the New York Public Library is open Monday–Satur-
day, 10–6.

Most visitors who come to New York have heard of 42nd Street
and include it among such "must-see" attractions as Fifth and
Park avenues, Central Park, or Rockefeller Center. While most
other sites are known for their elegance and charm, 42nd Street
has been notorious for its sleazy movie houses, slick shops,
and unsavory characters in and around the Times Square area
and besieged theater district. But 42nd Street is much more
than that. If you walk with us from its eastern end across Fifth
Avenue to the west (to Sixth Avenue, the Avenue of the Americas), you will discover artistic and aesthetic pleasure you may

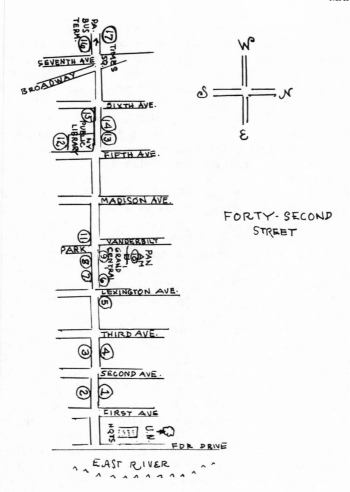

FORTY-SECOND
STREET

not ordinarily associate with this street. For here you will find
some of New York's grand landmarks, beautiful lobbies en-
hanced with murals or sculpture, indoor and outdoor garden
oases, and odd and unexpected architectural gems—from a
charming little church amid tall buildings to an unlikely Romanesque-style bank. So, come along with us to discover the
"other" 42nd Street.

Our first stop is the Ford Foundation Building (1), halfway between First and Second avenues on the north side of 42nd Street. (The official address is 320 East 43rd Street, although the entrance to the garden is from 42nd.) This tasteful, contemporary glass edifice is constructed around one of New York's most fabulous and spacious interior gardens, a 130-foot-high "greenhouse" that can be enjoyed by employees and visitors alike. (The garden is open to the public on weekdays during office hours.) All the interior windows in the building look out onto the spectacular greenery, rather than the usual cityscape. The one-third-acre oasis is a lush combination of tall trees, terraced shrubbery, ground-cover, and water plants gracing a tranquil pond. Although there are seasonal outbursts of brilliantly colored blossoms, the garden is mostly a subtle study of different intensities and shades of green. One can only wish that more urban corporate centers would create such luxuriant green spaces.

Directly opposite the Ford Foundation Building, on the other side of 42nd Street, is The Church of the Covenant (2), at 310 East 42nd. This delightful little church is somewhat dwarfed by the surrounding tall buildings of Tudor City, a 1920s complex of apartments in the American Tudor style. But it can hold its own; built in 1871, it has great charm, with its gabled peaked roof and nice proportions reminiscent of gentler times. To enter the church, you must climb some rather steep steps, which were added after the church found itself a full story above street level—when 42nd Street was lowered to construct the United Nations complex nearby. The inside is intimate and uncluttered; the unusually shaped sanctuary—more square than most—has pretty, circular stained glass windows, delicately carved traceries, and wooden arches. You can visit Monday–Friday, 9–12, or attend a Sunday service at 11 A.M. Telephone: (212) 697-3185.

Continue walking west on 42nd Street to the Daily News Building (3), at 220 (between Second and Third avenues). This fine 1930s art deco brick building (one of several art nouveau gems in the district) can best be seen from across the street, where you can appreciate the full impact of its unusual facade. Rows of brown brick spandrels and windows create a stunning striped pattern. We especially liked the bas reliefs around the entrance; they add decorative charm to the fairly stark architecture. Walk inside, where you will find the world's largest indoor globe—not a work of art, perhaps, but certainly a curiosity. The illuminated revolving globe, set into a recess in the floor, can mesmerize and instill a sense of wanderlust even in the most jaded viewers.

Across the street, at 219 (where you will get a good view of the Daily News Building) is what appears from the outside to be a rather undistinguished contemporary building (4). But, if you walk inside to the outer lobby, you'll find a mosaiclike wall panel that is worth a look. Called *Space and Movement*, this geometric work by the artist F. Bevilacqua features a variety of intermingling shapes against a black marble background.

And now for one of the highlights on this walking tour. The Chrysler Building (5) at 135 East 42nd (on the corner of Lexington) is certainly one of Manhattan's most beloved and recognizable skyscrapers. It is also one of its most vivid icons, having appeared in many paintings, photographs, movies, and other pictorial representations since its completion in 1930. It was the dream of the automobile magnate, Walter P. Chrysler, who wanted to create the world's tallest building. A secret contest ensued between his architect, William Van Allen, and H. Craig Severance, who was busy at work on the Bank of Manhattan on Wall Street. The latter assumed that he had won the competition; when, at the very last moment the dramatic stainless steel spire of the Chrysler Building was assembled and installed, adding some 123 feet to its height. Walter Chrysler's dream-come-true was shortlived, however. Ironically, the Empire State Building was completed only a few months later, dwarfing all the rest.

The Chrysler Building, now restored to its original splendor after some years of neglect, remains one of the city's most romantic and dazzling images—particularly at night, when the diamond shaped windows on its tapering tower are outlined in lights—a favorite site to native New Yorkers and visitors alike. The building reflects in many ways the automotive world it glorifies: from its largely stainless steel facade (it probably has more stainless steel that any other building in the city), to its winged gargoyles (reminiscent of ornaments on car hoods) and radiator caps at the corners resembling capped wheels. The lobby, once an automobile showroom, is an artistic gem. This tasteful interior is rich in color and texture, from the warm tones of deep red and buff African marble on the walls to the intricate inlaid wood patterns that form a subtle counterpoint Note especially the magnificent elevator doors and walls decorated in four different patterns of wood veneer in fanciful floral designs. The large 1930 ceiling mural (97 feet by 100 feet) by Edward Trumbull is representative of the art deco style in its theme as well as its style. Appropriately, it depicts the glories of transportation and hard work, ideas popular during the 1930s particularly with automobile magnates. (Apparently Trumbull used some of the workers in the building as models.)

And now we shift gears and go to the Grand Hyatt Hotel (6) next to Grand Central Terminal (which we will visit later), for a complete contrast in style. For this building is pure glitter from its mirrorlike glass facade—which reflects the surrounding buildings—to its razzle-dazzle interior. The 4-story lobby atrium is complete with Italian marble floors, giant bronzed pillars, fountains cascading noisily, gilded ceiling rods in diagonal patterns, huge circular stairways, mirrors galore and plants and flowers everywhere. Music and the bustling sounds of activity fill whatever vacuum is left after the overabundance besieging the senses.

Cross 42nd Street back to the south side, where you'll find one of our favorite old buildings, at 122 East. An unusually well-kept and attractive example of art deco architecture and interior design, the Chanin Building (7) is a delight to look at both inside and out. Before you enter you'll see on the front of the building some decorative carvings at the fourth floor level and sea monsters just below. But the major interest for us was the narrow lobby with its elegant Istrian marble and intricate bronzework. Even the little gateways that conceal firehoses are disguised with the most elegant designs, as are the elevator doors and mailboxes. This care for artistic detail within a building puts many contemporary buildings to shame. Note the jeweled clocks and the cubist bas reliefs executed by the sculptor René Chambellan.

On the same block, at 110 East 42nd, is another New York landmark building. This is the main office of the Home Savings Bank of America (formerly the Bowery Savings Bank) (8), which is built in the style of a Romanesque basilica. Here you might imagine you are in an Italian church rather than a bank, though you'll see many customers (dwarfed by the huge arching ceiling) doing business at old-fashioned polished counters. This massive room is 160 feet long and 65 feet high, and its proportions and grace make it unusually striking. Note the fine details of its marvelous marble-patterned floor, colored marble columns, and arches (the marble came from France and Italy) intercut with polished bronze. The marble floors are so intricately designed with geometric patterns that they might serve as examples for the hard-edged abstractionists of post-Mondrian days. Note the medieval-style carvings over the doorways that depict squirrels and eagles—symbols appropriate to a bank's ideals of thrift and strength. Some bright tapestries decorate the wing to the east. Don't miss a visit to this bank, which gives a taste of 1923 grandeur to old 42nd Street.

Immediately next door (west) of the bank is the entrance to the upper floors of the same building. Step in here to see the vaulted ceiling, which is deep blue tile work glistening with gold stars. It is a nice entranceway to a bank of elevator doors with carved bronze panels. As you might have guessed, the carvings depict bank employees at work.

Cross back on 42nd Street to one of the city's best loved, and much used, buildings, Grand Central Terminal (9). Designed in 1903–13, this building is one of the finest examples of Beaux Arts architecture in Manhattan. You will enjoy walking through the doors to the main room—though you can hardly call such a massive space a room. It is a vast concourse with many fine windows, arches, happenings, people, and bustle, topped by a vaulted ceiling some 125 feet high. The interior of this landmark is about to undergo substantial renovation.

You can enter the former Pan Am Building (10) that adjoins Grand Central either from within Grand Central or by turning onto the small street called Vanderbilt Avenue that forms the station's western boundary. Here you'll walk north for one block and enter the side door of the former Pan Am Building to see several sights of interest. Immediately within the side door is a golden metal thread sculpture that is uncommonly well set with light filtering through the glass onto it. This elegant sculpture, by Richard Lippold, is a combination sculpture and mobile and is unrelated to the rest of the lobby's decor.

Follow the streaming crowd toward the central lobby and you'll find yourself in a rather curious modern interior space that resembles a stage set for *Aida* on two levels. Large brilliantly gilded columns topped by crescents decorate the interior space, and each is hung with fern plantings in baskets. The effect is rather like imaginary palm trees; a sort of pseudo-Egyptian ambience pervades this bustling, very efficient lobby with its golden railed steps and escalators. Take one of them to the second floor lobby where more gold palms await you, and walk toward the back. Here you'll find yourself on a mezzanine with an interior view of Grand Central, and more escalators. Just above them is a massive wall decoration by the modernist artist, Josef Albers. One of the fathers of geometric abstraction, he assembled this design of red, white, and black stripes in a variety of combinations. Albers was a Bauhaus artist whose interests included combining art and architecture into geometric unity. A respected theorist, he completed this mural, called *Manhattan*, in 1963. Unfortunately, the mural seems to be quite unnoticed amid the golden decorations and scurrying crowds in the lobby.

Go back to 42nd Street and cross once more. At 120 East 42nd you'll find an unusually nice spot, a branch of the Whitney Museum of American Art (11) within the Philip Morris Building. On the corner of Park and 42nd, a very inviting art space (free entrance) features changing exhibitions of contemporary art (some borrowed from galleries in the city), though several works are on permanent display. This pleasing area has some tables and chairs for a comfortable rest and the chance to take in very interesting pieces of art (the exhibitions change frequently) in an informal and spacious setting. (Snacks may be had here at an espresso bar.) There is also an adjacent gallery with exhibitions on a specific theme; among the recent subjects were "Miniature Environments" (box sculptures) and works by

American realists Paul Cadmus and George Tooker. The Whitney is open from 11–6 Monday through Friday, Thursday to 7:30. Telephone: (212) 878-2550.

Your next stop is another major city landmark, the New York Public Library (12), the imposing building on the corner of Fifth Avenue and 42nd Street. You should visit the three floors of this library at your leisure, for it is filled with interesting sights, from the giant reading room to the special collection on the third floor. But on this outing, we suggest you walk up the broad stone steps between the famous lions (designed by Edward C. Potter in about 1901) and enter the lobby. Just behind it you'll find the Library's small exhibition space, where a charming series of exhibits is featured. Combining writing, pictures, and a particular subject, these shows often include unusually fine works. A recent example was an exhibition of baseball writing and pictures, and among the wide-ranging paintings were works by Raoul Dufy, George Bellows, and Claes Oldenburg. In the periodical room on the first floor you'll find a newly completed set of thirteen murals which depict New York's different architectural styles in trompe l'oeil by Richard Haas.

And if you take the elevator to the third floor you'll find ongoing exhibitions of prints and rare manuscripts that line the halls or are displayed in the hushed elegance of the special collection rooms. This library is one of New York's most important cultural treasures. The collections are so vast and varied that you will invariably find something of interest on display. Also note the WPA murals by Edward Laning dated 1940 on the third floor. Called *The History of the Recorded Word*, they are among Laning's many vivid works. *Prometheus* by the same artist can be seen on the ceiling of the Reading Room. Telephone: (212) 869-8089.

After leaving the library cross 42nd Street to 11 West 42nd, about halfway up the block going west. This is a well-kept and attractive building called Salmon Towers (13). It houses a number of different organizations. Note the attractive entranceway, with its carvings depicting the twelve months of the year and sculptures of classical figures representing the professions. Inside is a highly polished interior. Take the elevator to the fourth floor, where you'll be surprised by a two-floor renovation for the NYU Center for Continuing Education. Their carefully decorated area makes a tasteful and elegant backdrop for the trompe l'oeil paintings by Richard Haas. Depicting various scenes around 42nd Street in a muted palette of beiges and pale blues, they are curious visual surprises at the end of each short corridor. Don't miss the little café, which pictures Central Park. Each corridor symbolizes another street with a view. We found this to be an ingenious setting for classrooms and a nice melding of contemporary art and architecture.

Practically next door to this building is the CUNY Graduate Center (14) at 33 West 42nd. You will not need to go upstairs to see any art here; everything is on ground level, beginning with two large sculptures flanking the entrance. These rather rusted contemporary works are by Linda Cunningham; they are called *War Memorial III.* Elongated, twisted metal shapes, they are rough-edged, cast bronze abstractions. Inside you'll come upon a large, rather dank space that resembles a parking garage, but which houses a series of contemporary sculptures in a sculpture mall. Very large, modern works were on display when we visited. Despite its rather forbidding cold environment, the mall is a good large space for sculpture.

End your walk with a visit directly across 42nd Street to Bryant Park (15). The newly renovated Bryant Park, just behind the library, is now a delightful, European-style park, with well-kept grass, plantings, kiosks, ballustrades, rows of trees, a working fountain, and small green chairs dotted across the lawn in the London style. There are five statues; on the terrace behind the library is perhaps the most intriguing: a Buddhalike bronze portrait by Jo Davidson of his friend Gertrude Stein, one of the few women so honored in New York.

Other statues include likenesses of Goethe by Karl Fischer; William Cullen Bryant by Herbert Adams and architect Thomas Hastings; William Earl Dodge by John Quincy Adams Ward; and Brazilian statesman José Bonidacio de Andrada e Silva, a life-size statue by José Otavia Correia Lima. This nice center-city space is a cool, tree-lined place for a rest, and, despite some recent low points in its history, we expect a new atmosphere will soon prevail here.

You could venture farther west, however, into a presently

tawdry area best known for its seediness and movie marquees. If you wish to brave several unattractive blocks of Times Square, you'll find a large collection of public art at the Port Authority Bus Terminal (16), between Eighth and Ninth avenues. George Segal's well-known *Commuters* (1980) is a bronze sculpture with white patina showing three realistic, tired-looking figures, who are almost lost among the sixty million passengers rushing by each year. J. Estevan Perez is represented by *Constructivist Space Drawing* (1981), which consists of fifteen fired porcelain enamel panels along a wall on the B level. Probably the most popular work is George Rhoads's *42nd Street Ballroom* (1983), a delightful kinetic sculpture in the South Wing. Also in the South Wing is a series of twelve silk-screen double-faced banners by Richard Anuszkiewicz, called *Complimentary Gothic, I* (1984).

Just across the street is a nice old church, The Church of the Holy Cross (17). Here, in a quiet atmosphere of stained glass and marble, you'll come across several works designed by Louis Comfort Tiffany, including the two mosaic panels that flank the center altar and, on the right of the entrance, a glass work depicting St. John the Baptist.

... And in Addition

- New York Public Library: Tours of current exhibits (usually held at 12:30 and at 2:30) and tours of Central Research Library building (usually at 11 and 2), each lasting about one hour, Monday–Saturday; free. For information, call (212) 930-0911 or 869-8089; for information on exhibits or general information, call (212) 930-0800. Library workshops on basic library skills: afternoons and evenings call (212) 340-0944.
- Whitney Museum at Philip Morris: film programs in connection with current exhibits (free, on first-come, first-served basis), usually at 6:30 on Wednesdays, held in Philip Morris Auditorium (which holds about 60 people). Call (212) 878-2550 for information.
- CUNY Graduate Center has regular concerts and lectures. Call (212) 642-1600 for information.
- United Nations gardens and public spaces (between 44th and

48th streets and First Avenue). Among the outdoor sculptures to see are Barbara Hepworth's bronze Hammarskjöld Memorial called *Single Form* (1964), Fritz Cremer's *The Rising Man* (1975), Anton Augustinčić's *Peace* (1954), and Zurab Tseretelli's *Good Defeats Evil* (1990), a variation on St. George and the Dragon, recently donated by the USSR. It is made of Soviet and American missile parts. The garden along the East River, which contains the most impressive collection of hybrid tea roses anywhere in Manhattan, is also a pleasant place for walking.

- Intar Latin America (420 West 42nd Street, 2nd floor): gallery specializing in art from the Americas, particularly contemporary works. Telephone: (212) 695-6134.
- "Neon for Forty-second Street," by Stephen Antonakos is a blue and red swirl of neon above a building at 440 West 42nd Street.
- International Center of Photography at 1133 Avenue of the Americas (43rd Street). Telephone: (212) 768-4680.
- Just south of 42nd Street are three sites where you can see contemporary sculpture:
1. On Third Avenue at 200 East 42nd, you'll find Jan Peter Stern's "Windward" (1961), a geometric bronze abstraction outside the building.
2. In the lobby of 99 Park Avenue (between 39th and 40th streets) is "Seeking Freedom," a stainless steel modern globe with a blue bird perched in the center, by Lisa Amundsen.
3. Directly across the street, in the lobby of 90 Park Avenue, are three impressive works by Bert Schwartz. Based on Biblical themes, these are fiberglass and stained glass abstractions, one with a fountain 30 feet high.

13

Arts in Process

Soho and Tribeca Studios, Ateliers, and Galleries

HOW TO GET THERE
Subway: *E train to Spring Street, or N or R train to Prince Street, or #6 train to Spring Street.*
SUGGESTED TIMES
Afternoon and by appointment, Tuesday–Sunday. If you wish to make appointments with individual artists listed, call them during business hours at least two days in advance.

The art of making art seems somewhat mysterious to most of us. We see finished products glossily displayed in galleries and museums, well lit, carefully framed behind glass, on display in elegant surroundings. Where are the artists who make it? How do they go about? Why do they do what they do?

To answer these questions, come along with us on an art-in-process walk. Here you will see art happening, as well as being displayed as a finished product. On this walk there will be few explanatory notes (and prices) pinned to walls; instead, you can ask questions of the artists themselves. We will be visiting workshops and studios where the city craftspersons and artists do their work. And then when you enter nearby galleries you might find you have a whole new understanding of what you are seeing. We chose Soho and Tribeca for our art-in-process walk. Here one of the city's largest concentrations of creative

111

people in the visual arts live and work and exhibit. Among
their studios and workshops are some of New York's best
known galleries and alternative museums. We found the narrow streets with their jumble of galleries and the off-beat environment invigorating and off-beat, from the scale of the buildings to the people on the streets. It is one of the city's most
individual neighborhoods.

It's always amazing how the arrival of the artists and galleries
changes an area. Soho was once the heart of Manhattan's manufacturing district. Today you'll find many of New York's leading
artists and craftspersons in this downtown area (Soho is a nick-
name for South of Houston) and in Tribeca (Triangle Below

Canal). Along narrow cobblestone streets filled with the rumble of trucks are the giant spaces both artists and their galleries need. Lofts in old manufacturing buildings (many with unusual architectural details and cast-iron fronts) were first converted to studios and galleries by artists during the abstract expressionist era. Looking for space there they could work on oversized canvases and sculpture, artists found Soho's unpartitioned manufacturing space and "away-from-it-all" charm perfect. The city legalized lofts for artists some years ago. By the late 1960s, giant galleries had sprung up, and the epicenter of New York's avant-garde art world was to be found south of Houston instead of in the posh Upper East Side.

But, as so often happens, the artists' colony was followed by trendy boutiques and restaurants, as well as dozens of commercial enterprises. Today high rents have driven many in the art world south once again—this time to Tribeca. So far, the Franklin Street area has several concentrations of workshops, and many of the city's avant-garde artists and museums call this area home. Both regions are "mixed bags," but well worth a visit. Nowhere else in the city will you find such a concentration of creative energy in a small area.

It should be added here that we are inviting you into the workshops and studios of a tiny segment of the area's artistic population. Obviously their output is in no way representative or indicative of every style or trend. Some is abstract, some more figurative. Each has its own raison d'être, and we've made no judgments about what you'll like and what you'll think is either dull or shocking. We hope, by the way, that since these creative people were good enough to open their doors to us, that you'll be polite enough to say that everything you see is at least interesting.

Note: Before embarking on this walk, please read ahead and decide whether you would like to make appointments with any artists. They must be telephoned first for an appointment. Call them several days in advance, and plan your walk around the hours you set up. The other stops along our route are open to public visits at the hours listed.

Our first stop is the InterArt Center (1) at 167 Spring Street.

113

This combination tapestry workshop and exhibition space provides lectures and classes about a variety of crafts. Most interesting is the weaving room, where the fiber art is made. Here giant Gobelin-style looms and bright colored weavings can be seen. Adjacent space houses not-for-profit galleries. Telephone (212) 431-7500.

You are now in the heart of artistic Soho. We expect you will dip into galleries as you go along these busy streets. The old warehouses and manufacturing buildings that they have taken over provide magnificent, spacious surroundings. Don't forget to visit 2nd-floor galleries as well as those you can look into from the street.

Continue east on Spring Street to Greene Street and turn left. At 110 Greene Street you'll find the Sculptor's Guild (2), which features art by contemporary sculptors in a variety of styles. In addition to this nice upstairs exhibition space, the Guild has shows at other sites in New York and around the world, including a recent exhibition in Kyoto. Don't miss occasional works on display in the hallways of this building. Telephone: (212) 431-5669

Walk north on Greene Street to Prince Street, where you will turn right. Cross over as you near Broadway. On the southwest corner is a trompe l'oeil mural (3) by Richard Haas that was sponsored by City Walls, Inc., in an effort to enliven the city's drab outdoor surfaces. This witty mural reproduces in paint some of the architectural details of the building.

Walk east a few steps to Broadway and turn right. Here is a major museum block. At 593 Broadway is a new Soho addition. (see Artwalk #11).The Museum for African Art (4), which recently moved from the Upper East Side, has elegant new quarters here. You will not want to miss this collection and its changing shows. The Museum is described on page 96. Hours: Tuesday–Friday: 10:30 to 5:30; Saturday: noon to 8:00; Sunday: noon to 6 P.M. Telephone: (212) 966-1313.

Almost next door you'll find the New Museum of Contemporary Art (5). Here is an alternative space which specializes in mixed media installations and various avant-garde happenings. Recent shows included *The Appearance of Sound* by Martha

Fleming and Lyne Lapointe, and an installation by Erica Rothenberg called *Have You Attacked America Today?* The museum is open Wednesday, Thursday, and Sunday, 12–6, and Friday and Saturday, 12–8. Telephone: (212) 219-1355.

Your next—and a major—stop is at 575 Broadway, the marvelous new additional home of the Guggenheim Museum Soho (6). This is the downtown branch of the illustrious Solomon Guggenheim Museum on Fifth Avenue (described on page 47). Here in an elegantly renovated old Soho warehouse the museum brings smaller shows and a lively collection of events for the downtown area. Recent exhibitions have included paintings by Chagall, sculpture by Brancusi, Kandinsky watercolors, "Industrial Elegance," and a show called "Robert Morris: The Mind/Body Problem." Hours: Sunday, Wednesday, Thursday, Friday: 11–6 P.M.; Saturday: 11–8. Telephone: (212) 423-3500.

Upon leaving the Guggenheim Soho, cross the street to The Alternative Museum (7), upstairs at 594 Broadway. (And don't miss the many galleries in this building and all along this block both upstairs and at street level.) The focus here is on showing less established artists in an open atmosphere. Recent events include multimedia and politically-oriented exhibitions. Telephone: (212) 226-4444.

Nearby is the giant loft studio of Paul Vazquez (8), an artist currently at work on a series of large diptychs and triptychs called the "Paradox Series." You will enjoy a visit with this personable artist, who will be happy to talk about his enigmatic, semiabstract acrylics, which are a combination of geometric forms and anthropomorphic figures. Telephone: (212) 274-0307.

Walk to Spring Street and turn left, continuing east to Lafayette Street. A new and charming addition at 72 Spring Street is the Children's Museum of the Arts (9). Among their delightful and eclectic offerings for kids from five to ten years old are classes in giant animal sculpture, mobile making, and a sculpture garden workshop using found objects. There are ongoing exhibitions by children from around the world. Hours: Tuesday–Sunday 9–5; Thursday till 7. Telephone: (212) 274-0986.

Walk north on Lafayette to the corner at 55 Prince Street for

115

an interesting visit to a sculpture casting studio. The Ranier Sculpture Casting workshop (10) is a busy place providing cast ing facilities for professionals and nonprofessionals alike Works being cast when we visited ranged from tiny, realisti figurines to bold abstractions. If you have never seen the intri cate casting process, you will enjoy observing firsthand it many stages. Only small works are cast here; Ranieri operate a much larger facility outside the city. Telephone: (212) 982 5150.

Head south one and one half blocks back to Broome Stree and turn right. Walk to Crosby Street and make another righ turn. At 54 Crosby you'll find the studio of Arturo Di Modic (11). Arturo di Modica, the sculptor, will show visitors aroun by appointment. He prefers to be called one or two days i advance; it is best to reach him in the morning.

Di Modica is a native of Sicily who has been in New Yor for several years. His studio attests to his facility in just abou every sculpture medium. He employs assistants for his man projects, and we think you'll find his very busy studio ex tremely interesting. He will show you the various stages of hi work, beginning with drawn plans for commissions, throug small plaster models, up to huge bronze or marble sculpture (see page 18). Di Modica has hopes of a "Renaissance" work shop environment, but finds the American public infuriatingl indifferent to art; recently he "dumped" eight tons of sculptur on Fifth Avenue to counteract what he termed "media indif ference."

His works are exuberant, with suggestive organic forms, ofte representing natural shapes of animals and human beings. Glis tening marble and bronze surfaces are interspersed with rough plaster works; we recommend this visit for those who find tex tures and sculptural shapes intriguing. And Di Modica is genial host who will talk about his work easily. Telephone (212) 966-9068.

Return to Broome Street and walk west until you reach Woos ter Street. Turn left and walk south to 35 Wooster. Here is th elegant Drawing Center (12) with its columned facade and row of sleek Corinthian columns and gleaming wood floors. Th

allery shows the works of emerging artists who are not con-
ected with dealers and have not yet had solo shows. About
fty artists are carefully selected from some fifteen hundred
ntries to exhibit in one of the center's three annual contempo-
ary shows. (A fourth annual exhibit, held from April to July,
eatures historic works.) A recent show was based on a surreal-
st game called "exquisite cadaver," in which artists each added
o a single work unaware of other contributions. Contemporary
rawing is examined in its many interpretations—from col-
ages, charcoal drawings, photos, found objects to installations
sing different materials such as paper, string, wire, powdered
raphite, acrylic, sand, beeswax, oil, and pen and ink. The
rawing Center is open Tuesday–Saturday, 11–6, and Wednes-
ay, 11–8. Telephone: (212) 219-2166.

Further along on the same street (if you're still feeling ener-
etic) at 141 Wooster is one of the centers for the avant-garde
howings of the DIA Center for the Arts (13). Here you'll find
hanging exhibitions of the latest in the visual arts, as well as
ectures, symposia and publications. For some time, they have
een exhibiting Walter De Maria's "The New York Earth
oom," an environmental, literally earth-filled work. As of this
vriting, the same artist is also being shown at another DIA
enue at 393 West Broadway (see below). DIA's headquarters
re at 548 West 22nd Street (where you can visit a conceptual
ooftop installation by Dan Graham made of geometric glass
orms), and 155 Mercer Street. Telephone for information on
ll DIA sites: (212) 473-8072.

From Wooster Street, walk one block west (left) on Houston
treet to West Broadway, a major thoroughfare for boutiques,
alleries, and shops. At 393 West Broadway, amid a cluster of
oth serious galleries and commercial kitsch is another DIA
ocation (14). At this writing they were presenting a show called
The Broken Kilometer."

You've now completed half of this Soho/Tribeca walk. If
ou're feeling energetic and have time to spare, you might want
o continue to Tribeca. Although Tribeca may not yet be the
lamorous spot that Soho is, it is a genuine artists' community
vith many studios, and some unusual museums, and galleries.
lthough it is a bit of a walk, we encourage you to continue.

117

Walk south on West Broadway for several blocks until you come to the "V" formed by Varick and West Broadway, and Franklin Street. Turn right (west) on Franklin, to another of our favorite stops, the Franklin Street Potters (15) at 151 Franklin. This bright, cheerful, and attractive working studio is churning with activity. Seven busy potters work here (Judy Jackson and Emily Pearlman are the two full-time artisans), and there are different styles, techniques, and works to look at. Some of the potters use high-fire clay and glaze, while others use low-fire clay and glaze (which produce brighter colors). Visitors are welcome to come in and browse and watch the artists at work. The ambience is relaxed, friendly, and very productive. In the oven room at the back are three kilns to bake the pottery; you'll also see a kick wheel and electric wheel. The two full-time potters mix all their glazes from scratch and use a full ton of clay every couple of months. The hands-on atmosphere is so appealing in this workshop that you'll feel like rolling up your sleeves and digging in yourself. The Franklin Street Potters is open Monday–Friday, 10–6. During the weekend we were told that someone is usually there working after 12 noon, but we recommend that you phone first if you plan to come then. Telephone: (212) 431-7631.

Continue west on Franklin, turn the corner at Hudson Street (left), and walk two blocks to Worth Street. Go left, to 11 Worth Street, the working studio of sculptor Bill Barrett (16). We were told by both the artist and his studio assistant that there is usually someone in the studio during the day and that it is not necessary to make an appointment to visit; however, to be sure we suggest you telephone first. Bill Barrett is a Santa Fe/New York sculptor who usually works in aluminum and bronze. His massive welded metal constructions can be seen in various cities as well as in New York. (On Staten Island a large aluminum graffiti-inspired sculpture is on display at New Dorp High School.) Although Barrett does much of his work—especially his casting and foundry work—elsewhere, here at his Tribeca studio you can see models, works in progress, as well as finished works. We found him a friendly host, though there is less hands-on atmosphere here than in some of our other studio visits. Telephone: (212) 431–5591.

Our next three stops will give you an idea of the most current
and avant-garde art in process these days. Three "alternative"
exhibition spaces are within one block of each other.

From Bill Barrett's studio, continue east on Worth to West
Broadway (less than a block), go north two blocks, and cross
West Broadway to 112 Franklin, The Franklin Furnace (17),
which calls itself the "belly button" of Tribeca. The goal of this
unusual archive/museum/art center is to collect, preserve, and
interpret so-called "throw-away" avant-garde art of the past,
while continuing to foster art of the present and future. The
motley items in their archives and on display include artist-
produced books, magazines, records, tapes, unusual artworks
in nontraditional forms (both permanent and ephemeral), and
installations. You might see antique postcards, odd newsletters
signed with thumbprints, or other fairly ordinary objects rendered unique by their particular treatment or interpretation.
Recent exhibits (which change monthly) have included such
eclectic items as a series of booklets on the adventures of monkeys and men; the personal experiences of a wealthy avant-
garde beach community as expressed through images, texts,
and objects; and life-size cutouts of famous contemporary political figures. In addition, Franklin Furnace produces original
off-beat performances using different mediums—from taped or
live conversations, special audiovisual effects, moving images,
movement, vocal duets, and slides to dramatic scenes on all
sorts of contemporary topics and multimedia artist performances. The Furnace is open Tuesday–Saturday, 12–6. Telephone: (212) 925-4671.

A very short walk left on Church Street and around the block
to the corner of White Street will take you to our next stop, the
Alternative Museum (18), at 17 White Street. The focus here is
on showing nonestablished artists in an open atmosphere,
where new ideas can be presented in an uncommercial way.
This nonprofit organization is operated by a cooperative group
of artists. The results are fresh, innovative exhibits, as well
as poetry readings, workshops, and concerts. There are two
exhibition galleries—the Main and the Matrix galleries—where
you may see thematic shows or one-person shows by as yet
unknown artists. Typical of their unusual offerings is a recent

119

show called *Mon Rêve* (My Dream), a record of Haiti since
Duvalier by folk artists and others. A permanent collection of
representative works by more than 70 artists is on display on
a rotating basis, but many of the exhibits come from outside
(including foreign countries). Hours: Tuesday–Saturday, 11–6.
Telephone: (212) 966-4444.

And finally, our last stop is Artists Space (19), at 223 West
Broadway, just up the street. This popular and well-established
gallery offers another exhibition space for innovative and eclec
tic art and architecture. Recent shows have included a particu
larly interesting and unusual architectural exhibit, "London
Project," which featured drawings, collages, models, installa
tions, and silkscreen prints of that city. Among the concepts
explored were the condition of the contemporary city, time
telling methods, the vision of the city as expressed through
classical literature, and London's symbols of power as seen
through its buildings. More recently, in order to raise funds,
Artists Space has turned itself into a temporary miniature gol
course with each hole designed by a different artist. Gallery
hours are Tuesday–Saturday, 11–6. Telephone: (212) 226-3970

. . . And in Addition
You are invited to visit the following artists' studios and work
shops (outside of this immediate Soho area) if you call first to
make an appointment:

- Diana Carulli, a specialist in fabric and wire sculpture and
  batik, on Van Dam Street. Telephone: (212) 255-6312.
- Darrell Nettles, East 10th Street. This artist's studio is a tidy
  place where he makes large, geometric woven and painted
  canvas stuctures on wooden bases. Telephone: (212) 473-
  4910.
- Claire Heimarck, West 37th Street. This abstract artist works
  on paper in a variety of media and has a press in her studio
  Telephone: (212) 239-4825.
- A. C. Hollingsworth, Grand Street. This painter, teacher, and
  raconteur's fifth floor walk-up on the edge of Soho is filled
  with his bright-colored, semiabstract works and collected ar
  tifacts. He is a genial host who will talk about his own work

and that of other African-American artists, and will share with you his wide acquaintance with such artists as Romare Bearden and Hale Woodruff. Telephone: (212) 281-3234.

- Greg Wyatt, the sculptor-in-residence at the Cathedral of St. John the Divine, works and teaches in a wonderful studio in the crypt below the church. See page 167.
- P.S. 1 in Long Island City, Queens (see page 202).
- Diana Soorikian, West 14th Street. Large, semiabstract works fill this inviting studio in the heart of the wholesale meat district where the artist works (and a number of films have been shot).
- If you are interested in painting your own pottery, you might want to visit the studio of Emily Goodman at 31 West 21st Street in Chelsea. Here you can decorate your own pottery creations and have them glazed and fired.
- To visit the New York Experimental Glass Workshop (647 Fulton Street in Brooklyn) see page 219.
- The Drawing Center: lectures, concerts, and programs including one on care and conservation of art.
- The Franklin Furnace, Alternative Museum, and Artist Space: all offer every sort of contemporary cultural affair.
- American Craft Museum (see page 138).
- If you are interested in performance art, check Art in General at 79 Walker Street. Telephone: (212) 219-0473.
- The Clocktower at 108 Leonard Street for recent art exhibitions by local artists. Telephone: (212) 233-1096.
- Storefront for Art and Architecture, 97 Kenmare St. changing exhibitions. Don't miss the puzzle-shaped and pivoting doors and windows in this deconstructed storefront designed by artist Vito Acconci and architect Stephen Holl. Telephone: (212) 431-5795.
- Greenwich House Pottery, 16 Jones Street (Greenwich Village): Another busy pottery workshop, this one is part of an active community center that features many different classes in various kinds of art and music. Telephone: (212) 242-4106.

14

Midtown Oases—
Atria and Outdoor Art

Part I, East Side

HOW TO GET THERE
Subway: #6 train to 51 Street or E or F train to Lexington–Third Avenue station.
Bus: Fifth Avenue bus downtown or Madison Avenue bus up town (M1, 2, 3, 4).

SUGGESTED TIMES
Check individual listings, but note that all atria and lobbie, are open during the week; some are open daily; others are closed on weekends. Your best bet is to take this walk during the week, preferably during business hours.

Even if you're a native New Yorker, you probably think of Man hattan as a vast collection of stone and steel buildings sur rounded by streets and sidewalks. True, there's Central Park but are there other urban oases with trees? And, better yet, with art in them? Well, surprisingly, even to us, we have found many right in the heart of midtown, and we've devised two walks (or one very long walk!) that will take you from one lovely spot to another, from oases with trees and potted flowers that change with the season to waterfalls and modern sculptures.

You'll see some exciting outdoor art and indoor atria. And there are benches aplenty to sit on. In fact, this is an unusually relaxing artwalk, because the serenity of these little spots invites you to pause and contemplate both nature and sculpture, and to listen to the sound of rushing waterfalls instead of honking horns.

We have divided this artwalk into two sections, because there are so many places to visit in midtown. On one day you can explore the oases on the East Side; and, making an imaginary line down the center of Fifth Avenue, on another day enjoy the West Side. Or, if you are a particularly energetic person, you can do both walks in one day.

Our first stop—and one of our favorites—is Greenacre Park (1) on 51st Street, between Second and Third avenues. This intimate Japanese-style urban garden is a tranquil respite from the city's noise and confusion. The gentle sounds you hear are those of a rushing brook, a fountain cascading over an abstract granite sculpture, and a graceful 25-foot waterfall. Even though this park is tiny—60 feet by 100 feet—it creates the impression of spaciousness. The plantings are well tended, yet naturalistic and understated (in the Japanese manner) and, unless you arrive during lunchtime, you will not find this park crowded. Here you can sit amid the greenery and contemplate, read, or have a snack (as many do) before starting your walk. There are tables and chairs on the main level, a raised platform in the shade, and discreet lights for night-time use.

From Greenacre Park walk west to Third Avenue and then south to 50th Street. The Crystal Pavilion (2) at 805 Third Avenue is another world from the quiet oasis you've just left, for this is a bustling, glittering rendezvous spot with shops, galleries, cafés, and small restaurants, as well as places just to sit and rest. The setting is aggressively contemporary and "glitzy," with its massive three-level shiny stainless steel columns, neon lights, glass elevators, and granite. It's an impressive space, one that shows the fascination of many modern architects for volume and light. Its waterfall, sunny alcove, and plants (in large commercial plots) tend to soften its somewhat hard-boiled look and make the decor less forbidding. The Crystal Pavilion is open Monday–Saturday, 7:30 A.M. to 11 P.M.

Walk down to 777 Third Avenue between 48th and 49th streets. Here, a graceful, swirling 15-foot high stainless steel sculpture adds interest to the otherwise anonymous contempo rary building it adorns. Entitled *contrappunto* (3), this light airy 1963 work by Beverly Pepper consists of two separate parts: the upper portion, rotated by a motor, suspends from the actual building and reacts to the stationary lower portion forming a sort of sculptural counterpoint.

Walk south on Third Avenue to 711 Third Avenue (between 45th and 46th streets). The lobby is decorated by a large wrap around 1956 Hans Hoffmann mosaic (4) in his customary, brilliant primary colors and geometric abstract shapes.

From here it's a short hop to our next stop, Park Avenue Atrium (5), which can be entered from Lexington Avenue or 45th or 46th streets (the building has three official addresses) Like the Crystal Pavilion, this modern New York atrium is big splashy, and jazzy, from its lighted see-through elevators that rush you up and down at top speed, to the tiers of greenery festooned over aluminum balconies on each floor. A huge sus pended contemporary sculpture, *Winged Gamma* (1981), by Richard Lippold extends over several stories, dominating the scene. Its long steel rays complement the stark, modern deco and add interest to the futuristic interior. Unfortunately, the seating area is not especially inviting, for you are offered only uncomfortable granite benches set in the usual ficus trees in large tubs. But the overall scene and the flurry of people coming and going are fascinating to watch. The Park Avenue Atrium is open from 8 A.M. to 6 P.M. Monday–Friday.

Exit to Park Avenue and begin walking up the avenue, past some of New York's fanciest corporate addresses. Between 46th and 47th streets, in front of 245 Park Avenue, you'll see a giant contemporary black fiberglass sculpture in the shape of inter locking serpentine forms (or doughnut-shaped parts, de pending on your point of view). Entitled *Performance Machine Big O's* (6), it was created by Lowell Jones in 1985 and very much embodies the twentieth century's fascination and love affair with machinery. This unusual kinetic sculpture operated by solar energy takes four hours to complete one rotation which means that unless you have time and patience you won' notice its movement.

Walk one block north to the Chem Court Building (7) at Park

Avenue and 47th Street, the headquarters of Chemical Bank. Before entering this massive building (which takes up a full block), note a bronze figure of a man hailing a cab at the front entrance. This amusingly realistic sculpture called *Taxi!* (1983) by Seward Johnson, Jr., blends in with the people rushing in and out of the building and might pass unobserved. When you first walk inside the building you are stunned by the sheer size and abundance of everything: from the immense atrium with its glass and geometric steel supports to the staggering number of plants. The three-storied greenhouse (which measures 12,500 square feet) features all sorts of greenery, from large-scale versions of common household plants—which look exotic because of their size and lushness—to olive trees, vines, and Chinese evergreens. A large waterfall adds pleasant background sounds. Unlike other public atria in the area, Chem Court is open 24 hours daily.

Leaving the imposing Chem Court, walk north to Park and 50th Street where you'll find St. Bartholomew's Church (8), affectionately known as "St. Bart's" in the community. This charming Romanesque-style church is virtually dwarfed by its towering neighbors and contrasts sharply with its surroundings. Note its graceful curved lines and ornate carved portico (sculpted by Daniel Chester French and Philip Martiny and modeled after a church in the south of France). Its delightful enclosed garden is reminiscent of those found in English country parsonages and provides a welcome respite in this urban setting. Within the garden is a bronze sculpture, *The Four Generations*, by the Mexican sculptor Francisco Zuniga, now depicting three barefoot Mexican peasant women (a fourth was stolen some years ago). There was a time when the future of St. Bartholomew was also in jeopardy, as some of New York's most aggressive real estate developers had their eye on this prime site. Conservationists and the community rallied and, with its future more secure, the church seems to hold its own in this unlikely spot.

Just one block north on Park is a nice sunken outdoor plaza in front of the Rudin Management Building (9) at 345 Park. This is a popular picnic spot for those who work in the neighborhood and the site of frequent summer lunch-hour concerts.

125

(We once heard an excellent jazz group there.) The surroundings are pleasant and the people-watching first rate on this busy street corner. Here, too, as in the case of so many new corporate building complexes, contemporary sculptures grace interior and exterior spaces. On one end of the plaza you'll find *Dinoceras* (1921), a 12-foot-high bronze work by Robert Cook. This curious structure resembles the intertwining bones of a prehistoric animal (the dinoceras lived in North America during the Eocene period) and was modeled in beeswax, of all things! In the lobby of the building is a less exotic but, nonetheless interesting rose marble work by Luis Sanguino depicting an amorous couple, not surprisingly called *Amor*.

(We recommend a quick detour to 50th Street. You'll find the Heron Building at 70 East 50th Street, a recent addition to the East Side; of particular note is the small, rather fascinating plaza that ornaments the lobby. Here, set in a kind of radical perspective is a three dimensional trompe l'oeil, columned plaza and fountain that functions both as a witty send-up of classical architecture and a spatial extension of the lobby.)

Walk up Park to 52nd Street and west, to the Park Avenue Plaza (10), at 55 East 52nd Street, another dazzling modern building. A walk-through arcade between 52nd and 53rd streets, this somewhat stark green marble atrium is also a place for sitting. (There are tables and chairs at each end.) Its especially high ceiling gives it a feeling of great spaciousness, which is reduced to a more human scale by the various potted plants and flowers arranged diagonally. A waterfall—the inevitable ingredient in many modern interior gardens—adds interest to the high east wall and ubiquitous ficus trees adorn each end. Next to the atrium you can enjoy an arcade wih several trendy shops and cafés. Park Avenue Plaza is open daily from 8 A.M. to 10 P.M.

Walk east again to Lexington Avenue, to the corner of 53rd Street. At 599 Lexington Avenue, a large, typical, Frank Stella work is the center of attraction. Entitled *Salta Nel Mio Sacco* (11), it consists of jagged cutout painted forms in brilliant colors.

Just north is another modern New York landmark, the Citi-corp Building, with its contemporary church, St. Peter's Lutheran Church (12). This light-filled, glass space houses an impressive Louise Nevelson construction in its Erol Beker Chapel of the Good Shepherd.

Turn west and, on your way back across 54th Street toward Park Avenue, you might stop at Lever House (13) (Park Avenue and 54th Street). There you will find a variety of changing exhibitions in the main lobby, including group shows, sculpture, and community art events, although sometimes the massive lobby is empty.

At 520 Madison Avenue and 53rd Street you'll find an art-filled lobby (14). These are the headquarters of Continental Illinois, whose otherwise ordinary lobby contains six large contemporary works of art. Most prominent among them is another Frank Stella, his *Estoril* (1981), a giant bright-colored, hard-edged mixed-media affair on etched magnesium. This work is permanently on display, while the other five paintings change every six months or so, and you can go back on other occasions for a fresh look. (In fact, this particular walk is recommended in different seasons, for the plantings in the various gardens, as well as the pictures, change frequently.) Don't miss the lovely waterfall. The lobby is open during business hours only.

As you walk north on Madison Avenue, stop into the lobby of the Dillon Read Building (15) at 54th Street. Here, at 535 Madison Avenue, is a fine Miró tapestry in a dark, dreary lobby. The bright woven forms (recognizably Miró in shape and color) brighten the dark gray walls of the lobby. Outside there is a tiny plaza, replete with fountain and greenery and ivy walls—one of the city's little vest-pocket oases.

Just down the street at 527 Madison (at 53rd) is an evocative bronze sculpture by an English artist, Raymond Mason. Called "The Crowd," its many figures are huddled together against the outside world.

A small hop up Madison will take you to another interesting modern walk-through, the brand-new Park Avenue Tower (16), at 65 East 55th, connecting 54th and 55th streets and Park and Madison avenues. Particularly unusual about this space are the attractive gray and rose marble panels on the giant walls that create a different style of decor from the somewhat predictable waterfalls, steel columns, lights, and potted ficus trees. The kaleidoscope effects resulting from these different marble designs are quite stunning in the posh lobby.

Up one block, off Madison Avenue at 60 East 56th Street there is a tiny lobby graced by an appealing Anton Refregier mosaic (18). It consists of many small tile designs held together by a decorative grid of iron rods. Compared to some of the giant, brash works found in our newest lobbies, this seems an intimate, delicate ornament.

To make a quick detour, walk to 500 Park Avenue at 59th Street. Here in the lobby (the entrance is on 59th Street) is a very large, bold, horizontal abstract painting by Mimi Thompson. Called *One-Headed Landscape* (20), Thompson's work features fluorescent paint motifs on canvas in an expressionistic style.

Walk to Madison and head south to 57th Street. Our next stop has been one of New York's favorites. On the corner of 57th (officially 590 Madison) is the famous lobby and garden of I.B.M. (21), just recently sold. When I.B.M. opened its "state-of-the-art" public space, New Yorkers heaved a collective sigh of relief—at last a place to stop in midtown and rest, look at art, and even buy a snack. It is truly a delightful oasis and we hope will continue to be so. The tall, graceful bamboo trees of the indoor garden rise over tables and benches and always-changing displays of flowers and decorative plants. The atrium has an asymmetrical shape, and you'll wonder if you are actually indoors or out; the atrium is open all winter and it is always popular, like the favorite reading or "hanging-out" spot on a college campus.

In the outdoor part of the former I.B.M. complex, you'll find a granite, stainless steel, and water sculpture/fountain, *Levitated Mass* (1982), by Michael Heizer. You can sit on the edges of this massive and low, horizontal piece and watch city life pass by. In the center of the flat, abstract work is an 11-ton boulder that seems to be rising from the surrounding water, creating the illusion of weightlessness.

Here you may exit and walk to Fifth Avenue. At 745 Fifth Avenue, between 57th and 58th Streets, be sure not to pass by

745 Fifth Avenue, a 1930s building midblock. Here you'll find an unusual painted lobby ceiling from the art deco era. It is the work of Arthur Covey, who made a brightly colored, mosaic-style, semiabstract picture of Manhattan Island filled with bridges, street scenes, skyscrapers, and rushing trains.

If, instead of exiting at Madison Avenue you walk right through I.B.M.'s interior garden area, you will come into the adjoining Trump Plaza (22). Some people consider this fairly new addition to the New York scene to be an example of unbridled "glitz," tacky, overdone, and symptomatic of conspicuous consumption. On the other hand, you won't want to miss this controversial site, a curious blend of beauty and excess. Here the glamorous salmon pink marble walls are so warm in tone and spectacular in texture that they almost overwhelm you. The centerpieces of this lobby are its fancy escalators and multistoried waterfall (80 feet high). Its rushing noise, the frequent musical entertainment (live pop), and the hundreds of gawking tourists make this a very noisy place indeed. Although this is public space, there is an aura of bustle and commerce about it; dozens of very pricey shops abut the atrium, and it is difficult to find a place to sit down. Although there is one marble bench, it is often decorated with potted flowers. What is most worth looking at here is the opulent decor of the 1980s, a strange mixture of Renaissance marble and contemporary space. Open daily 8 A.M. to 10 P.M.

Exit on Fifth Avenue and turn immediately to your left. On the corner of 56th, at 717 Fifth Avenue, you'll see the Corning Glass Building. Inside the lobby is a glass abstraction by the noted geometric artist Josef Albers, *Two Structural Constellations* (23), made in 1958. Part of a series known as constellation studies that explore form through the connecting of points, this mural is a three-dimensional work. The linear design is made of white Vermont marble and gold leaf (echoing the marble in the massive lobby).

On leaving the building, walk south on Fifth Avenue to 693 Fifth Avenue (between 55th and 54th Streets) to the Takashimaya department store. Inside is the surprising and elegant Gallery at Takashimaya (24), one of the city's newest and most inviting exhibition spaces. Designed by Kevin Roche, this two

129

story gallery features seven annual shows of contemporary Asian and American arts of unusually high quality. Open Monday through Saturday 10–6 (Thursday until 8). Telephone: (212) 350-0115.

Your last East Side oases are just around the corner on East 53rd Street. These are two different vest-pocket parks that will delight you: first, you'll come to a tiny open space decorated with a large and fascinating graffiti-laden section of the Berlin Wall (25). To its west you'll discover Paley Park (26). This pretty little spot is one of the earliest vest-pocket parks in Manhattan, and a good place to rest and prepare yourself for the West Side.

15

Midtown Oases—
Atria and Outdoor Art

Part II—West Side

HOW TO GET THERE

Subway: E or F train to Fifth Avenue and 53rd Street station.
Bus: Fifth Avenue bus downtown or Madison Avenue bus up-
town (M 1, 2, 3, 4).

SUGGESTED TIMES

Check individual listings, but note that all atria and lobbies
are open during the week; some are open daily, others are
closed on weekends. We recommend taking this walk during
the week.

If you have completed Part I of this walk, you'll find yourself
at Paley Park at 53rd Street and Fifth Avenue. You might begin
the second half—the West Side section of the walk—by stroll-
ing down New York's favorite avenue, noting its fine shops and
two distinguished churches (St. Thomas at 53rd Street and St.
Patrick's at 51st). At 666 Fifth Avenue in a passageway between
52nd and 53rd streets you will want to see Isamu Noguchi's
(1955–57) *Ceiling and Waterfall* (1). Here, in a dark walk-
through is an aluminum and stainless steel merging of light,
sound, and water (all familiar themes in Noguchi's mature
work). It consists of a series of standing forms that resemble
wave shapes, not unlike the raked Japanese gardens turned

131

vertically. Ingenious lighting and the gently curved ceiling panels give the entire passage a faintly otherworldly quality, while the sounds of the trickling waterfall mask the honking horns outside.

Walk one block south to 51st Street, to another corporate headquarters: Olympic Towers (2). This building includes an arcade between 51st and 52nd streets. You'll find a collection of chairs to rest in the shade of palms and schefflera trees. In the center of the arcade there is a high dome where skylights brighten a two-story waterfall into a square pool below. You can eat here at a small café-bar and listen to piano music (competing with the rushing water for your attention). The arcade is open from 7 A.M. to midnight daily, but don't go on Sunday nights when the waterfall is shut down.

Exit the arcade on the 51st Street side and go back to Fifth Avenue, to find yourself in New York's most famous urban oasis of all: Rockefeller Center. Depending on how much time you have, you might prefer to devote more than just a few moments of a long walk to this special spot. Here you can ice skate in season, eat, take a tour, walk through the underground passageways (filled with shops), visit the NBC studios, attend Radio City Music Hall—we could go on and on with the things to do at Rockefeller Center. If, however, you want to keep your eye only on the theme of this walk, note the major sculptures that ornament (and are indeed an integral part of the design of) this masterpiece of urban planning. Walking south on Fifth Avenue you'll come first to 636 Fifth Avenue, where a large glass bas relief decorates the front of the entrance. Called *Youth Leading Industry* (3), it was designed by Attilio Piccirilli in about 1936. The design, showing a young male guiding a charioteer that symbolizes commerce and industry, is in the idealistic and dramatic 1930s style that pervades much of the Center's art. It is made of glass block (then a recent development), which can be illuminated from behind.

At the entrance to 630 Fifth Avenue you'll find one of the city's most famous statues: Lee Lawrie's 15-foot-high bronze statue of *Atlas* (4). Made in 1937, the giant, muscular figure holding a globe symbolizes the spirit of enthusiasm and promise of the Rockefeller complex when it was built in the 1930s.

The statue, which is the equivalent of four stories of the building behind it, fills the entrance court and harmonizes with the architecture around it.

Continuing south, at 626 Fifth, you'll find another bronze work, this time a bas relief made by the late Giacomo Manzù pictures *The Italian Immigrant and Italia* (5). It was completed in about 1965 to decorate the entrance to Palazzo d'Italia. Manzù's sculpture depicts a sheaf of wheat and grapevines and below, a barefoot mother and child, arrived at last in America.

Cross 50th Street to the next building of the Center complex, number 620. Here you'll see the gilded bronze relief called *Industries of the British Commonwealth* (6), an overdoor panel decoration by Paul Jennewein. Its companion piece is an overdoor panel on the corner of 49th Street, *The Friendship of France and the United States* (7) by Alfred Janniot; you'll find it over the entrance of La Maison Francaise at 610 Fifth.

But in between these ornate decorations you'll enjoy visiting New York's favorite garden: the Channel Gardens of Rockefeller Center (8). Here, in an inviting walkway to the skating rink and other seasonal pleasures, are the ever-changing flower arrangements and topiary specialties that draw over 50 million visitors a year. In the center of the plantings are six statues: these fountainhead figures were made about 1935 by René Paul Chambellan, who made many other works for Rockefeller Center. Here the Nereids riding the backs of dolphins and the Tritons are part of a series of fountains and mirrored pools that are charming to look at, and also symbolize such admirable qualities as Thought, Imagination, Will, Energy, Alertness, and Leadership. Plantings around the statues are so carefully maintained that the Channel Gardens are often thought to be exceptional examples of the combining of art, nature, and urban planning.

Now as you leave Fifth Avenue to walk west, take a look at the skating rink restaurant from its high overlooking walls. Before you reach Rockefeller Plaza, a small interior street that divides the block between Fifth and Sixth (Avenue of the Americas), note another famous Rockefeller Center statue (9), *Prometheus* (1934) by Paul Manship. The golden bronze figure sits picturesquely in front of a splashing low fountain and the famous collection of flags; its half reclining form rests on a granite mountainlike pedestal, symbolizing earth, and within a large ring decorated with zodiac signs, representing heaven. Prometheus holds aloft a flame as he flies; his suspension, the splashing fountains, and flags waving in the wind seem to fill this urban spot with electrifying motion. Across Rockefeller Plaza is another Lee Lawrie artwork: over the doorway to 30 Rockefeller Plaza is a vast 1933 panel of molded glass, called *Wisdom with Light and Sound* (10). Made of some 240 glass blocks, it floods the lobby with light and decorates the street side with its ingenious design. The huge figure of "Wisdom" (above) traces—with the aid of a compass—the cycles of "Light" and "Sound" (below). Don't miss this example of 1930s design and ethos.

Inside the building on the west wall you'll find José Maria Sert's 1937 "American Progress" mural called *Triumph of Man's Accomplishment Through Physical and Mental Labor.* Just to the north on Rockefeller Plaza is our last major sculpture of the Center. Here, over number 50, is an interesting example of "early" Isamu Noguchi. There are examples of his work in its abstract form in several of our walks, but here you'll find a 1940 work, one of his last figurative sculptures. Called *News* (11), this stainless steel work adorns the Associated Press Building (hence its subject) and was the winner of a competition held by the builders. It represents newsmen at their work; careful examination will disclose notepads, wirephoto and tele-type machines, and cameras, but its overall impression is of curving, massive bodies and planes. The abstraction of these forms was soon to appear in Noguchi's later work.

Continue west to Sixth Avenue, where more of Rockefeller Center's art decorates the buildings and plazas. At 49th and Sixth (1250 Sixth Avenue) you'll enjoy the mosaics (12) on the outside of the entrance. Representing Poverty, the Arts, Fear, Thought, and Hygiene (a truly American collection!), these mosaics were made in 1933 by Barry Faulkner in a typically art deco style. Their bright colors are still gleaming.

If you cross the avenue and walk one block south to 48th Street, you'll find the Celanese Building. In the walkway between 47th and 48th streets there is a rather spectacular sculpture by the Egyptian artist, Ibram Lassaw. Entitled *Pantheon*

(13), its abstract forms are a visual counterpart to the urban environment. Lassaw is one of the most widely shown of contemporary sculptors and an original member of the early group of abstractionists in New York. (Nearby, at 228 West 47th Street, by the way, in the lobby of the Hotel Edison, are some bright, nouveau art deco murals of New York by Kenneth Gore.)

Our next stop is one of our favorites; walk one block north to the McGraw-Hill Building (14) at 49th Street. Here you'll first spot their sunken courtyard with its modern stainless steel sun dial. Called Sun Triangle, this 50-foot-high work was designed by Athelstan Spilhaus, an oceanographer and meteorologist. It is accompanied by maps embedded in the plaza floor. This building has more pleasures in store for you. In the lobby are thirty-two cast bas reliefs by Hildreth Meiere and eleven art deco designs called, Radio and TV Encompassing the Earth. Of particular interest in the McGraw-Hill lobby are three cheerful, characteristic Stuart Davis tapestries. Their bright geometric designs and typically hard-edged patterns lend real personality to this otherwise undistinguished lobby space. You won't want to miss these. And you must make sure to visit McGraw-Hill's wonderful little park, behind the major part of the building. Here is one of our favorite urban oases: the Water Tunnel garden park. It has Japanese-style trellises, hanging plants, locust trees, benches, and the lovely sound of rushing water. Its piece de resistance is the water tunnel itself, a walk-through waterfall, truly a delight to experience and to contemplate.

Just across 50th Street is the Time-Life Building (15), noted for its plain, but spacious outdoor plaza. It features fountains and low walls for sunning, and has long been a favorite of lunchers and sun worshipers. In the plaza a large blue contemporary sculpture ornaments the space. Curved Cube (1972), by William Crovello, looks like a three-dimensional symbol, a letter or number from some obscure alphabet. It is said to have been inspired by classical Japanese calligraphy—in fact, the artist did study in Japan for some years. Curved Cube was one of six large sculptures placed around the city by The Association for a Better New York. Inside the lobby are several notable artworks: a mural in bronze and two shades of Carrara glass by Josef Albers made in 1961 and a giant wall-sized Fritz Glarner

135

painting called *Broadway Rhythms*. Both are in the abstract geometric style that grew out of Piet Mondrian's interest in angular spatial patterns. The Glarner is filled with pulsating small squares that suggest the dynamic motion of the city center.

From here it is a short hop to the impressive Equitable Center (16), which, like Rockefeller Center, combines art, restaurants, shops, and corporate offices. Located in a spacious, airy complex between 51st and 52nd streets and Sixth and Seventh avenues, this imposing center is a real treasury of artworks, including the PaineWebber Gallery (with rotating exhibits), as well as its permanent collection of murals, paintings, and sculptures by such important artists as Roy Lichtenstein, Sandro Chia, Thomas Hart Benton, and Sol Lewitt. The PaineWebber Gallery shows a variety of interesting art—usually with a particular theme—and it is a large and inviting space. The lobby of the Equitable Center itself features several works, including a massive Lichtenstein called *Mural with Blue Brushstroke* (1984–85).

Created on site, this mural is named for the bold brush stroke resembling falling water that is its central focus. Surrounding it in the painting are other pop images in bright colors in the unmistakable style of Lichtenstein. Just below this monumental work is *Atrium Furnishment* (1984–85), an innovative semicircular dark marble sculpture/seating area surrounding a massive table and plants. By Scott Burton, whose works often combine architecture, sculpture, and furniture, it was conceived for this spot, and its shapes reflect those of its surroundings. You'll find two other environmental works by Scott Burton in the plaza outside: *Urban Plaza North* and *Urban Plaza South* (1985–86). Geometrically shaped stools, tables, and benches made of gray-green granite are lined up on the sidewalk, looking like large, stylized stone mushrooms. Although not particularly comfortable looking, they nonetheless make an architectural/sculptural statement and provide a resting area on a busy city street.

Perhaps the best known work on permanent display at the Equitable Center is Thomas Hart Benton's *America Today*

(1930). The ten individually named panels are painted in tempera on linen. They represent in figurative idiom the social and economic life of the nation as observed by Benton on his many travels cross country during the 1920s. Here are lively and bold interpretations of urban life, workers, and industrial scenes. While most panels depict American life in optimistic and exuberant terms, one of its most effective, *Outreaching Hands*, is especially poignant in its portrayal of a poorhouse and breadlines during the Depression. Originally commissioned by the New School for Social Research in 1930, this early Works Progress Administration (W.P.A.) piece was purchased and then restored by the Equitable during the mid-1980s.

In the corridors of the Equitable you'll find Paul Manship's *Day* (1938), a dynamic bronze statue featuring a figure in leaping motion. Part of a series called *The Moods of Time*, this kinetic work contrasts with the more abstract works inside and outside. In the lobby ceiling high above the elevators is Agnes Denes's intriguing *Hypersphere: The Earth in the Shape of the Universe* (1986), an environmental work showing the earth with its seven continents. A great feeling of space and breadth is created with the use of glass panels, mirrors, and plantings.

The Equitable Center also displays art in its outdoor spaces. An attractive galleria between 51st and 52nd streets features other works worth seeing. Two appealing animal sculptures in bronze add whimsy to these corporate headquarters: *Hare on Bell* (1983) and *Young Elephant* (1984), both by the British sculptor Barry Flanagan. They are a favorite with children and are engaging in their originality and sense of movement. The hare is shown dancing on top of an elephant; in the other work, a hare jumps over a bell. Both sculptures contrast sharply with the strong element of abstract design of the works displayed in the grand, granite atrium inside and the large Sol Lewitt wall drawings behind. These six huge building decorations called *Wall Drawing: Bands of Lines in Four Colors and Four Directions Separated by Gray Bands* (1984–85) show horizontal, vertical, and diagonal lines in primary colors and are typical of the artist's minimal, and somewhat static, style.

Don't miss Sandro Chia's massive and colorful mural *Palio*

(1985–86), located just inside Palio Restaurant, which is part of the Equitable complex. (See page 90 for more details.)

Go east on 52nd Street, back to Sixth Avenue and turn left. Here, between 52nd and 53rd streets you'll find one of the city's latest additions to its outdoor art: a brand-new group of three works by Jim Dine called *Looking Toward the Avenue* (17). These large figures are grouped (two together at 52nd and one at 53rd Street); they are all variations on the Venus de Milo theme. Dine, one of the first pop artists, has here reverted to a theme that interested him back in the 1970s. The statues are a definite asset to the bland building behind them. Made of green bronze they are 14, 18, and 23 feet high, respectively. (It may amuse you to known that the figures have caused a great deal of complaint from passersby, who find the statues objectionable.) We think you will enjoy these modern versions of an antique theme.

Cross Sixth Avenue at 52nd Street and walk a short way on 52nd east, toward Fifth Avenue. Your eye will soon be caught by a most unusual plaza on the north side of 52nd, and opening through the block to 53rd. This is an interesting combination of art, architecture, and plantings forming the E. F. Hutton garden (18) plaza of the Deutsche Bank Building. Built in an unusual "Aztec/Egyptian temple"—postmodern style, the columns and arches are of a pinkish granite, surrounded with benches and a centerpiece sculpture called *Lapstrake* by native Texan Jesus Bautista Moroles. Made in 1987, this striking piece of art is also rather primitive in style; it is a vertical mass of alternating slabs of granite, some rough, some smooth, suggesting primitive ruins in some distant place. It rises like an ancient column among the pathways and potted plantings of this very interesting public space. Inside the building you'll find the Lobby Gallery, an elegant exhibition space that presents a new show every six weeks.

Walk through the Deutsche Bank's vest-pocket park to 53rd Street, turn right and at 40 West 53rd Street, you'll find the new location of the American Craft Museum (19). A visit here will likely challenge many a person's idea of the nature of "crafts." This elegant, sophisticated and quite new exhibition space displays traditional as well as contemporary crafts in an innovative fashion. You'll find works in a variety of styles, historic periods, and media—including clay, metal, glass, fiber, and wood; on a given day you might chance upon an exhibit of antique quilts or bold glass works. A recent show featured the amazing basketlike sculptures of fiber artist John McQueen. The museum also has a permanent collection that focuses on post-World War II crafts. A full agenda of educational programs, lectures, and special events is available to the public. The American Craft Museum is open Tuesday from 10–8 and Wednesday–Sunday from 10–5. There is an entrance fee. Telephone: (212) 956-3535.

Almost directly across the street you come to our last stop on this artwalk, the famed Museum of Modern Art (20). One of the world's preeminent collections of contemporary art, it is perhaps a fitting completion to this walk. The sculpture garden here is a major section of the museum that combines both art and garden space in a unique and inviting way. It is likely that an art lover in New York will already have the MOMA (as it is known) on his or her list. But if you want to cap off your artwalk in style, perhaps another visit (just to the garden this time?) will be in order at the end of your walk. Whenever you visit the museum, however, be sure to see the garden and enjoy the fine examples of sculpture set among the trees and slates of this idyllic spot.

. . . And in Addition

- International Center for Photography Midtown (I.C.P.), 1133 Avenue of the Americas: changing photographic exhibits. Telephone: (212) 768-4680.
- New York Telephone, 1095 Avenue of the Americas: eclectic exhibitions. Telephone: (212) 395-2295.
- At 9 West 57th Street, between Fifth and Sixth avenues, in the lobby of the Solow Building, examples from the owner's collection are exhibited. Recent displays have included a Miró exhibit and a giant bronze *Titan* by Marcus Lupertz.
- At the Plaza Hotel, 59th Street entrance, off of Fifth Avenue ask to see a Paul Gauguin flower painting in an office to the right of the door.

- The Urban Center, 457 Madison Avenue, houses the head-quarters of the Municipal Art Society and their gallery. They have frequent exhibitions relating to urban life, public art etc. Telephone: (212) 935-3960.
- Inside the newly restored Coty Building at 714 Fifth Avenue, near 56th Street, you'll find three lovely windows made in 1912 by the famous glass craftsman, René Lalique.
- Steinway Hall at 109 West 57th Street: Here in opulent, old-world splendor amidst dozens of shiny grand pianos, is the Steinway art collection, featuring massive rhetorical paint-ings of an era long past. All with musical subjects, they in-clude work by illustrators Rockwell Kent and N. C. Wyeth and numerous other artists bearing titles such as "Beethoven in Nature," "Das Rheingold," "Tristan und Isolde," and an unforgettable Schubertian "Erl King." Telephone: (212) 246-1100.
- If it's three o'clock on a Tuesday and you are in the vicinity of 53rd Street and Park Avenue, take a ten minute guided tour of Philip Johnson's and Mies van der Rohe's Seagram Building. (See the Four Seasons Restaurant, p. 88.) An inter-est in historic receptacles of glass and pewter will be re-warded. The only other artwork visible to the public are two nice tapestries by Miró, though there is also a giant red and orange diagrammatic mural of the distilling process by Her-bert Matter. (A list of the glass collection is available on the fifth floor.)

16

An Auction Outing

HOW TO GET THERE
Subway: Subway stops for the Upper East Side are at 86th Street and Lexington Avenue or 68th and Lexington (4, 5, or 6 train).
Bus: For Sotheby's take the First or Second avenue (M15) bus, or the 72nd Street crosstown (M30, M72) bus.

SUGGESTED TIMES
You can visit an auction house to attend an auction or to view the art that will be sold at a variety of times. See individual auction house hours that follow.

On this artwalk we propose to take you to two of New York's finest auction houses—or three, if you wish to make the optional loop.

If you've never experienced a fine art auction, you have a real treat in store. For, in addition to providing you with the rare opportunity to view works that may not be seen elsewhere, auctions are a form of theater. At center stage of these live performances are the artworks or objects being considered by the audience—international art collectors, museum curators, dealers, art lovers, or simply observers—while the auctioneer in stentorian tones announces the bids. The battles for items are not loud or raucous—indeed, bidders hold up their paddles in silence, while others phone them in—but the atmosphere can be charged with electricity, especially when prices escalate at a dizzying rate, leaving everyone reeling in suspense. The pace is quick, as the bidding surges from one "lot" to the next, with hardly a moment's hesitation (sometimes as many as 100 lots are sold per hour).

In our view, attending an auction is an entertaining and informative way to spend a morning or afternoon, whether you are buying, looking, or just soaking up the atmosphere, and you can learn a great deal about today's art market. Contrary to popular belief, not everything sold at auction is wildly expensive. Indeed, part of the fun and challenge is that you can still find great bargains, especially in the decorative arts (granted, less frequently in the fine arts arena). And, while most museums charge an entrance fee, gallery viewing at auction houses, as well as most New York auctions themselves, are free—unless you buy a catalog or get carried away in your bidding!

New York has its fair share of first-rate auction houses—from famous institutions that sponsor some of the

AUCTION HOUSES on the UPPER EAST SIDE

most dazzling sales in the international art market to more modest but still important houses, where you can find a wide variety of items in terms of both quality and price.

You may wonder where the auction houses get their fine art. Much of it comes from private collectors who have decided to sell off major works. Some art comes from museums that want to exchange gifts that have been gathering dust in their cellars (because they already own a similar work). You'll see many famous names from marquises to museums to oil tycoons in the small print of the catalog. Similarly, the buyers are often the same museums, trading up or plugging a hole in their collections, or wealthy investors and dealers bidding on behalf of anonymous international collectors.

On this auction outing you will sample two of Manhattan's most distinguished auction houses. One, the famed Sotheby's (with auction houses on four continents), is known worldwide for its elegant and high-quality auctions of European and American paintings, sculpture, and drawings, from Old Masters and impressionists to modern and contemporary works, as well as all sorts of decorative arts. The other—Christie's East—is an offshoot of its internationally acclaimed parent, Christie's (which can be found on 59th and Park in Manhattan, as well as in locations throughout the world). Here on 67th Street, paintings, prints, photographs, sculpture, and furniture are sold at more accessible prices (about 80 percent of the items are sold for under $5,000). We chose these two houses because we felt they were representative of the types of auction houses found in our area—and also because the walk from one to the other is pleasant and not too long.

You can plan your outing in one of two ways: if you're interested in attending a particular type of auction, you should call Sotheby's and Christie's East ahead of time to find out what kind of art is being auctioned and when, so you can plan accordingly. Or, if you suddenly find you have a free day, you can go on the spur of the moment, taking your chances as to what you'll find. Keep in mind that before each auction the items to be sold are put on display for several days, where they can be examined carefully, up close. At the presale, catalogs are available free of charge for consultation: at the sale, there's a charge for them, anywhere from $7.00 to $30.00. In order to bid you are given a paddle, which you get when you register at the entrance (free of charge). And, if you plan to buy, check ahead as to what method of payment will be accepted (neither Sotheby's nor Christie's East accepts credit cards). Although we cannot promise that world records will be broken at the auction block on the day you go, we can assure you that you'll enjoy your adventure.

From the moment you step into Sotheby's chic East Side building at York and 72nd Street, you're aware you're in the world of art as high finance. The plush carpets, uniformed guards, and elegantly dressed customers all denote the rarefied world of the collector—not just any collector, but the likely purchaser of Picassos or Old Masters or Jasper Johns. The bustle of commerce mixes with the fabulous collections of art, and everyone seems to talk in whispers. The constantly changing shows and subsequent auctions require a lot of moving of pictures and objets d'art, and the galleries are filled with future buyers, honest-to-goodness art lovers, and dealers, dealers, dealers.

Down on the lowest level from the lobby is a giant exhibition space. Here you'll find the art items that will soon be put on the auction block. These may include an impressive collection of paintings by the Masters, which you can walk around and examine for free, in a museumlike but uncrowded, relaxed atmosphere. You can also consult the catalogs hanging on each wall and find out how much the management expects each item to bring at auction (a bonus not available at museums). Stylish young women answer your questions with alacrity.

On the second level, up a flight of plushly carpeted stairs, you'll find a long desk, another exhibition hall, and the famous auction room. Here the world of high finance meets the world of art. You are given a large paddle with a number on it, you can buy a catalog, and take a seat (free admission). Up in front you'll see an auctioneer who speaks with polite and noncommittal tone, selling art in increments of $100 or $10,000. A bank of telephone bid receivers faces the audience and occasionally bids on behalf of the unseen collector on the phone. With studied lack of emotion, the auctioneer bangs down his gavel every few moments and quietly says something like, "Sold, for $45,000, to bidder number such and such" (though it should be added that many works go for far less). You shouldn't miss this taste of the art scene. As far removed as it can be from the little studios and workshops of the artists themselves (see Artwalk 13), it nevertheless represents the rarefied heights of success that some artists dream about (and few attain in their own lifetimes). It does seem rather hard to make the connection, though, between this scene and the artist's act of creation. Nonetheless, the international firm of Sotheby's (with auction houses in cities from London to Tokyo, Madrid to Beverly Hills, and Milan to St. Moritz) is still supposed to be flourishing, after riding the crest of the wave of "art as investment."

Among recent exhibitions and auctions held here were Southeast Asian art, contemporary prints, Victorian paintings, ancient artifacts, modern paintings, and a world of decorative art from rare jewelry to antique furniture and Persian rugs. You will find information for planning your visit to coincide with the kind of art of most interest to you in the Sunday New York Times (Arts and Leisure section) or by calling at Sotheby's: (212) 606-7000. The hours for exhibitions of art to be sold are Tuesday–Saturday, 10–5, and occasional Sundays. Exhibitions close at 3 P.M. on the day preceding the auction. The auctions themselves are held at 10:15 A.M. and 2 P.M. (You can wander in during the auction and wander out again at will.)

In addition to the scene just described, Sotheby's is also running a slightly less exalted set of auctions called Sotheby's Arcade in the same building. Here you'll find lower prices and items that might not interest the most serious investors or biggest museums. Nevertheless, if you actually plan to buy something at a reasonable price at one of these auctions, you would be advised to go to the Arcade. Viewing hours are the same; auctions at 2 P.M.

From Sotheby's find your way to Christie's East, at 219 East 67th, between Second and Third avenues. (We suggest you walk down Second or Third avenues to get there.) The atmosphere at Christie's East is more low key and relaxed than at Sotheby's, no doubt because the stakes are not quite as high. The building, although not as elegant or spacious, is still roomy enough to include two exhibition galleries and a good-sized auction hall—all filled to the brim with artworks, "objets," and furniture. But, regardless of the unpretentious surroundings, you're still reminded at every turn that you're in a world-class auction house—from the high-quality sale items on display, to wall charts showing the Christie "empire" extending the world over like an octopus with mighty tentacles. (Don't miss the pictorial chronicles on the wall near the entrance outlining the history of the dynasty from its beginnings in the eighteenth century.)

The auctions correspond thematically to those at the pricier Christie's on Park Avenue, although they are held on different days. Estates are often sold, which can result in an eclectic mix of artworks or "objets"—from fine paintings and prints to coins, stamps, furniture, antique jewelry, rugs, furniture, or unusual collectibles such as toys and dolls. You might well fall in love with a unique object and decide to bid on it for there is great choice and the prices are not astronomical. On one of our last visits we attended an auction featuring American paintings, watercolors, drawings, and sculpture, many of which were going for relatively modest sums (under $1,000). The hall was filled to capacity and the gallant auctioneer had to speak over a constant hum of conversation, as people were comparing notes on the various lots. The atmosphere was far less daunting than at Sotheby's, although the bidding was equally brisk. Other recent auctions at Christie's East have featured glass and ceramic objects, animation art and "Disneyrama," and twentieth-century decorative arts, including art nouveau and art deco.

Viewing at Christie's East is Tuesday–Saturday, 10–5; Sunday, 1–5; days preceding sales, 10–2; Monday, 10–5; or by appointment. Sales are held usually on Tuesday. Call (212) 606-0400.

And now, depending on your energy and time, you can either return home or visit the William Doyle Galleries at 175 East 87th Street, for a slightly different atmosphere. Here is a more cluttered and pleasantly inviting auction house that might remind you of nineteenth-century London (or how you imagine it). There is a mix of grand pianos, giant Victorian art on the walls, and bustle that makes the place appealing. People at the auction are definitely there to buy; it does not attract the same clientele, but more likely interior decorators or others looking for a piece of the past that they can afford. Recent auctions included mostly furniture, decorations, and silver, but some had paintings and sculpture as well. Among the most interesting were an auction of art nouveau and art deco works, a French Empire auction, and a sale of Belle Epoque decorative arts.

Exhibition hours are Saturday, 10–5; Sunday, 12–5; Monday, 9–7:30; Tuesday, 9–2. Auctions take place every other Wednesday, from 10 A.M. to 4 P.M., and occasional evenings. Call (212) 427-2730, or for recorded 24-hour telephone announcement of events, (212) 427-4885.

Perhaps you will return home from this artwalk with an original work of art in hand!

... And in Addition

- Sotheby's has a series of lectures and seminars that are of very high quality. Recent examples included a series on Georgia O'Keeffe and Alfred Stieglitz, a fine arts conservation seminar, and a travel seminar to Italy on Futurism. Call (212) 606-7822 for information.

- Christie's East has panel discussions and seminars on a variety of art-related topics; open to the public, free of charge on a first-come, first-served basis. Call (212) 606-0440.

- Other auction houses to visit in Manhattan: Christie's, 502 Park Avenue at 59th Street, (212) 546-1000. Swann Galleries, 104 East 25th Street, (212) 254-4710. Tepper Galleries, 110 East 25th Street, (212) 677-5300.

17

Exploring Central Park and Its Surroundings

A Treasure Hunt for Children

HOW TO GET THERE

Subway: #6 train to 68th Street (Hunter College Station) and walk west to Fifth Avenue and south to 64th Street.

Bus: Fifth Avenue downtown (M1, 2, 3, 4) bus or Madison Avenue uptown (M1, 2, 3, 4) bus; from West Side take 66th–67th Street crosstown bus (M66).

SUGGESTED TIMES

Even though the park is open from dawn to 1 A.M. you should visit only during the day. The zoo is open from 10 A.M. to 4:30 P.M. daily; note that during the spring, summer and fall months, the park drives are closed to motorized vehicles from 10 A.M. to 3 P.M. daily and on weekends. For museums, check individual listings. For general information on the park, telephone (212) 397-3156.

Central Park, in the heart of Manhattan, is a cherished recreational resource for New Yorkers. Here you can engage in many an activity, from biking, boating, and carriage and horseback rides to roller and ice skating, running, ball playing, or birding. You can attend cultural events during summer months—outdoor concerts, "Shakespeare in the Park," or even the opera

148

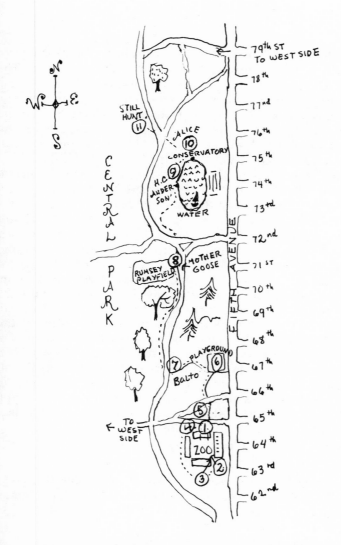

But, in addition, Central Park is also a wonderful outdoor sculpture park with a collection of interesting, unusual, and sometimes charming statues that coexist with the usual equestrian and heroic pieces found in public places. These works are all nestled within the leafy 843 acres of rolling terrain that make up the park. Many of these statues are particularly appealing

to children, who delight in seeing favorite storybook characters
or easily recognizable animals rendered in stone or bronze. This
free outdoor exhibition is a wonderful place to introduce young
children to sculpture; for, unlike more inhibiting and confining
museum settings, here they can walk right up to each sculpture,
touch it, and even climb up on it. (*Alice in Wonderland*, stop
10, is a particularly popular spot for children to do just that.)

This artwalk—designed primarily for younger children (although all readers will enjoy it)—covers the area in and around
the Central Park Zoo at 64th Street and Fifth Avenue, north to
76th Street, and the West Side portion between 80th and 81st
streets. Later, after you leave the park, you can continue your
treasure hunt in the West Side neighborhood as far north as
91st Street, for the treat of an "animal sculpture" playground.
For practical reasons, we have divided this artwalk into two
sections: East Side and West Side. (The full walk may be too
long for small children.) Note that most of the animal sculptures
in the park are inside or near the zoo; others are also easily
reached on foot. To make the walk more amusing for young-
sters, you might have them "find" the sculptures listed here.
Using our descriptions (and, perhaps, armed with a map of
Central Park, available at the information center near the entrance to the zoo), you might ask them to look for a sculpture
that fits a certain description and location, rather than simply
pointing it out. Most children love treasure hunts, and these
are all treasures worth hunting for.

You will be searching for the following:

EAST SIDE
1. A clock with a group of animal musicians (monkeys, bear, elephant, goat, kangaroo, penguins, hippopotamus)
2. A dancing goat surrounded by frogs
3. A great tigress with cubs
4. A dancing bear with five small frogs
4. An animal gate
6. An arched bridge
7. A heroic Siberian husky dog
8. Mother Goose with some of her friends (Humpty Dumpty, Mother Hubbard, Little Bo-Peep, and Old King Cole)

9. The fairy tale author Hans Christian Andersen with his ugly duckling
10. Alice in Wonderland and her friends
11. A fierce stalking panther

WEST SIDE
1. A fifteenth-century Polish king on horseback
2. Four characters from Shakespeare
3. Herbs and flowers descended from Shakespeare's own garden
4. Six wild creatures and Teddy Roosevelt with his guides, all decorating a museum
5. A small stone squirrel eating an acorn
6. A hands-on museum just for children
7. A stone family group on a park bench
8. A flock of stone sheep

Please keep in mind that this is in no way a comprehensive guide to all of Central Park's statues; these might appeal most to the smallest and youngest of artwalkers.

East Side
Begin your walk at the Central Park Zoo, at Fifth Avenue and 64th Street. At the southern entrance, above the arched brick gate, you will see the delightful *Delacorte clock* (1964–65) by Andrea Spadini (1). Commissioned by the philanthropist George T. Delacorte—who was fascinated by the animated clocks he had seen in Europe—it features a motley collection of eight animals. At the top two bronze *monkeys* strike a bell, while a group of six "musicians" play their instruments and dance in circles below them. A *bear* plays a tambourine, an *elephant* the accordion, a *goat* the pipes, a *kangaroo* with baby the horn, a *penguin* the drum. But our favorite is the *hippopotamus* who, amazingly, plays the violin—and with great gusto! A complete performance can be heard on the hour, when you'll be treated to the tunes of nursery rhymes; a shorter version plays on the half hour. Children love to watch the figures dancing above, and the gate is often bustling with eager anticipation just before the performances.

From here you can enter the zoo, where, in addition to the

many live animals, you and the children will also find two bronze animal groupings: *Dancing Goat* (c. 1935), located in a niche near the Zoo Café, and *Tigress and Cubs* (1866), next to the real monkey display.

Dancing Goat (2) is part of a pair of fountain statues by Frederick George Richard Roth. (You'll see its counterpart, *Honey Bear*, as you leave the zoo.) The fanciful 6-foot goat balances on its hind legs in a humanlike position, as water sprays from the mouths of surrounding frogs at its feet. Whereas the goat is depicted in a whimsical fairy tale-like way, *Tigress and Cubs* (3) is a bold, gripping work. The artist, Auguste Cain, who worked in Paris, created what is certainly a fine heroic statue—animal or not. The larger than life-size tigress proudly holds in her mouth a dead peacock, its long tail hanging down to the ground while her two cubs leap about at her feet. Cain was able to capture an expression of pure triumph on the face of his heroine.

As you leave the zoo, look for *Honey Bear* (c. 1935) (4) on your left, just past the Delacorte clock. Like the goat, this charming bear also stands on his hind legs with his head thrown back, while the five frogs at his feet recycle the fountain's water. Unlike *Tigress and Cubs*, this happy work is one of fantasy and humor rather than realism.

Next you'll walk under the overpass (to the 65th Street Transverse) where, immediately to the right, you'll find the Lehman Children's Zoo (5). Its gates (1960–61), by the sculptor Paul Manship, celebrate the joyous effects of music on all creatures, humans and animals alike. On either side of the gate two boys are shown playing the pipes of Pan, while a central male figure is dancing with abandon, surrounded by two *goats* and assorted *birds*. These birds, all different, are perched merrily atop the decorative bronze swirling arches that form the gate.

As you leave the zoo heading north you'll soon find yourself at a small and unusually charming children's playground (6). By artistic use of wood, stone pavilions, and an arched bridge reminiscent of a Japanese garden, the designers of this playground (adjacent to Fifth Avenue at 67th Street) have created the feel of environmental sculpture. The natural boulders that adjoin the playground and the unusually pretty plantings help make this an especially appealing spot.

And now you'll come to one of the park's most beloved statues. From the playground walk along the path bearing to your left at the fork. You'll find *Balto* (7) (1925), New York's only commemoration of man's best friend. And what a heroic tale is Balto's! The Siberian husky led a team of dogs on a long trek through Arctic blizzards, carrying diphtheria serum to desperate, epidemic-ridden Nome, Alaska, in 1925. Because of this brave dog who "never once faltered" on the arduous journey, the mission was successful—all except for poor Balto, who died shortly after from overexertion. To celebrate his incredible courage and loyalty, a committee commissioned Frederick G. R. Roth to create a commemorative statue. This realistic piece is a dramatic vision of heroic determination. The larger than life-size bronze dog is shown panting, eyes fixed upon the trail ahead of him, legs apart, ready to continue the journey. His harness is attached to his back. He sits atop a rough boulder in a naturalistic setting, and there is an impressive plaque below him describing his deeds. Generations of young admirers have climbed on him, stroked, and hugged him. As a result, the patina has worn in places, adding to the impression of the roughness of his voyage.

On leaving Balto, walk alongside the main roadway heading north. To the left of the road near the Rumsey Playfield is a 1938 carved granite statue of *Mother Goose* (8) looking much the way we might imagine her (also by the sculptor Frederick G. R. Roth). This Mother Goose is an energetic figure, cape flying, witchlike hat on her head, and a giant basket clutched in her hand. On the sides of the statue are some old favorites of every child who has been read to or has looked at some of the most familiar pictures in children's literature. Among the characters—Humpty Dumpty, Mother Hubbard, Little Bo-Peep, Old King Cole. Mother Goose is a bit scary—and children will love her.

To get to the Conservatory Water—a lovely pond next on the agenda—you must cross the 72nd Street Drive. Here, near 72nd Street and Fifth, is a particularly pleasant part of the park for small children to visit. They will find children sailing model boats across the water and an atmosphere of calm and orderliness reminiscent of a French park. Here also are two of the city's favorite sculptures.

On the west bank of the pond is the legendary statue of *Hans Christian Andersen* (9), made in bronze by Georg Lober and installed in 1956. Ever since, this 8-foot-tall portrait of the great Danish writer (with one of his familiar characters) has attracted children by the thousands, who like to sit on the open book in his lap, climb on his head, and otherwise show their affection. Among the Andersen tales that inspired the work are the story of the Ugly Duckling, and in fact, a sculpted duckling sits at the statue's feet. From May to September on Saturdays one or another of Andersen's (and other writers') stories are told for children at this site. The statue is surrounded by steps and a feeling of space, as it overlooks the Conservatory Water; it makes a fine place to stop for a story yourself.

On the north side of the same pond is another city landmark for children (and adults) of all ages. The group of *Alice in Wonderland and her friends* (10), by José de Creeft can be found in an alcove near Fifth Avenue and 75th Street. Seated atop a great toadstool, Alice is seen surrounded by the Mad Hatter, the March Hare, the Dormouse, and the Cheshire Cat. The scale of this bronze tableau is such that children climb all over it and explore. "Alice" fanciers will notice that she and her friends vaguely resemble the characters in the John Tenniel original 1865 *Alice* edition, which inspired the sculptor.

From "Alice"—and for a change of pace—walk to 76th Street and the East Drive where you'll find a vivid, bold bronze *panther* stalking its prey. Crouching on a rocky outcropping amid the foliage, he looks as though he is about to spring on you. Called *Still Hunt*(11), this is the gripping 1881–83 work of the American sculptor Edward Kemeys, who was best known for his animal sculptures, especially those of wild animals. Unlike some of the other animal sculptors of his day, he had no interest in representing the animals literally. *Still Hunt* is intentionally rough in the way it is finished, and not completely accurate anatomically. But you'll find it dramatically conveys the idea of a panther about to pounce on its next victim.

A little farther north is one of the newest additions to Central

'ark's sculpture collection, a trio of bears. Like their counter-
)arts at the Children's Zoo, these three are friendly-looking,
:limb-on-type bronzes. The work of Paul Manship, they are the
:enterpiece of the refurbished playground at Fifth Avenue and
'9th Street, called the Pat Hoffman Friedman Playground. And
:xpected soon is a set of animal gates to be installed at the 85th
itreet playground, just north of the Metropolitan Museum on
'ifth Avenue.

Finally, behind the Metropolitan Museum, is *Cleopatra's
Needle*, an Egyptian obelisk that is more than thirty-five hun-
lred years old.

Charming murals by Ludwig Bemelmans, author of *Made-
eine* will also delight children in this neighborhood. See walk
.0 for description of Café Carlyle.

This ends our children's East Side treasure hunt. If you're
;ame to discover additional pleasures, continue on to the West
iide.

Vest Side
'rom *Still Hunt* head northwest toward Belvedere Lake, to find
<ing Jagiello (1939) (1), a gripping heroic equestrian statue.
['his over-life-size work was the creation of the Polish sculptor
itanislaw Ostrowski. It represents a famous fifteenth-century
'olish warrior who united Lithuanian and Polish territories.
fere he is dramatically portrayed, standing straight in his stir-
ups, with two swords in hand, symbolizing his military suc-
:esses. The statue was first seen at the Polish Pavilion at the
.939 World's Fair in New York, an appropriately timely work
)f defiance and patriotism during the early war years in Europe.

Follow the main path, bearing left, to "Shakespeare territory"
n the Park. You'll find the celebrated Delacorte Theater, home
)f Shakespeare in the Park, a venerable New York tradition,
he romantic-looking storybook Belvedere Castle in the back-
;round, and just beyond, the delightful Shakespeare Garden.
\t the entrance to the theater are two groups of bronze statues (2).
fou should immediately recognize one as *Romeo and Juliet*
1977) in romantic embrace and, if you're up on your Shake-
:peare, perhaps identify the other, *The Tempest* (1966). Both
ire by the sculptor Milton Hebald and express very different

155

moods. While *Romeo and Juliet* is lyrical in spirit, *The Tempes[* is turbulent, animated, and wild. The smooth surfaces of th[former contrast sharply with the rough texture of the group i[*Tempest* depicting Prospero and Miranda.

The *Shakespeare Garden* (3) on a hill below Belvedere Castl[contains hawthorne and mulberry trees descended from th[very plantings Shakespeare once tended. There are over 12[plants, all mentioned in his plays: delphiniums, primroses, an[columbines, as well as sundry herbs. The plantings are tende[

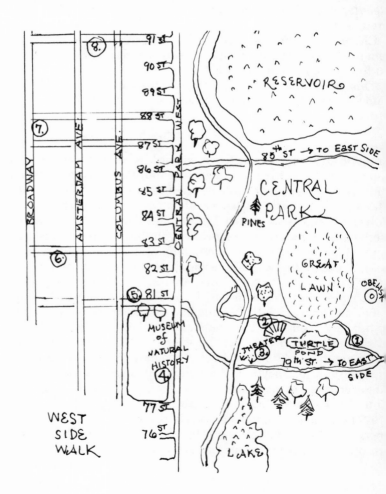

but natural looking, and the setting is perfect for a spring picnic.

Exit Central Park at 77th Street, where you'll find yourself directly in front of the imposing American Museum of Natural History (4), one of New York's most important cultural institutions. If you look beyond the grand architecture, you'll find all sorts of interesting details that may pique children's fancy, including many dramatic animal decorations. In fact, on either side of the Central Park entrance, is a "bestiary" your children will enjoy discovering. Look for a collection of bas relief granite *bears, bison, moose, rams, lions,* and other wild beasts. Have them spot the large *eagle* over the portico, as well as a group of *eagles* on the turret above. On a different note you will enjoy the impressive memorial to Theodore Roosevelt, centered on a fine equestrian statue (c. 1940)—also directly in front of the museum. A great naturalist and conservationist, T.R. is somewhat rheortically depicted as an explorer-hunter on his horse, flanked by two guides—an African and an American Indian.

The sculptor, James Earle Fraser, a personal friend of the president, was known for his animal and Western themes. (He also designed the nickel coin that showed a buffalo on one side and an Indian on the other.) In the rotunda of the Roosevelt Memorial you'll see more works commemorating the colorful life of this energetic president, including murals picturing his African explorations and the building of the Panama Canal during his presidency. From here you can enter the museum, where, in addition to its world-famous natural history exhibits, you'll find one of the city's best collections of primitive art. Comprehensive cultural displays on Eskimo, Asian, African, and American peoples with costumes and arts and crafts are among the fine exhibitions. You can enjoy entirely re-created village scenes (such as a wedding in an Indian village), models of a traditional Japanese home, African masks, and many examples of primitive art. This large museum (which occupies about four city blocks) contains more than anyone can see on one visit, especially if the not-to-be-missed Hayden Planetarium is included. (Here, sky shows, films, and panoramic slides will almost transport you and the children to the heavens above. Shows are held daily, usually in the afternoons, but there are always permanent astronomical displays on view.)

157

The American Museum of Natural History is open daily
10–4:45; Wednesday until 8; Sundays and holidays, 10–5. Dis
cretionary entrance fee. Phone: (212) 769-5100. For information
on the Hayden Planetarium, call (212) 769-5920. There is an
entrance fee.

Upon leaving the Museum, turn left onto 81st Street, and
walk to number 25 between Central Park West and Columbus
Avenue. Have your children spot a small stone *squirrel* (5) in
medallion bas relief on the third floor between two windows
(He's busily eating an acorn.) This is the kind of decorative
detail that adds charm to many otherwise nondescript build
ings in New York.

From here it's a fairly short walk to the Children's Museum
of Manhattan (6), at 212 West 83rd Street, between Broadway
and Amsterdam Avenue. A relatively new place (founded in
1973), it is filled with innovative exhibits and events where
children are encouraged to participate, as well as to observe
learn, and have fun. There is a main exhibition hall, including
the "Brainarium," with films, magical patterns, games, and so
called activity station; an up-to-the-minute media station com
plete with the latest of equipment, studios, and videos to in
spire today's youngest communications generation; an early
childhood center with activities for the tiniest tots; a well
lighted, airy art studio for everything from painting, sculpting
and etching, to weaving, calligraphy, and bookmaking; a nature
and pet center (a miniversion of some of the exhibits at the
Museum of Natural History); and a photography studio, collec
tion rooms, greenhouses, outdoor gardens, and a roof garden
Here, children of all ages can explore art, science, and nature
throughout the four floors of exhibits, studios, and activity cen
ters. It's a very busy, bustling place, so come prepared. Hours
Tuesday–Sunday, 10–5; Friday, 2–5; closed on holidays. Small
admission fee. Telephone: (212) 721-1234.

If energy level is not a problem for you or the children, end
your outing at a special children's playground at West 91st
Street. But we have something else for you to see en route: a
whimsical and very lifelike statue in the courtyard of the Mon
tana Building, at 247 West 87th Street (on Broadway, between
87th and 88th streets). Called *Park Bench* (7), this bronze work

by Bruno Lucchesi realistically depicts a family group—grandparents, mother, and small child—sitting on a park bench. Here at the Montana their bench is located on a sort of dais well above ground level, so that you can look up to the sculpture.

It's a short distance from here to the last stop on this walk. Don't fail to take your small fry to Constantino Nivola's Children's Playground (8) at 91st Street between Columbus and Amsterdam avenues. Here, on an ordinary city block, is a charming collection of stone *sheep*, just the size for small children to enjoy. Nivola, a native of Sardinia, specializes in children's sculpture, and the sheep on 91st Street are a delightful addition to the city. Of several different colors, these rough-textured, woolly-looking creatures are fanciful, sturdy, and obviously popular with small kids. Nivola is a leading exponent of this kind of environmental sculpture for playgrounds.

... And in Addition
Central Park sponsors many activities that are of interest to children and adults alike:
- Puppet shows (nominal fees): Marionette theater at the Swedish Cottage. Telephone: (212) 988-9093.
  Handpuppets at Heckscher House. Telephone: (212) 397-3163.
- Story-Telling: at Hans Christian Andersen statue, Saturday mornings from 11 A.M. to 12 noon, May–September. Telephone: (212) 397-3156.
- Park tours: on weekends, free of charge. Call (212) 397-3156 for information.

18

University and Cathedral Walk

Art on the Columbia Campus and nearby St. John the Divine

HOW TO GET THERE
Subway: #1 train to 116th Street station
Bus: Broadway M104 bus.

SUGGESTED TIMES
It may be more fun to visit the campus while the college is in session and the students are milling around, that is, during the academic year. Weekdays are more lively than weekends.

In the heart of uptown Manhattan you'll find the campus of Columbia University hospitably housing a number of interesting sculptures. Set amid the walkways and hedges of the lovely college campus is a great variety of artworks—each separately placed to enhance the buildings behind it or the courtyard around it. We suggest that you arrive at the 116th Street entrance to the campus and walk directly through the large gates into the center of the campus. From there you can follow this brief walking tour to see the highlights of the sculpture collection. While you are on your artwalk you might also step into several of the buildings that house museum collections or student art shows. But our main focus in this walk is on the outdoor art, which is almost always accessible and is particularly enjoyable to see on a nice spring day, when the campus is filled with students lolling about the grounds (and sometimes sitting on the sculptures).

Begin your walk at the main entrance at Broadway and 116th Street; here you will find the first of Columbia's outdoor art-works. Forming the pylons to the main gate are two tall, imposing statues. One represents *Letters* and the other, *Science* (1). They date to about 1915 and 1925, respectively, and were made by the sculptor Charles Keck. Their granite forms are properly dignified for the entrance to a great university. *Letters* (on the

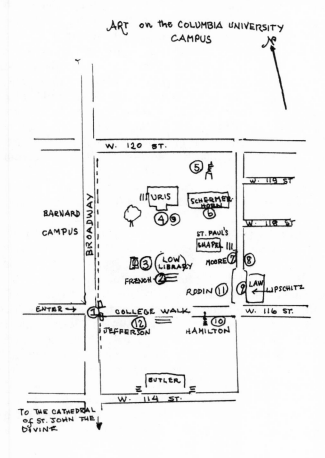

ART on the COLUMBIA UNIVERSITY CAMPUS

south side) is a classically draped female figure holding an open book across her chest, while *Science* is a male figure holding a compass and a globe. Both are in the classical style of early nineteenth-century institutional sculpture that personified the arts and sciences as idealized ancient Greeks serenely standing atop pedestals.

Walk in through the gates to the wide central space of Columbia's campus. On your left is Low Library, now home to a variety of short-term exhibitions and events. (The Library itself has moved across the campus.) On the wide steps of Low Library is perhaps Columbia's best known sculpture, *Alma Mater* (2) by Daniel Chester French. Representing the university and welcoming its students to the campus, *Alma Mater* is a graceful seated bronze figure with a book (signifying knowledge) lying open in her lap. (The statue is an idealized representation of Columbia's seal.) French conceived of the *Alma Mater* as a "gracious figure" that would have "an attitude of welcome to the youths who should choose Columbia as their College," and it has indeed seen many such students come and go, demonstrate upon it, and even bomb it in the 1960s. *Alma Mater* wears a laurel wreath and also has an owl in the folds of her robe. She holds a scepter made of shafts of wheat in one hand. Her symmetrically upraised arms are well designed to lead the eye to McKim, Mead and White's graceful Low Library building behind her.

After climbing the steps and visiting the inside of Low's fine rotunda, where there are occasional exhibits, you will exit at the same front door and turn to your right. In the landscaped area to the west of the Library (Lewiston Lawn), you'll find one of Columbia's favorite works of art. This is *The Great God Pan* (3), a reclining bronze figure on a granite pedestal surrounded by shrubbery. *The Great God Pan* (1894–99) was made by the sculptor George Gray Barnard and was, in its day, the largest bronze work ever cast in one piece in the United States. While Pan was not designed for the campus (but was a gift from the Alfred Corning Clark family who had commissioned it for another site), it is an unmistakable landmark on the campus. *The Great God Pan* (half goat, half man) is seen lying on a rock, playing his pipe and gazing slyly at the world. His body is powerful, his face, with its goat ears and mass of curls, rather sardonic. This pagan nature god is certainly not your run-of-the-mill university sculpture and should not be missed.

Walk around Low Library until it is behind you. You'll next come upon a distinctly different type of sculpture, a twentieth-century work called *Curl* (1968) (4), by the sculptor Clement Meadmore. Made of giant twists of black-painted steel, it is 12 feet high and is a hollow squared tube twisted into a series of curved forms. Meadmore, a native of Australia, views public sculpture as a "bridge between human scale and architectural scale," and here his *Curl* sits directly in front of the Columbia Business School's vertical modern building. Curiously, it is also a kind of reclining piece and makes a nice contrast with the *Great God Pan* who stretches out on one elbow nearby.

From this point walk north, alongside Uris Hall, toward the School of Engineering (Mudd Hall). In the cemented plaza area there you'll find *Le Marteleur* (5), a bronze work made in 1886 by a Belgian artist named Constantin-Emile Meunier. Though from a distance the strong figure (larger than life-size) seems quite abstract in form, up close you'll find it's a fairly realistic, socially conscious work celebrating the modern laborer. *Le Marteleur* (which means a metal worker or hammerer) is one of Meunier's works calling attention to the world's workers as noble, handsome, proud men. The figure here carries pincers for pouring molten metal; he wears a leather apron and a worker's cap. Slightly out of place on this patrician campus, he makes a strong statement not only as a work of art, but also in his positioning between the School of Business and the School of Engineering.

Here you will turn back (south) toward the center of the campus again and come to Schermerhorn Hall on your left. In this building on the eighth floor (take the elevator) you'll find a small museum housing visiting collections. Called the Miriam and Ira D. Wallach Art Gallery (6), the museum holds exhibitions of interest to the public, as well as to the students and faculty who work in the building. When we were there recently they were showing a very elegant sampling of master drawings from the Julius S. Held collection. Among the works were fine pieces by Tiepolo, Watteau, and Benjamin West, to name only three. Exhibitions here change regularly. For information, you can call (212) 854-7288.

On leaving this building continue south. On your left there is an overpass crossing Amsterdam Avenue at 117th Street, and here you'll see Henry Moore's (1967) work called *Three Way Piece* (7). This large bronze sculpture is 7 feet high and is a collection of abstract forms, quite distinct from the more traditional (and earlier) Moore works—such as the reclining figures at Lincoln Center. The shapes, however, are recognizably Moore-like, as is the smooth bronze finish.

Nearby, across the overpass, is a contemporary (1973–79) but very different work, *Tightrope Walker* (8) by the sculptor Kees Verkade. While Moore's sculpture is purely abstract in form, Verkade's is a more realistic, allegorical work. It is imaginative and fun to look at. Two acrobats are balancing atop one another, their arms outstretched as though they were walking a tightrope. Though the work is made of bronze, it was modeled with bits of clay and has the rough texture of long, knobby limbs we might associate with the tinier Giacometti sculptures. It is a tribute to "Wild Bill" Donovan, the war hero Columbia alumnus, who was known for his daring. *The Tightrope Walker* can be seen from below, by the way, if you wish to go down to the lower level.

Our next artwork is *Bellerophon Taming Pegasus* (9), by Jacques Lipchitz. This giant work (over 40 feet tall), which towers over the entrance to the Law School, might be enjoyed better from a distance. You might wish to back up over the bridge to get a better view. Created between 1964 and 1967, it is a quintessential Lipchitz design with its twisted shapes, wings, outstretched limbs, and grouping of forms. You can see the winged horse Pegasus, with Bellerophon trying to tame him by pulling him downward from his ascent toward Heaven. Particularly typical of this sculptor's style is the horse's face with its bulging eyes and contorted shape. A similar Lipchitz work, by the way, can be seen on the wall of the New York State Theater in Lincoln Center (see page 42).

Back on College Walk (the main artery through the campus to 116th Street), you'll spot a more traditional work on your left as you head toward Broadway. In front of Hamilton Hall you find, appropriately, a *statue of Alexander Hamilton* (10), made in 1908 by William Ordway Partridge. The bronze statue shows Hamilton making a speech, his hand on his heart, his eyes intense. Hamilton, one of the most illustrious students at the college, has a companion piece also by Partridge in a statue of Thomas Jefferson (see below). Partridge was an American sculptor whose work was characterized by a somewhat impressionistic style, rather than the classical toga-draped or naturalistic statues of so many other late-nineteenth-century-early-twentieth-century American sculptors.

In front of the philosophy building on the right of College walk is a familiar statue: Rodin's *The Thinker* (11). Auguste Rodin originally sculpted this famous work in 1880, but as is well known, it has been cast and recast numerous times. This casting of *The Thinker* was made in 1930. Certainly it would be hard to find a more suitable site for it, even though Rodin originally made it for the Pantheon in Paris. *The Thinker* has been interpreted in various ways, even by its own creator, who originally modeled a "poet-artist" brooding over man's condition. Later he said it was "a social symbol," representing the "fertile thought" of humble people. In any case, you'll enjoy seeing it in New York's own university environment.

As we mentioned, a statue of *Thomas Jefferson* (12) is the last stop on our artwalk. You'll see a work by William Ordway Partridge representing Jefferson in front of the Graduate School of Journalism, which is on the south side of College Walk. Made in 1914, it too celebrates the thinker, for Jefferson is shown as an intellectual with wrinkled brow, and serious expression. Like the Hamilton statue, this one is also somewhat impressionistic, but it has the familiar details of likeness and dress. The statue was given as a gift to the university by the Joseph Pulitzer family.

This completes the outdoor tour, but visits to various departments and to Barnard College across Broadway will allow you to see additional exhibits. For example, you'll find architectural displays at the Architecture School, film exhibitions at the Fine Arts Department, or Middle Eastern art or student works in the appropriate buildings. To find out what's showing where, you can go to the visitors' office in Dodge Hall, just on your left as you enter the campus gates.

And now for a visit to America's largest Gothic cathedral and one of New York's major attractions. From the Columbia University campus it's a short walk to the Cathedral Church of St. John the Divine, at Amsterdam Avenue and 112th Street.

Begun in 1892, this extraordinary structure is still not completed. (Its predecessors in the Middle Ages took at least as long, if not longer, to be built, some never to be finished at all.) A bustling community unto itself, the St. John the Divine compound is populated with artists, artisans, construction workers, church people, and visitors moving about its vast expanses, busily engaged in various activities. As an art lover you'll enjoy wandering around and seeing the many individual chapels, the stained glass windows, the lovely rose window, the stone carvings, the great bronze doors, tapestries, arches, columns, and other architectural details.

The seven chapels—each honoring a distinct ethnic group—are filled with art objects of interest. Two have impressive works by the noted sculptor Gutzon Borglum. In St. Columba's Chapel (dedicated to people of Celtic descent) are Borglum's figures representing influential personages in the English Church. St. Saviour's Chapel (dedicated to Eastern Orthodoxy) includes over fifty of his carvings. (You'll find additional works by this artist in other parts of the church.) Here, too, you will see many ancient icons of great beauty. St. Ambrose's Chapel (the "French Chapel") is graced with a statue of a pious Joan of Arc by Anna Huntington, and the Italianate St. Ambrose's Chapel contains fine Renaissance paintings by Giovanni di Paolo, Simone Martini, and the School of Paolo Veronese.

The cathedral's stained glass windows are particularly appealing for their deep, intense color. Their style varies from faux-medieval to more modern. They represent many different areas of human endeavor, some surprising in a church setting. One of the bays is dedicated to sports, and you can identify a wide variety of activities, from bowling to auto racing and swimming. There are bay windows that depict the arts, education, the law, motherhood, medicine, and the press, as well as vignettes from history and the Bible. You shouldn't miss the magnificent rose window at the end, composed in a more traditional vein.

Rare tapestries are among the church's greatest treasures. There are two sets, both dating from the seventeenth century and depicting scenes from the New Testament. Those hanging in the nave, based on designs painted by Raphael in 1513, were made in England. The other group, called "The Barberini Tapestries," was woven in Rome on the Papal looms founded by Cardinal Barberini. As you walk about you will be struck by the remarkable wood and stone carvings and statues that adorn portals, niches, altars, pulpits, and columns throughout. There are also constantly changing exhibitions of contemporary art. Among the unfinished portions of the church are the still empty niches that await future works of art.

If you are interested in learning about the church's many treasures in greater detail you might want to take a guided tour or pick up one of the guidebooks available in the attractive gift shop inside the church.

Outside the church is a tiny (but charming) Biblical garden with plants mentioned in the Bible, and a courtyard with a fountain decorated in giraffe and crab motifs. If you have children in tow (and even if you don't), you won't want to miss the Children's Sculpture Garden. The garden's Peace Fountain was designed by sculptor Greg Wyatt in 1985 (see below). This is one sculpture garden where children are encouraged to touch the art works and even to splash around the fountain. Surrounding the dramatic Biblical figures that form the center of the fountain are some 120 small bronze sculptures designed by children for a series of contests over the years. There is also a nice seating area where one can relax and take in the scene.

One of our favorite parts of this visit is to the crypt of the Cathedral, where a well-known sculptor, Greg Wyatt, has been sculptor-in-residence for over ten years. After your descent into the depths of the Cathedral, Mr. Wyatt's studio-workshop will surprise and delight you. Here, in a brightly lighted, two story space, giant sculptures take form, proceeding through the many and various stages that come before their casting in bronze.

You will find Mr. Wyatt a most informative and helpful guide to the work going on here. He uses the space for both Cathedral projects and his own commissions—among them many major monuments for public and corporate buildings. (You will see his large statue in the Cathedral's garden, the "Peace Fountain," in various casted stages and parts on the shelves in the studio.) Mr. Wyatt's graceful, complex, figurative works begin as small plaster sculptures; they are transformed in this studio into the giant forms that in a later stage will be covered by a wax cast preparatory to being taken to the foundry to become the monumental bronze statuary we see in public spaces.

Of particular interest here, too, is the apprenticeship program that the sculptor encourages. Students from various city high schools and art programs are at work here under the most inviting conditions (except for the plaster-dust filled air; we do not recommend sculpture studios to visitors with respiratory problems). This environment brings students together with the artist and the process in a way that is most unusual today, though it is a time-honored tradition since medieval days. As for those of us who know little about the process, this is an ideal place to begin.

To visit Mr. Wyatt's studio you must telephone for an appointment. Telephone: (212) 662-4479. The guard in the kiosk at the south side driveway of the Cathedral will give you directions to the crypt.

Having visited the inside of the Cathedral, you should be sure to see the stone-carving workshop on the north side of the building. Here for many years the stone carvings of the figures, pediments, cornices, and other parts of the Cathedral have been cut from limestone and other giant blocks of stone.

Although today the additions to the facade have come to a halt until further donations are received, the stone work continues on other commissions for buildings across the country. The vast workshop areas include gargantuan cutting wheels for marble, storage of huge blocks of limestone, wheels and saws and other tools of the trade, and in the smaller areas, people at work at the more delicate tasks of hand carving and polishing. (Again, we do not recommend this very dusty environment to those with respiratory problems.)

This visit is more or less inspiring depending on what is

being worked on at the time you arrive. The recent slow-down in building and the interruption in the work on the facade of the Cathedral itself have left the stone workshop rather forlorn, but probably not for long. We know of few such workshops in New York, and a visit to see the stonecutters, sculptors, and the process itself is always interesting.

To visit you should call the public relations office of the Cathedral at (212) 678-6888 for an appointment. You will find the workshop outside of the Cathedral on the north side.

Many concerts and other special events are held at St. John the Divine. Tours are offered regularly at 11 and 2 on weekdays and 12:30 on Sundays, but you are welcome to walk around at will except during services. The church is open daily, 7–5. Telephone: (212) 316-7540.

. . . And in Addition

- Riverside Church, at 490 Riverside Drive, has some wonderful stone carvings, stained glass windows, paintings and a cloister, as well as a 392-foot bell tower. Don't miss Jacob Epstein's *Christ in Majesty* in the nave on the second floor gallery and his *Madonna and Child* in the court next to the cloister. Telephone: (212) 222-5900.

- Nicholas Roerich Museum, at 319 West 107th Street (Riverside Drive), is an unusual, odd, small museum devoted to the works of Nicholas Roerich, an artist, anthropologist, philosopher, traveler to the Far East, and nominee for the Nobel Peace Prize. Telephone: (212) 864-7752.

- Grant's Tomb, Riverside Drive at West 122 Street: this pompous memorial, now being refurbished, has an interesting display concerning Grant's life inside. Outdoors there is an unusual artistic feature: the recent benches adorned with bright mosaic tile designs surround the monument and depict myriad images of city life. They were made by residents of the community and are filled with cheerful energy and good humor.

19

Walking Down
Medieval Garden Paths

The Cloisters

HOW TO GET THERE
Subway: A train to 190th Street and Overlook Terrace; exit by elevator and walk through the park.
Bus: M4 Madison Avenue (Fort Tryon Park—The Cloisters).
Car: West Side Drive (Henry Hudson Parkway) north to first exit after George Washington Bridge. Follow signs. Parking on premises.

SUGGESTED TIMES
Obviously, the best time to visit is during the week, when the museum is less crowded (although you might meet groups of school children). Hours: Tuesday–Sunday, 9:30–5:15, from March–October; Tuesday–Sunday, 9:30–4:45, from November–February. Closed New Year's Day, Thanksgiving, and Christmas. There is a fee.

Among the particularly magical parts of the Cloisters (the Metropolitan's medieval-style museum in northern Manhattan) are the gardens. While the pleasures of visiting the museum's medieval architecture and seeing its exquisite collection of fine art from the Middle Ages may be well known to New York's museumgoers, its gardens are in themselves well worth a special trip. The arcades of five cloisters have been reconstructed with the original stones and integrated into the museum's architecture; four cloisters surround their own unusual gardens. These spots are extraordinarily evocative; in fact, it is hard to believe you have to exit into the twentieth century when you leave.

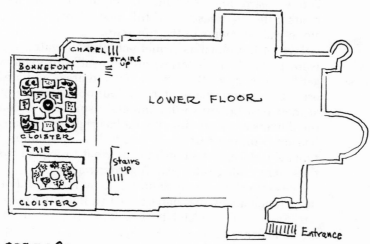

THE CLOISTERS

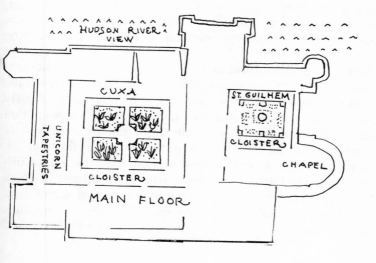

Though they are small, as gardens go, they are so filled with architectural, sculptural, and botanical interest that you might spend many hours walking round and round, or dreamily sitting on a bench imagining you are in thirteenth-century France, perhaps, or a member of a twelfth-century Cistercian order. Dimly heard medieval music sounds as you walk, and of course, the art treasures of this distant past await you in the stone-walled rooms of the museum.

Two of the cloisters (square-columned walkways that once were parts of monasteries) are enjoyable to visit even out of garden season, for they are in covered areas and are kept flowering throughout the winter. All four of the cloister gardens are at their best in late spring and early summer, of course, when the flowers are blooming, the herbs bright and green, the espaliers leafy on their trellises. The following thumbnail descriptions should give you an idea of what to expect from each of these (chronologically listed) gardenwalks,

The earliest cloister is Saint-Guilhem le Desert. Formerly part of a French abbey that dates back to a Benedictine order in 804 A.D., Saint-Guilhem Cloister was built in 1206. Its stone pillars are topped by capitals (the decorative carved tops) whose designs are based on the spiny leaf of the acanthus plant. But there are many additional patterns carved on these columns, including a wonderful series of faces, flowers, entwined vines, and elegant foliage. There are small holes drilled into these designs in intricate honeycomb patterns, and no two columns seem the same.

Some of the sculptural decoration can be traced to ancient Roman design (still in evidence in southern France). This cloister surrounds an indoor garden that is planted fully in early spring. When we saw it last in winter, the flowers were potted and neatly arranged. The architectural details occasionally seem to imitate the very shapes of the leaves and flowers.

Almost directly across the central room from the Saint-Guilhem le Desert Cloister is the wonderful Saint Michel de Cuxa Cloister, a beautiful spot both in winter and in spring and summer, when it is ablaze with flowers. This cloister was in a Benedictine abbey first built in 878, though the cloister itself is from the twelfth-century. From an area northeast of the Pyrenees, it forms the central part of the framework of the Cloister museum and is appropriately gracious and inviting. Its original function as a communal place for monks to walk, meditate, read, or take part in processionals can be readily imagined. The lovely stone walks surrounded by archways and columns open onto a sunlit garden of individual bedded flowers and plants. Each column is carved with typically medieval gargoyles, two-headed animals, or two-bodied monsters. You will want to spend time examining this garden and its cloisters, and perhaps sitting on a bench enjoying the ambience of quiet and beauty.

On the lower level of the museum you'll find the Bonnefont Cloister, a purely outdoor garden walkway. Its origins are in the south of France, near Toulouse. The cloister, with its slender graceful columns in rows of twos, comes from the late thirteenth–early fourteenth century. Cistercian monks once walked through these cloisters, and the very simple design of the architecture and limited amount of sculptural pattern represent their ascetism. (Decoration was not meant to draw attention away from devotion to duty and God.) Of particular garden interest here is the herb garden, a favorite among New Yorkers. More than 250 species of plants that were grown in the Middle Ages are cultivated in this outdoor space. In the center is a charming little well. The herbs are grown in raised planting beds with fences around them. Among our particular favorites here are the trained espaliers, growing against lattices in the sunlight. Anyone with an interest in gardening will find this cloister irresistible.

Finally, the fourth cloister, also on the lower level, is the Trie Cloister, from a Carmelite building in the Bigorre region of southern France. Reassembled with parts of several other cloisters, this small outdoor garden arcade is of particular interest if you look at the Unicorn Tapestries in the museum. The garden contains samples of the very plants woven into the design of the tapestries some five centuries ago. (Information at the cloisters will identify them for you.) Part of the charm of this garden is the sight of the red tile roof surrounding it and the fruit trees set among the flowers. This garden, of course, is also only cultivated during growing months.

Though obviously you will get more pleasure out of this medieval garden walk in the growing season, even in wintertime it is nice to wander about the unkempt cloisters outdoors, to see the view of the Hudson, and to contemplate the beauty of the architecture and sculptural designs in the indoor gardens.

Among the many treasures you will want to enjoy in the museum while you are there are the Unicorn Tapestries, the stained glass in the Boppard Room, the wonderful altarpiece by the fifteenth-century painter Robert Campin, and our particular favorites, the medieval wood sculptures. Children, by the way, will enjoy this walk; there are numerous crenellated walls, dark staircases, impressive and picturesque statues that they'll love, and even medieval playing cards on display.

A visit to the Cloisters is perhaps the closest you can get to being in France while in Manhattan. We found the combination of art, history, and flowering plants an irresistible delight.

. . . And in Addition

Many events of interest are held at the Cloisters; among them are gallery talks on such subjects as medieval imagery, tapestries, gardens of the Middle Ages, and colors in use in Medieval France. There are many concerts of medieval music played on early instruments. You will also find demonstrations of how medieval art was made, including such techniques as enameling and miniature painting. There is a guide to the gardens in which each plant is labeled and described. For information on all these events, including guided tours, call (212) 923-3700. If you feel the need for additional exercise, you might wish to leave the Cloisters by way of Fort Tryon Park and walk south through this very pleasant park with its terrific views of the Hudson and New Jersey's palisades.

THE BRONX

An Art/Nature Walk Through an Elegant River Estate

Wave Hill

HOW TO GET THERE

Subway: #1 train to 231st Street. Switch to BX 10 or 7 bus at northwest corner of 231st Street and Broadway. Walk across parkway bridge and turn left. Walk to 249th Street, turn right at Independence Avenue, and follow signs to Wave Hill gate. Or A train to 207th Street; switch to BX 100 bus at 221st and Ishman streets (Broadway corner) to 252nd Street and walk to 249th Street, as above.

Car: Take the West Side Highway (Henry Hudson Parkway) up to Riverdale. After the Henry Hudson Bridge toll booths, take 246th Street exit. Drive on the parallel road north to 252nd Street, where you turn left and go over the highway. Take a left and drive south on the parallel road to 249th Street and turn right. Wave Hill is straight down the hill. Limited parking on the grounds and street parking.

SUGGESTED TIMES

We recommend weekdays (when Wave Hill is free and never crowded), although the estate is open seven days a week, all year, 9:30–4:30 except for Christmas and New Year's Day. In summer, the hours are extended. Note: Glyndor House Gallery is open Tuesday–Sunday, 10—4:30; Wave Hill House Gallery is open Tuesday—Saturday, 10—4:30. The greenhouses are open only from 10—noon and 2—4.

Wave Hill (675 West 253rd Street at Sycamore Avenue) is one of New York City's less known gems. Although familiar to some, this rare botanical garden/art environmental center comes as a real surprise to most first-time visitors. Its picturesque setting high above the Hudson, with remarkable views on all sides, its formal gardens, vast rolling lawns dotted with huge old trees and environmental sculptures, and its acres of woodlands, make this 28-acre park a unique spot. And as you stroll by its two stately manor houses set in the plantings, you'll imagine you're enjoying a day at a private estate, miles away from the city.

In fact, in the past Wave Hill was the country home of several prominent New Yorkers. From the time the first of its two houses was built in 1848 by the jurist William Lewis Morris,

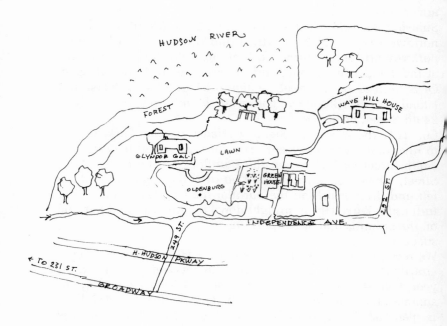

it was occupied by illustrious people who often entertained members of New York society. As a boy, Teddy Roosevelt spent a summer here with his family, where it is said he learned to appreciate nature—birds in particular. William Makepeace Thackeray visited on occasion; Mark Twain lived here from 1901 to 1903 (and even built a treehouse on the grounds); and Arturo Toscanini occupied the house from 1942 to 1945. In the 1950s it was home to the head of the British delegation to the United Nations, and visitors included the Queen Mother, Anthony Eden, Harold MacMillan, and Konrad Adenauer. Most proprietors of Wave Hill were interested in preserving the incredible natural site from profiteering land developers and in further enhancing it with both formal and naturalistic landscaping. The financier George Perkins, who moved in during the 1890s, was particularly successful in securing Wave Hill's future. (A conservationist, he also led the movement to preserve the palisades and organized the Palisades Interstate Park.) He expanded the estate, adding greenhouses, gardens, orchards, pergolas, and terraces. Working with a landscape gardener from Vienna, he created an English landscape—style garden, mingling formal with informal plantings, and rare trees and shrubs with more common species. Many of these plantings still remain. In 1960 the Perkins family deeded the estate to New York City to become an environmental center for the enjoyment of everyone.

Today, Wave Hill (also called Wave Hill Center for Environmental Studies) is and does many things. It sponsors indoor and outdoor art shows (particularly outdoor sculpture shows throughout the vast grounds), horticultural exhibits, chamber music concerts, drama and arts festivals, and outdoor dance performances. There are ecological programs, lectures, craft workshops, and such special events as hawk watches and maple sugaring. And it is a place in which to enjoy both the thousands of remarkable plant specimens in the formal and wild gardens and the contemporary art scattered throughout the impressive grounds. A walk through this peaceful oasis will appeal to nature and art lovers alike, as well as to those who just want to get away from the chaos and noise of the city.

From the moment you walk through the gates, past the small

179

parking area, and onto the meandering brick walkway, you know you're in a very special place—for the landscape has a feeling of space, with breathtaking views and grand vistas. At the same time it has intimacy and charm, unlike most institutional botanic gardens. The plantings have been designed on a small scale, so as to create a more personal environment, in keeping with Wave Hill's tradition as a private estate. And there is an atmosphere of peacefulness and ease. On nice days you might well see people sitting in the grass or in comfortable wooden armchairs scattered about in the lawn, enjoying the view, contemplating a work of art, reading, or just relaxing. Others may be sketching, photographing, or wandering among the various gardens.

Directly in front of the entrance is a nineteenth-century stone-columned pergola, a perfect lookout point to the Hudson and the palisades. To the right of the entrance is an enchanting flower garden, one of a collection of distinct plantings. This particularly luxuriant one combines old-fashioned varieties with less familiar plants, creating a carefree, romantic look. You will frequently see people examining the flowers with book in hand, admiring the colors and combinations, which are clearly the work of an artist (in fact, John Nally, who redesigned this garden, had worked as a print maker). Behind the flowers are the conservatory and greenhouses, with many exotic plants; an enclosed herb garden, with over one hundred varieties; a "wild" garden, with perennials and shrubs of different sizes and shapes arranged in a naturalistic way; an aquatic garden surrounded by shaded, trellised walkways; and more expanses of lawns and forests beyond.

As you wander from one garden to the next, you'll see contemporary outdoor sculptures in the grassy areas. Most of them are temporary exhibits that are shown for only a few months at a time, although two are on long-term loan: Claes Oldenburg's Standing Mitt with Ball (1973), a whimsical steel and lead baseball mitt holding a wooden ball; and Robert Irwin's Wave Hill Wood, remaining from his 1987 exhibition at Wave Hill. Irwin's group of ceremonial stone markers is set apart. The series of statuary begins at the roadside, continues across a grassy field, and ends in a wooded trail. The wanderer is invited to leave the road and experience both art and nature more intimately. In fact, the works shown at Wave Hill are commissioned and then installed in such a way as to harmonize with their surroundings; their materials and shapes blend with the natural landscape.

The works exhibited indoors are also of an environmental nature. They are shown in the two manor houses, Wave Hill House and Glyndor House. The older of these, Wave Hill House, is a handsome nineteenth-century fieldstone building with white shutters, ivied halls, and a vast terrace overlooking the river. Inside are several gallery rooms. One recent exhibit consisted of bold black and white wall drawings of plant life by Mike Glier. Next to the gallery space is Armor Hall, where chamber music is performed frequently. At Wave Hill House you can pick up a map of the area, as well as sundry pieces of literature and brochures relating to exhibits and subjects of horticultural interest. One series of pamphlets gives detailed information on conifers (among the most ancient plants on earth), with a self-guided tour among Wave Hill's varied and rich collection. (All the conifers on the grounds are labeled.)

Glyndor House, the other indoor gallery, is a red brick Georgian Revival-style house built in the 1920s. The exhibition space here is particularly appealing and bright; the airy white-walled rooms with their delicate moldings and gleaming wide-board wood floors provide an ideal setting. When we last visited we viewed a contemporary sculpture show of natural wood pieces by the abstract artist, Jene Highstein; his larger pieces were being exhibited outside in the lawns.

We recommend you visit Wave Hill during the week, if possible, when it is rarely busy. Obviously, the gardens are best seen during the flowering season, but a walk through the grounds on a crisp, clear winter day can be a real joy.

... And in Addition
- Near Wave Hill alongside the Henry Hudson Parkway at 250th Street is a 15-foot-high environmental work called *Past, Present, Future* by contemporary sculptor Vivienne Thaul Wechter.
- For further information on the wide variety of special events at Wave Hill, such as exhibits, concerts, lectures, classes, and so on, call (212) 549-3200.

21

Botanical Delights, Indoors and Out

New York (Bronx) Botanical Garden Walk

HOW TO GET THERE

Subway: D train to Bedford Park Boulevard Station or #4 train to Bedford Park Boulevard Lehman College station. Then take BX17 bus eastbound or walk eight blocks east.

Bus: Regular bus service from Manhattan, Westchester, and the Bronx. Call for information: (212) 220-8700.

Car: Get on Bronx River Parkway north, either from the Cross Bronx expressway (Route 95) or from the Triborough Bridge and the Bruckner Expressway (Route 278). Follow signs for Botanical Garden (after the Bronx Zoo). Parking on premises (small fee).

SUGGESTED TIMES

Spring is the most beautiful time to visit, but gardens are open year-round. We recommend weekdays.

It's a cold, bleak, and gray February morning and you're wondering if spring will ever come. Or perhaps it's a muggy, noisy New York summer day and you're feeling hot and bothered. A visit to the New York Botanical Garden in the Bronx, where you are transported to a special world, will lift your spirits at any time of the year. For here, in this wonderful and vast oasis of natural beauty, all sorts of plants and flowers grow, bloom and proliferate during much of the year—whether inside the grand Conservatory (where spring becomes a reality, starting in early February) or throughout the bucolic 250 acres of meadows, woodlands, ponds, brooks, hills, and gardens. In this environment you will not only feel a sense of peace and relaxation—away from the cares of the surrounding city—but also of joy in the discovery of their wonderful gardens.

The New York Botanical Garden—one of the largest and most important in the country—was the creation of Dr. Nathaniel Lord Britton, a young American botanist. While on his honeymoon in England in 1889, he and his bride visited the Royal Botanic Gardens at Kew outside of London. They were so inspired and enthused by what they saw that they were able to

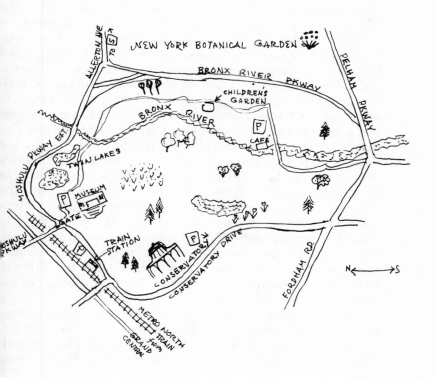

convince the "Torrey Botanical Club" in New York to create a
similar public institution for botany and horticulture within
the newly formed Bronx Park.

The resulting complex is very grand indeed, encompassing
the famous Enid A. Haupt Conservatory (presently closed for
extensive renovation), as well as a wide variety of outdoor gar
dens and several imposing buildings housing a library, a charm
ing botanical shop, classrooms, and administrative offices. One
of the main attractions throughout the year is the Conservatory
an elegant Victorian greenhouse ambitiously patterned after the
Palmer House at Kew Gardens (1844) and the Crystal Palace at
Hyde Park in London (1851). Its eleven galleries, which sur
round a courtyard with two reflecting pools, are a delight to
wander through; here you will experience a variety of habitats
climates, and collections of plants—from historic, to thematic
to old-fashioned, English spring gardens. At the entrance of the
Conservatory is the splendid Victorian-style Palm Court, a 90
foot-high central domed pavilion that contains over three thou
sand species of palms of different sizes and shapes. Some gal
leries are devoted to changing displays of flowers and plants
including exuberant spring flowers in the most brilliant colors
patterns, and combinations that cheered us up on one particu
larly grim wintry day. Other galleries concentrate on very spe
cial permanent exhibits; among our favorites are two galleries
devoted to new and old world desert plants, where you can see
the endlessly fascinating masses of cacti (some of which are
very old) with their fantastic shapes and textures, as well as
the subtly shaded sagebrushes and exotic bushes from the
American desert. Another favorite is a mysterious primeval fern
forest with cascading waterfall, orchids, and mosses. You can
view this display from a skywalk above, but walking through
it makes you feel as if you're in an exotic jungle. As you wander
from one room to the next, you will experience the different
environmental habitats and climates—from the dry heat of the
desert to the torrid tropics.

Surrounding the conservatory are several inspiring gardens
that should be visited during the appropriate seasons. The for
mal Bechtel Memorial Rose Garden is a particular pleasure with
its geometric designs formed by crisscrossing paths amid rose

beds containing over two hundred varieties of rose bushes. The Jane Watson Irwin Garden with its collections of flowering perennials, ornamental grasses, and bulbs is systematically arranged to produce a colorfully pleasing effect. The Armand G. Erpf is a compass garden, where the points of the compass are made of granite cobblestones surrounded by Victorian plantings. There is a small, elegant herb garden containing over eighty varieties of herbs. A sensational rock garden where you will find masses of plants from rocky and mountainous regions of the world is interspersed with giant boulders to create an alpine habitat. The native plant garden features wildflowers and other indigenous plants of our region growing abundantly along with forest trees, a limestone outcropping, marshy meadow, and sandy strip of New Jersey Pine Barrens. And throughout these varied gardens are avenues of bulb displays, hills of daffodils, circular beds of crocuses, and masses of azaleas and rhododendrons—truly a feast to the eye! If you're not feeling too tired, you might walk through parts of the Hemlock Forest, 40 acres of virgin forest that cuts through the middle of the garden. This unique woodland is supposedly the only section remaining of the original forest that once covered all of New York City.

After you have taken in all this natural beauty, you might want to browse in the Shop-in-the-Garden, an original little store located in the giant Museum Building (open 10–5, Tuesday–Sunday). And in the same building is the impressive library (open to the public for research) with over 190,000 volumes of plant science literature (some dating from the thirteenth century). It is considered one of the best of its kind. The library is open 11–6, Monday–Thursday, and 11–4, Friday and Saturday.

The New York Botanical Garden is open Tuesday–Sunday, 8–6 (summer hours are 10–7); there is an admission charge, and there is a charge for parking. The Conservatory is presently being renovated; call for update on its reopening. There are guided tours on weekends from 10:30 to 3:30. You can get information or make arrangements by phoning (212) 220-8747. The general information number for the Garden is (212) 220-8700.

. . . And in Addition

- For occasional lectures, classes, and symposia on botany
  horticulture, ecology, and landscape design at the New York
  Botanical Garden telephone (212) 220-8700. For guided tour
  on weekends: (212) 220-8747.
- Lehman College, Bedford Park Boulevard West, (212) 960
  8211: changing art and photographic exhibits.
- Bronx Museum of the Arts, 851 Grand Concourse at 161 St.
  (212) 681-6000: changing exhibitions of modern painting
  photography, and sculpture, as well as community art show
  can be seen here and at satellite galleries throughout th
  Bronx.
- A Tom Otterness bronze sculpture called "Double Foot" i
  a new addition to Roberto Clemente State Park, near Yanke
  Stadium. These giant, melded together feet, are adorned b
  tiny sculpted figures.
- Bronx Central Post Office, Grand Concourse and 149th Street
  On the walls inside are a series of murals celebrating Americ
  at work by Ben Shahn and his wife, Bernarda Bryson. Amon
  the colorful scenes are farmers planting their fields and engi
  neers surveying sites. One vignette depicts Walt Whitma
  speaking before a group of workers and their families, appar
  ently discussing his poetry.
- In the elevated IRT station for the #6 train at East Tremon
  Avenue and Williamsbridge Road there is a stained glas
  triptych by the noted artist Romare Bearden. The recentl
  installed 9′ × 6′ work, "City of Glass," depicts a luminou
  city.

QUEENS

22

Flushing Meadows

An Outdoor Gallery of Sculpture

HOW TO GET THERE
*Subway: #7 train to either Willets Point-Shea Stadium station
or 111th Street station.*
*Car: Take Queens-Midtown Tunnel and the Long Island Ex-
pressway (Route 495) or the Triborough Bridge and the Grand
Central Parkway. Exit at Shea Stadium and follow signs into
park. Parking on premises.*
SUGGESTED TIMES
*The park is open all the time, year round. No admission fee.
Telephone: (718) 699-6722. Queens Museum: open Tues-
day–Friday, 10–5; Saturday and Sunday, noon–5:30. Closed
Mondays.*

Perhaps you've noticed a massive metal unisphere alongside
the Grand Central Parkway or Long Island Expressway, while
driving to Long Island. Or perhaps you've passed some large,
looming structures on your way to a sports event at Shea Stadium or the National Tennis Center. If you've never ventured
into Flushing Meadows we invite you to discover an intriguing
world—and not just the world represented by the giant unisphere. For the vast grounds (nearly 1,300 acres) at Flushing
Meadows Park, once the scene of two World's Fairs—in 1939
and 1964—are filled with sculptures, pavilions, and odd aban-
doned structures from those events. Some of these relics are

surprisingly good works, others merely forlorn curiosities, but you'll enjoy exploring them, as well as seeing more recent outdoor sculptures. And in a mall in the middle of the park you'll find the Queens Museum, with its worthwhile, albeit eclectic, exhibits and permanent collections—including its one-of-a-kind enormous geophysical panorama of New York City.

For a change of pace, we propose you bike, rather than walk, from one spot to the next. Bicycles can be rented for a modest fee at nearby Meadow Lake, and the flat terrain throughout the grounds is ideal. On your "art bike ride" you will enjoy riding through the vast park (now mostly a giant playground) with its expanses of lawns, rows of trees, lakes, and recreational facilities—a zoo, children's farm, game fields, and picnic areas. But you will expecially be amused by the odd artworks interspersed here and there.

From the bike rental booth, take the path across the lawn toward the unisphere. Our first statue is a traditional one: a bronze *George Washington* (1) standing on a pedestal and looking appropriately presidential. It is by Donald De Lue, a well-known sculptor of works celebrating patriotic themes. (Another work by De Lue, *Rocket Thrower*, is next on our route.)

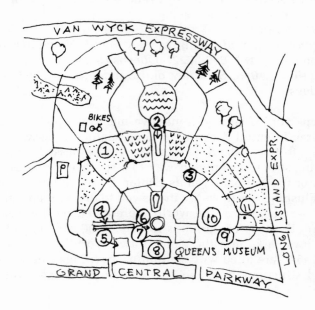

Nearby you'll find a small group (unfortunately only here temporarily) of distinctly untraditional sculptures bearing neither artists' names nor titles. These intriguing works include a chopping block, a giant propeller, an egg, and a carved tree within a circle of surrounding trees. (The site for these off-beat works is ideal; it seems a shame that more of the vast grounds are not used as temporary homes for contemporary works of this kind.)

You'll find *Rocket Thrower* (2), a more realistic statue, east of the unisphere, where it graced the Court of Nations at the 1964 World's Fair. Its creator, De Lue, was an American who specialized in the large symbolic figures that were so popular in the first half of this century. His *Rocket Thrower* is a giant male figure reaching dramatically into the sky to launch an arc-shaped object through a collection of stars, symbolizing space. It suggests reaching into the unknown.

Our next sculpture stands alone in a green field; it is an unusual and evocative memento of the past—the very distant past. Unlike people from other parts of the world, Americans are unused to spotting antiquities in their parklands. Here in Flushing Meadows you'll see the *Column of Jerash* (3), a gift from Jordan given to the World's Fair by King Hussein. Built originally by the Romans in 120 A.D., it was transported to Queens to ornament the Jordanian Pavilion, now long gone. It remains here in this unlikely spot—a lone, but very elegant column from a group of classical ruins known as "The Whispering Columns of Jerash" for the sound of the wind rustling among them.

Facing the unisphere (between Shea Stadium and the unisphere) is another striking sculpture: *Freedom of the Human Spirit* (4) by Marshall Fredericks. It is a green bronze statue of a man and woman reaching up to the sky. Three geese are poised to fly around them. Representational but symbolic in concept, Frederick's work joins the De Lue and de Rivera works (next on your route) in attempting to capture the optimism of the World's Fair and its theme of exploration and spiritual freedom.

To the left of the museum is José de Rivera's *Free Form* (5), one of the most interesting sculptures in the park. A polished, curving metal construction, it resembles a giant boomerang. The nonfunctioning sculpture was meant to revolve, and the City hopes to repair its motor soon. It is made of granite and steel (de Rivera did much of his own forging and hammering). *Free Form* is well named; it soars into the sky like a free-flying bird. With their similar themes, #2, #4, and this de Rivera work make an excellent contrast in styles for the student of twentieth-century sculpture.

The centerpiece for the park is undeniably the *Unisphere* (6), the monumental steel globe that still dominates the entire area. Built for the 1964 World's Fair (a gift from U.S. Steel), the unisphere gives a see-through vision of the earth, its continents in place with giant latitude and longitude lines forming a grid of steel. While it may not precisely be deemed "art," it is nonetheless a striking construction. It is best viewed from a slight distance, though you will probably enjoy walking (or riding your bike) up to it, to experience its size and design more closely. Among the statistics you might consider are the following: the unisphere is 140 feet high, 120 feet in diameter, and it weighs 700,000 pounds.

Between the Queens Museum and the unisphere you'll find an empty pool that once decorated the World's Fair of 1964 and was ornamented by a picturesque fountain, *Armillary Sphere* (7), designed by the sculptor Paul Manship. Manship's fountain was made up of fanciful versions of the twelve signs of the zodiac, but over the years, some of the zodiac figures disappeared. Aries the Ram and Taurus the Bull, each 2 feet high, were just recently recovered and will perhaps be reinstated by the time you take this walk. The fountain was originally donated by the Fair to New York to honor the city's three hundredth birthday. (Unfortunately today it no longer functions as a fountain.)

The Queens Museum (8) is a lively and "au courant" place that houses a variety of interesting exhibitions and events. Among recent shows were "Television's Impact on Contemporary Art," "Classical Myth and Imagery in Contemporary Art," "New British Painting," "The Pattern and Decoration Movement," and an exhibition of Keith Haring works. In addition to these current themes, the museum has devoted exhibitions to

"Remembering the Future: The 1964 World's Fair" and "Classical Sculpture from Ancient Greece." Dozens of events take place at the museum, from workshops to films, lectures to celebrations. If you wish to coordinate your Flushing Meadows outing with a particular exhibition, call (718) 592-5555 for information.

No matter what the current exhibition is at the museum, you can always see the *Panorama*, a must-see exhibition upstairs in the small building. (Children will particularly enjoy this construction, as will any and all New Yorkers or New York enthusiasts.) The world's largest architectural scale model, this extraordinary structure shows all five boroughs of the city in precise and fascinating detail. Built at a scale of 1 inch to 100 feet, it includes every important building in the city and is constantly updated. Originally constructed as the featured exhibit of the New York City Pavilion at the 1964 World's Fair, the *Panorama* was an immediate success; it still is a major tourist attraction and teaching tool for the city's children (various neighborhoods can be lighted and studied). Over 865,000 buildings are represented, as well as the city's rivers, hills, bridges, and trees. The total panorama covers more than 9,000 square feet. A flyer at the museum will give you many more precise and interesting details.

To the right, a short distance from the museum, you'll find the *Time Capsule* (9), where items from 1964 were saved. Another reminder of the 1964 World's Fair is the New York State Pavilion (10), now a big, empty circular space with an intriguing floor that will particularly entice children and residents of New York State. Almost all of an enormous mosaic map of the State of New York still covers the pavilion's floor. It is so detailed that you can probably spot your old hometown or the route you take to the Adirondacks in the still-bright mosaic bits that make up this very unusual floor. (There is also an echo here—a reminder of the dilapidated state of the old World's Fair buildings that remain.)

Our final stop is the *Marble Bench* (11) commemorating the site of the Vatican Pavilion in the 1964 World's Fair. A circular bench and a dais made of granite, the pavilion once exhibited

Michelangelo's *Pietà*. But today it is merely a nice resting spot, which you might welcome after your long bike ride.

. . . And in Addition

- Queens Botanical Garden, at 43-50 Main Street and Dahlia Avenue, is a pleasant 38-acre park (once a dumping ground), of which about half is dedicated to formal plantings. You'll enjoy the Perkins Memorial Rose Collection (with its more than four thousand bushes), a rock garden, herb garden, and specialized garden for birds and bees. There is even a fragrance garden for the blind. In spring, flowering cherry trees, crabapples, and thousands of bright tulips add their magic, while in fall you can enjoy a wonderful display of colorful chrysanthemums. Queens Botanical Garden is a small but attractive spot to visit, with flat terrain for easy walking. The Garden also sponsors a variety of year-round workshops on such topics as Japanese-style dish gardens and hanging gardens for indoor or outdoor use. Telephone: (718) 886-3800.
- Queens College, CUNY, at Reeves-Melbourne Avenue and Kissena Boulevard. In the impressive new Paul Klapper Library, visit the Frances Godwin and Joseph Ternbach Museum with its permanent collection of European art, ancient glass, oriental and Egyptian art, and W.P.A. prints. Changing exhibitions feature drawings, paintings, and sculpture. Hours: Monday and Wednesday, 9–8; Tuesday, Thursday, 9–6; Friday, 9–5. No admission fee. Telephone: (718) 520-7049.

In addition, Queens College sponsors concerts, theater, film, lectures, etcetera, many of which are held at Rathaus Recital Hall. Telephone: (718) 520-7340.

- Queens Borough Public Library, at 155-06 Roosevelt Avenue, Flushing, sponsors workshops on crafts and visual arts, such as silk screening. Telephone: (718) 520-9842.
- Queens Borough Public Library Branch in Richmond Hill, at 118-14 Hillside Avenue. A 1938 mural by Social Realist painter Philip Evergood graces the main reading room. Called "The Story of Richmond Hill," the work illustrates

life in Queens in a somewhat caricature-like mode. On the left is an upbeat, jolly, urban scene; on the right, a far more somber one; and in the middle are the city planners and idealists who are caught in between.

- St. John's University, at Grand Central and Utopia Parkways, visit the Chung-Cheng Art Gallery in Sun Yat-sen Hall. Here you'll find works by local and Chinese artists, as well as a permanent collection of paintings, calligraphy, and other oriental arts. Open Monday–Friday, 10–8; weekends, 10–4. Telephone: (718) 990-6161, ext. 6582.
- Marine Air Terminal at La Guardia Airport in Flushing deserves a visit, especially if you're interested in WPA art. Here you'll see James Brook's huge (237-foot) mural *Flight* within the rotunda. Completed in 1942, this bold work was painted over during the 1950s, but finally restored in the early 1980s.

23

Exploring Long Island City, Queens' "Left Bank"

The Noguchi Museum and Socrates Sculpture Park

HOW TO GET THERE

Subway: N train to Broadway. Walk several blocks (west) toward the Manhattan skyline to Vernon Boulevard.

Bus: From Manhattan there is a shuttle bus on Saturdays that leaves from midtown (from the Asia Society at Park Avenue and 70th Street) every hour on the half hour, from 11:30 to 3:30 and returns on the hour. For seasonal changes and fares, call (718) 204-7088.

Car: From the Queensboro Bridge, take the first right turn possible (Crescent Street) and another right on 43rd Avenue. Go to the end of 43rd Avenue and take another right on Vernon Boulevard. Turn right off Vernon Boulevard at 33rd Road. Entrance to the Noguchi Museum is on the left at 32-37 Vernon Boulevard. Easy parking on the street.

SUGGESTED TIMES

Note that the Noguchi Museum is open only on Wednesdays and Saturdays from 11 to 6 April–November. There is a small entrance fee. Socrates Park is open daily, 10 to sunset, seven days a week.

Perhaps the most unlikely setting for an artwalk and truly memorable aesthetic experience is a visit to the bleak industrial area of Long Island City that lies just south of the Queens end of the 59th Street Bridge. Here, amid old warehouses and uniden-

THE ISAMU NOGUCHI GARDEN MUSEUM and SOCRATES SCULPTURE PARK

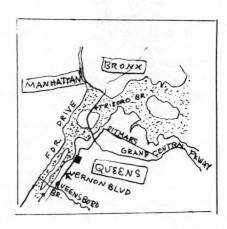

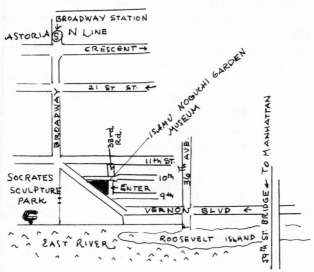

tifiable blocks of buildings, are two wonderful spots to visit—only a few blocks from one another. You will find yourself in this neighborhood very quickly after you exit from the Queensboro (59th Street) Bridge; you may be surprised to discover fine art in this decidedly commercial neighborhood.

Here, however, are two sculpture sites within a short distance of one another. Your first stop will be the Isamu Noguchi Museum and Sculpture Garden (32-37 Vernon Boulevard)—a veritable shrine devoted to the works of one of the twentieth century's most influential and best known sculptors. In a setting of careful calm and contemplation, including a sculpture garden filled with Noguchi's characteristic Japanese stone figurations, you can see the evolution of his art, from early figurative pieces to his most recent stone monoliths. The experience is an introspective one.

And in one of the curious juxtapositions of art sites in our many-faceted city, you'll find just blocks away, at the Socrates Sculpture Park, a collection of contemporary sculpture that is truly astounding in its freewheeling originality—some of it good, some fascinating, some quite awful. This most current collection sits on city-owned land on the banks of the East River. The seminal influences of such sculptors as Noguchi—the willingness to leave subject and representation behind in search of other truths—is evident everywhere, though there is nothing among these giant sculptures that vaguely reflects Noguchi's works themselves. Instead, you'll find changing exhibitions of vast and original works and—of particular interest—the artists themselves can often be seen working at their pieces in this unlikely, weedy field. You may wander at will through the towering constructions, waterside assemblages, and huge forms that are temporarily housed here.

The sculptures at the Noguchi Museum are mostly on permanent display, while those at Socrates Park change once or twice a year.

The Noguchi Museum and Sculpture Garden is about the best disguised art center we've discovered on our wanderings through the city. Set into blocks of old warehouses, it appears to be another nondescript, rectangular building, but on closer

inspection you'll see the angles of a contemporary-style building nestling into its triangular city block. Noguchi wanted a
home for his works that would be congenial to their style and
to his concepts of art's relationship to its surroundings. "These
are private sculptures," he said, "a dialogue between myself
and the primary matter of the universe."

And what you will find at the museum are some 350 works
that demonstate the great Japanese sculptor's spiritual presence, as well as his evolving use of stone and other natural
materials. The sculpture garden—walled off—brings traditional
Asian design to the twentieth century. In these delicate stone
works, trickling water fountains, abstract shapes, and patterns
catch the light and do indeed give you the sensation of being
very far away from both Manhattan and the twentieth century.

Yet Noguchi was, in fact, a quintessentially twentieth-century artist. His search was for abstract realities or what he called
"the brilliance of matter" that will turn "stone into the music
of the spheres." Everywhere—in the rough stone pillars, the
delicate marble pieces, the rounded basalt mounds, the intricate black metal abstractions—you sense the sculptor's preoc-
cupation with pure form and its relationship to the space
around it. Under the artist's own direction, the museum has
laid out works in a logical progression. In addition to the sculptures themselves, the museum includes many plans, drawings,
and photographs of Noguchi's contributions in other places
throughout the world. Among the fascinating examples are a
photograph of a marble spiral for children ("to show how the
idea of play relates to sculpture"), a dance set designed for
Martha Graham ("the stage remained my main testing ground
for many years"), and whole city plazas in detailed planning
drawings—a particularly fascinating addition to the works
themselves; they are a testament to his continuing interest in
sculpture outside the studio. Among the oddities we enjoyed
were paper lanterns and a musical weathervane designed by
the artist. But most of all you will come away with a sense of
the artist's serenity and spiritual presence that come through
these often highly abstract, monolithic works. Although this is
not art that is "easy" to understand for the layperson, it is
nevertheless an experience that will change the way the most

unreceptive observer of contemporary art looks at stone. You will have a new idea of how sculpture can both shape its surroundings and become a part of them.

The transposition to today's environmental sculpture is only a few blocks away. A short walk along Vernon Boulevard and the East River to 31st Street will take you to Socrates Park, New York's largest sculpture park. At first you might think this is an unlikely spot for an important outdoor exhibition space, surrounded as it is with warehouses, industrial buildings, and random vacant lots. But the breathtaking views of Manhattan's skyline directly across the river and the waterfront site provide a dramatic setting for the large, avant-garde works on display. In these raw, unmanicured 4½ acres you will probably see the boldest, most original, and certainly most massive sculptures anywhere in the city—from huge steel abstractions piercing the sky, to rough-hewn constructions in fantastic configurations, original structures atop floating barges, and waterfront sculptures.

The brain child of sculptor Mark di Suvero, Socrates Park—which he named in honor of the philosopher who "had a lot to teach [him]" and of the Greek community in nearby Astoria—was created in the mid-1980s from an eyesore lot filled with heaps of rubble. The idea was to provide a space for large-scale outdoor sculptures where the originality, vision, and creativity of the works were to be considered rather than the fame of the artists. Di Suvero was able to lease the property from the city for a nominal fee. Some ten years later it has become the city's newest public park. From the beginning the community was encouraged to participate actively in the project, to make it an integral part of its daily life. Local residents, including teenagers, were hired to clean and tend the lot (tons of rubble had to be hauled away) and to be involved in running the park. As the sign at the entrance says, "Elevation 7 feet, population friendly." And so it is. Socrates Park is a real part of the community, used not only as an exhibition space for outside artists, but also accessible to local would-be artists who may be inspired to add their own unsolicited works to those on display. People come here to walk, to contemplate, to observe, to play. According to di Suvero, "you're *expected* to touch" the works, much to the delight of the neighborhood children, who can't resist the temptation to use the place occasionally as a wonderful, almost surreal playground. A visitor may be lucky enough to observe artists at work preparing for future shows. In fact, one of the park's programs—the Outdoor Studio Program—asks its artists to create their sculptures right here on site over a few weeks' time, when they are available to discuss their work with the public. On several of our visits we met informally with some of these sculptors and their assistants, all busy at work nailing down massive wood constructions, hauling huge steel parts, or preparing the soil for a future foundation. Chain saws, tractors, and other heavy equipment are often used to produce the massive works and prepare for shows, and neighborhood residents are invited to help in the construction and installation.

There are one or two exhibits annually, each lasting for several months at a time. The inaugural show, held on September 28, 1986, featured works by sixteen artists including Mark di Suvero, Vito Acconci, Rosemarie Castoro, Lauren Ewing, Mel Edwards, Richard Mock, and Sal Romano. Since then, shows entitled "Sculpture: Walk On/Sit Down/Go Through," "Artists Choose Artists," "Sculptors Working," and "Sculpture City" have been on view. Some of the works included have been Robert Stackhouse's *East River Bones*, made from skeletons of sunken ships; Cristo Gianakos's *Styx*, a huge double ramp with a platform (perfect for climbing); Jody Pinto's *Watchtower for Hallett's Cove*, a tall wooden structure more likely to be found in the middle of a large field in a town in the Midwest; Malcolm Cochran's *Scrapyard Temple for Socrates*, whimsical granite pillars around which colorful coffee tins with their labels have been attached in drapelike fashion; and Alison Saar's *Fanning the Fire*, a totem-pole–like structure of wood, tin, and nails atop of which a stern-looking woman is holding a fan. Mark di Suvero (whose waterfront studio is literally next door) often displays his works here.

At each of the park's exhibition openings you are likely to see performances by musicians, actors, or dancers in and around the sculptures. Socrates Sculpture Park is open from

10 A.M. until sunset, seven days a week. Telephone: (718) 956-1819. There is no admission fee.

... And in Addition

- On leaving Socrates Park, we recommend you take a detour to P.S. 1 Museum at 46-01 21st Street, still in Long Island City. (This is not within walking distance, but you can get there by subway.) This alternative space par excellence is housed in a large, brick nineteenth-century building, which was once a school. Since its renovation in 1976, it has included working artists' studios, as well as galleries for innovative and unusual exhibits and some permanent installations. The thirty or so artists chosen to be in residence come from all over the world and usually stay for about a year. (Although most artists are not known to the general public, you might recognize an occasional name.) You can take a tour of the studios to see the artists at work and visit the first floor's eight galleries, where exhibitions change about every two months. Some recent shows have featured works by the Italian artist Michelangelo Pistoletto and the works of Austrian sculptor Franz West, including sculpture, film, collage, drawings, and assemblages created especially for P.S. 1 in collaboration with other Austrian artists. The permanent displays include James Turrell's *Meeting* (1980–86), a sky piece that can be seen daily (except in bad weather), immediately before, during, or after sunset; Alan Saret's *Fifth Solar Chthonic Wall Temple* (1976); and Richard Serra's *Untitled* (1976). Gallery hours: Wednesday–Sunday, 12–6. Telephone: (718) 784-2084 for admission fees and reservations, which are necessary for studio tours.
- Sculpture Installation at the Factory, 47-44 31st Street, Long Island City. (Although, as of this writing this installation is presently mired in litigation and may not exist much longer, we hope you get a chance to see it.) Set in an unlikely neighborhood of trucks and warehouses is an immense walk-in, interactive sculpture-environment that cannot fail to astonish the most jaded viewer (and delight children of all ages). A former furniture warehouse (some five thousand square yards) has been transformed into a one-of-a-kind of junk

sculpture-mosaic-video installation by three artists: Johnny Swing, John Carter, and J. J. Veronis and their five assistants. In this on-going project—some fifty tons of sculpture have already been positioned on floor, walls and ceilings. Such found objects as the side of a yellow school bus, water boilers, hub caps, working TVs, pipes, and bedsprings have been placed overhead and all around amid a vast three-dimensional tiled area which the artists hope to make into the largest mosaic in the world. Lighting, video, and cartoon and advertising figures complete the madcap environment. Don't miss the elevator—like none you've ever entered.

- The American Museum of the Moving Image, 35th Avenue at 36th Street, Astoria. Amid the movies, television, and video memorabilia and technology there are two works of nonelectronic art: a large, jolly, pseudo-Egyptian Red Grooms installation called "Tut's Fever" and a delightful five-piece jazz band carved of wood and found objects that served as props for a 1977 movie.
- You might also enjoy visiting another Noguchi garden in downtown Manhattan, at the Chase Manhattan Building. See page 15 for details.
- Queens Borough Public Library, Astoria Branch, 1401 Astoria Boulevard: here in the children's reading room you'll find W.P.A. murals created by Polish-born painter Max Spivak in 1938.
- Fisher Landau Center, 38-27 30th Street, Long Island City. Houses a 700-piece contemporary art collection. Telephone: (718) 937-0727.

BROOKLYN

24

Stained Glass in the Churches of Brooklyn Heights

HOW TO GET THERE
Subway: #2 and 3 trains, to Clark Street station.
Car: Take the Brooklyn Bridge and get in the right lane; take
the first exit, move directly to left lane, and take Cadman Plaza
exit (if you stay right, you will get on the Brooklyn-Queens
Expressway). Go straight through the first traffic light, and look
for a parking space. You are in the northern part of Brooklyn
Heights.
SUGGESTED TIMES
Sundays between 10 and 2, or weekdays during lunch hour.
Most of the sites on this walk are closed at other times. Bear
in mind that services may be going on, which should not pre-
vent you from quietly viewing the church windows. To be sure
of church and workshop hours, you might wish to make a few
phone calls before setting out.

Brooklyn Heights is an extraordinarily charming part of New
York City. It is a small jewel, both in its riverside setting and
its architectural style. A walk there is always fun, whether you
are a history buff or a riverboat watcher. But we found one of
the more unusual ways of enjoying this unique spot was by

BROOKLYN

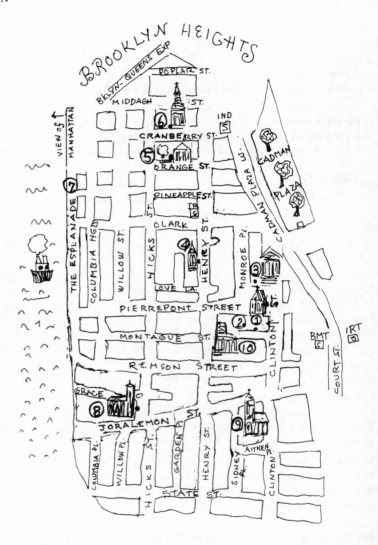

visiting some of its landmark churches with their remarkable
stained glass windows.

There are a dozen churches in the fifty-block historic region
of Brooklyn Heights and half of them date to the 1840s, when

208

Gothic Revival style dominated architecture. Along with wide-spread growth in religious fervor and in church building came a fascination with stained glass windows. In case you want to know a little bit about stained glass before you set out, here are a few notes about the history of this art form.

Stained glass came to this country with immigrants from Europe who were accustomed to its beauty in their churches. But the quality of glass made in this country was for a long time inferior to the European. The best windows were imported until American art glass became more common (between 1865 and 1900). Most of it was stock production; both colors and designs were premade and shipped off to new churches. This glass, still seen throughout the country, was chemically produced opaque or opalescent glass, a milky-textured, somewhat irides-cent glass that transmits very little light but both reflects and refracts light. It was, however, thoroughly American. In fact, much "stained glass" was actually painted glass; studios of glass painting were fashionable through the 1870s.

It was not until several American artists turned their attention to making "art" from glass in the European tradition—but with American taste—that stained glass became a full-fledged art form. John LaFarge, William J. Bolton, and William Holman Hunt were the new leaders in the field. All of them supplied windows for the churches of Brooklyn Heights, as you will see when you take this walk.

LaFarge, who perfected the opalescent glass technique begin-ning in 1875, precipitated the American revival in stained glass. Rather than trying to re-create the traditional medieval tech-nique, he went on to create a new technology and style. His opaque designs were done mostly in a kind of art nouveau genre. In all he created about three hundred windows. Later in his life he experimented with inserting real glass jewels into his windows (to provide translucent color in the otherwise wan productions). William J. Bolton, who worked with his brother John, had begun experimenting with this art from in 1842. His stained glass was much bolder in color than that produced by his contemporaries, as you will see at St. Ann and the Holy Trinity Episcopal Church on this walk.

But it was Louis Comfort Tiffany who transformed glass windows into a totally new art form in the United States. He opened his first workshop in 1878, experimenting with brilliant glass fragments, rather than the milky opaque glass then most fashionable. He created new colors (gold luster, Mazarin blue, aquamarine) and popularized their use in brilliantly colored scenes in his typically decorative art nouveau style. Using over five thousand different varieties and colors of glass, Tiffany's designs were not always original. Some were based on paintings by old masters (such as Doré, Raphael, and Ingres). You'll recognize his most common themes: peacocks, sailing ships, balustrades, and wisteria clusters. Frequently faces were painted in. His landscape windows (of which you will see several on this walk) were a particular trademark: many used landscape as religious symbolism. Tiffany became a style-setter; to have a Tiffany window or two was highly desirable, and churches by the dozen commissioned him. His workshops defined the public taste, as did his famous lamps and other glass objects (which were made from leftover glass pieces from his windows). You'll see examples at the First Unitarian Church among others on this walk. Other artists, like Holman Hunt and Otto Heinigke, shared in the stained glass phenomenon, but at the same time, workshops began factory-producing masses of inferior windows, which all but swamped the market. In fact, many churches designed for plain glass (such as Colonial churches) were refitted for opalescent scenes, which darkened the interiors and did not fit in with the architectural styles (see the First Unitarian Church, for example). It was not until the early 1900s that the secrets of European leaded stained glass were well understood by American craftsmen. The neo-Gothic architectural movement—which required real stained glass like its European ancestors—brought the traditional methods to American church windows (see The Cathedral of St. John the Divine in Manhattan, for example).

The tremendous surge in the building of churches in Brooklyn Heights took place just as the opalescent glass craze swept through. You will see different examples of both opalescent and painted glass on this walk, as well as a sample of modern stained glass (Our Lady of Lebanon Cathedral). So, without further comment, find the corner of Montague and Clinton streets on a bright Sunday morning and visit St. Ann and the Holy Trinity Episcopal Church (1).

The most remarkable features of this imposing, English Gothic church is its fabulous collection of sixty stained glass windows. (This church was known as Holy Trinity until it recently merged with St. Ann's.) Created by William J. Bolton with the help of his brother, John, during the period 1844–47, they are among the oldest such windows in the country, and are considered to be a national treasure. Bolton's use of bold color—unlike the more sentimental, flowery glass work of the time—attracted the architect Minard Lafever, who was then involved in the monumental Trinity Church. Lafever thought Bolton's stained glass windows would complement the Gothic traceries he was planning for this church. The Priory Studio, where the Bolton brothers designed, cut, painted, and fired the glass windows, was small, crowded, and not well equipped for such an undertaking, but they managed to complete their work successfully anyway.

The windows are considered by art historians to be among the best in the country. Their deep primary colors—particularly the reds and blues—are intensely vibrant, and their themes are depicted with feeling. Together they illustrate the story of the Bible in glass: on the clerestory windows are scenes from the Old Testament, while on the gallery windows are depictions of the New Testament. On the side aisles you'll see representations of the ancestors of Christ, including the Tree of Jesse. At the tops of windows the colors and forms seem brighter and designs conform to the shapes of the stone Gothic traceries.

To get an even better and closer view of the windows, we recommend you walk up the stairs (on either side) to the balcony. On both stairwells you'll notice some charming windows in a different style, whose attribution is not known. The stained glass seen up close creates an effect reminiscent of graphic art, with many small visible lines.

While viewing the interior of the church, you shouldn't miss the impressive carved reredo (the decorative wall behind the altar). There is also a bust of a certain John Howard Melish by William Zorach located in the vestibule.

Unfortunately, with the years the exterior of this fine church has suffered: the spire that Minard Lafever designed was removed in 1904 during the construction of the BMT subway, and the porous brownstone needs restructuring. Some of the windows are undergoing restoration. You might be interested in visiting the stained glass workshop (2) where this project is under way. It is around the corner, at 157 Montague Street, and we were told by the church's reverend that it may be visited by phoning first, (718) 875-6960. Here you will really begin to understand how stained glass is made.

Go left on Pierrepont Street, cross over to see the Church of the Savior (First Unitarian Church) (3), the dramatic sandstone Gothic edifice on the corner of Pierrepont and Monroe Place. This church has historic interest. In the early nineteenth century, a group of Unitarian merchants had come to New York from New England to seek their fortunes. Ostracized and criticized for their liberal beliefs, they decided to build a church on the site of a British fort dating from American Revolutionary times. They engaged Minard Lafever, the same architect who later designed Holy Trinity Church. The imposing Unitarian church, with its tall pinnacles and high central gable, was consecrated in 1844, making it the oldest church building in Brooklyn Heights. A series of illustrious and socially active ministers presided over this church, which has a long history of social activism.

To celebrate its fiftieth anniversary (in the 1890s), the church decided to commission the master stained glass artist Louis Comfort Tiffany to create a new set of windows. This decision was reached after some controversy from church members: some felt that the galleries within the sanctuary, which divided the upper and lower windows, were not well set up for stained glass. When the new stained glass windows were installed, the galleries still remained. The problem of accommodating both galleries and windows is apparent to visitors today; if you are walking around, you might find it difficult at first to see the lower windows because of the obstructed view. However, if you sit down in a nearby pew, or if you walk up to them, you can see them well.

The ten opalescent glass windows (eight are from the Tiffany studio) that make up this fiftieth anniversary series all embody the art nouveau style with its subtle colors, romantic nature scenes, and heroic figures draped in flowing garments. You might be able to spot some of the windows described next. Each of them has a name (bestowed by its donor) and a different theme. Some depict natural scenes: the Frothingham Window, the church's first landscape window, shows naturalistic forest views inspired by landscape frescoes found in the Church of San Vitale in Rome, while the Jessup-Stevenson Window depicts a romantic spring landscape with the inevitable flowering magnolia gracing the foreground. Others embody purely religious themes, such as the Woodward Window, a Tiffany window that shows the angel Raphael and the archangel Gabriel standing side by side. The White and Switzer windows are among those that embody Unitarian themes. The two non-Tiffany windows of this group, the Farley and Lord windows, were made by Alexander A. Locke, who had studied with John LaFarge.

The lovely rose window—enlivened with pure reds (due to the donor's curious dislike of blue!)—was added much later, in 1946, to celebrate the church's centennial. It pictures Christ proclaiming the eight Beatitudes, which are rendered in the eight surrounding panels. Designed by Charles J. Connick, another prominent artist of this genre, it was planned carefully so as not to clash with the existing windows. Telephone: (718) 624-5466.

Leaving the Unitarian church, stay on Pierrepont, bearing right, turn right on Henry, go halfway up the block and cross the street to 124 Henry Street, where you will find the First Presbyterian Church (4). Built in 1846, the First Presbyterian Church is an imposing brownstone building housing nine Tiffany glass windows and several by other stained glass artists. The high steeple rises ninety feet above the street to crown this sedate building. Sightlines for viewing the magnificent windows are unfortunately also interrupted here by the balcony construction, but nonetheless these are must-see windows for the stained glass enthusiast. The geometric windows made of small squares of lovely shades of blue, green, and brown, are particularly charming, not only as a contrast with the scenic and portrait windows, but as decorations in their own right (They remind us of Paul Klee's *Magic Squares*.) Tiffany's windows here are very nice; in particular you'll find a river scene that is reminiscent of the many landscapes by nineteenth-century American painters; it is the *River of Life* on the south wall. Religious symbolism in landscape was common in Tiffany's windows. Other windows on the south wall include *The Children's Window* by Maurice Cottier made in 1893 and three Tiffany works: *At Evening Time It Shall Be Light, Gratitude* and *Mary and Martha*. Over the pulpit, and of particular interest, is a mosaic glass design, Tiffany's *Alpha and Omega* window, which was a gift to the church by the nineteenth-century landscape artist Albert Bierstadt and his wife. On the north side, windows by Tiffany depict St. John, the Fisherman, the Guardian Angel, and the Angel of Victory. The courtyard contains several Celtic crosses. Telephone: (718) 624-3770.

Leaving the Presbyterian Church on Henry Street, turn left, and make another left onto Orange Street. The Plymouth Church of the Pilgrims (5) is on Orange Street., between Hicks and Henry. This famous Congregational Church has an illustrious history dating back to 1847, when it was founded by the influential and eloquent Henry Ward Beecher, who presided at its pulpit for some forty years. His fiery ministry was decidedly nontraditional and controversial. It included such dramatic episodes as the public "auction" of a slave girl to arouse antislavery sentiment throughout the nation. He also spoke out passionately for women's rights and temperance. Subsequent speakers who were heard here read like a "who's who" of abolitionists and other advocates of social reform: Wendell Phillips, John Greenleaf Whittier, William Lloyd Garrison, Horace Greeley, Clara Barton, Booker T. Washington, Mark Twain, Charles Dickens, and Martin Luther King, Jr., among others. Abraham Lincoln worshiped here (his pew, no. 89, is marked).

This large church, designed by the English architect, J. C. Wells, resembles a massive New England meeting house, with its austere dark-red brick exterior and lack of decoration. There is no steeple or tower. The spacious interior (which can hold ome two thousand people) includes a plain rectangular auditorium and balcony supported by graceful cast-iron columns surrounding the hall. The white walls and 80-foot-high ceiling add to the feeling of spaciousness.

There are two sets of windows to be seen at this site. In the sanctuary are nineteen memorial stained glass windows that, with their deep, rich colors, add interest and life to the otherwise stark interior. These interesting windows, designed by Frederick Stymetz Lamb, are unlike most church windows in that they represent the more secular theme of the "History of Puritanism and Its Influence Upon the Institutions and People of the Republic." with overtones of political, religious, and intellectual liberty. But to see the more remarkable stained glass windows in this church, you must go to the adjoining Hillis Hall, the social center (open after 12 on Sundays, or by inquiring). Here you'll see a collection of five Tiffany windows; the most impressive (in the center of the wall) represents the life of Christ. (Be sure to ask that the lights be turned on for better viewing of the windows, as they rest against a rather dark wall.)

If you can, wander around through the arcade in the rear connecting the church proper with the parish house. (On our first visit we were lucky enough to meet up with a pastor who, most obligingly, showed us through all the nooks and crannies.) You'll see a curious needlepoint version of Da Vinci's Last Supper as well as sundry portraits of past and present ministers.

Other things to see include portraits of Abraham Lincoln, and Harriet Beecher Stowe (Henry's equally famous sister), and a fragment of Plymouth Rock brought from Massachusetts in the 1840s. Upstairs, tucked away, is a nice but unidentified Renaissance painting of the Madonna and Child.

The handsome arcade garden—which is kept locked from the outside and can be entered only from inside the church compound—is centered around an imposing statue of Henry Ward Beecher in characteristic pose, by Gutzon Borglum. Telephone: (718) 624-7228.

After your visit, go right onto Hicks Street, turn the corner to Cranberry Street, and you'll find the Church of the Assumption (6). This Roman Catholic church is worth a quick look. Its

215

interior reveals an eclectic mixture of tastes and styles. It ha
decorative French-royal-style symbols such as the fleur de li
motif adorning the altar and dome, a painted ceiling, and vari
ous statuary throughout. The stained glass windows here ar
relatively modern. In our view the windows on the second tie
are more interesting than the somewhat ordinary ones at ey
level. The overall interior is light and attractive. Telephone
(718) 625-1161.

As you leave the church turn right, walk a couple of block
toward the river, turn left at Columbia Heights, and walk on
short block to the wonderful Esplanade (7). This 3,000-foc
pedestrian walkway overlooking Lower Manhattan Harbor prc
vides picture-postcard-perfect views of the skyline, includin
the Statue of Liberty and the Brooklyn Bridge. As you stro
along with other walkers and occasional joggers, you migh
find it difficult to realize that you are on a cantilevered terrac
perched over three levels of busy highways and the Brookly
docks below. This is a fine spot to take a breather. There ar
benches and a constantly changing scene for people-watcher
and for river-viewers.

Walk to the end of the Esplanade, go left on Remson Stree
to Hicks Street, where you'll turn right. In one block you'll fin
Grace Episcopal Church (8). The entrance is a little way dow
Grace Court, under one of many surrounding ancient trees. De
signed in 1847 by Richard Upjohn, Grace Church is an impos
ing yet charming Gothic Revival building of sandstone. Its inte
rior contains carved moldings and open wood vaulting. Th
stone piers replaced the original wooden ones in 1909.

Although most of the stained glass is unremarkable, there ar
three by Louis Comfort Tiffany and two by Holman Hunt. Th
typically subdued brownish and greenish tones of the stainec
glass of Grace Church make a subtle contrast with the brow
wooden vaulting. There is a particularly lovely rose windov
in this church; it seems more in the early European glass tradi
tion than in the pictorial nineteenth-century style that was s
popular in America. Telephone: (718) 624-1850 or 624-4030.

Leaving Grace Church, go back to Hicks and turn right. Tak
Hicks to Joralemon Street, to Sidney Place. At Aitken Plac
you'll see St. Charles Borromeo Church (9). This deep rec

painted church built in 1869 has a charming interior with decorative wood trim, as well as many statues of saints and stations of the cross. Though the stained glass windows are unremarkable, there are a series of small colored glass panels behind the altar that are unusually nice. And best of all is the ceiling. Divided into many sections by dark brown arches and moldings, it contains a series of pretty, stencil-like painted designs. The light-colored walls bear portraits and statuary. While the stained glass windows are rather ordinary, the overall feeling of this interior is harmonious and bright due to the nice architectural proportions and detailing. Telephone: (718) 625-1177.

Turn right on Sidney Place and at Joralemon Street go left to Henry Street. Turn right on Henry to Remsen Street, where you'll find Our Lady of Lebanon Cathedral (10). An entirely different artistic flavor permeates this very unusual church. Though it was also designed by Richard Upjohn (as the Congregational Church of the Pilgrims), it was acquired by Maronite Christians of the Lebanese community in 1944. The amalgam of Upjohn's architecture and Middle Eastern artistic traditions create a most unusual, but warm and engaging, interior. Upjohn, already well known for Gothic Revival churches, turned his attention to a Romanesque Revival design here, and this late-1846 building has a wide, spacious interior with slender columns and semicircular arches. Though the steeple disintegrated many years ago, the church still has a graceful overall design. To this the new congregation brought stained glass windows that are nearly primitive in their simplicity, suggesting Middle Eastern mosaic designs in colored glass. Their unusually brilliant colors are certainly incongruous in Upjohn's church, but they do suggest another time and place. So too does the charming mural of the Mediterranean over the altar and the calligraphic designs reminiscent of Arabic arabesques that edge the borders of the walls and ceilings. A curious addition are the west and south portals made from metal panels. These nautical designs were rescued from the ocean liner *Normandie*, which burned at its Hudson River pier in 1942.

While the windows of this church are certainly the brightest on our tour, they are perhaps the least suggestive of the American stained glass tradition; instead, they represent an attempt

217

to re-create a different and more ancient style of glasswork
There is little use of lead in them. The glass seems to be fused
without it, though the areas are cut into tiny squares to resemble
mosaic work. Telephone: (718) 624-9828.

... And in Addition

- Brooklyn Historical Society at 128 Pierrepont Street, Brook
  lyn Heights, conducts Saturday and Sunday afternoon his
  toric tours of the neighborhood, for which reservations are
  accepted. The Society also sponsors exhibitions and lectures
  Telephone: (718) 624-0890.
- Also in or near Brooklyn Heights are several notable sculp
  tures: Henry Ward Beecher by John Quincy Adams Ward can
  be seen at the south end of Cadman Plaza, the Brooklyn Wa
  Memorial with two classical figures by Charles Keck is a
  Cadman Plaza's north section, and at the intersection of
  Court and Montague streets you'll find Anneta Duveen's bus
  of Robert F. Kennedy.
- Antique shopping on Montague Street.
- If, after seeing the Brooklyn Heights churches described her
  you would like to see more stained glass windows, visit th
  following places in Manhattan (all contain windows by Loui
  Comfort Tiffany): Temple Emanu-El, Fifth Avenue and 65th
  Street; St. Michael's Episcopal Church, Amsterdam and 99th
  Street; YWCA, 53rd and Lexington Avenue (610 Lexington
  Avenue); Episcopal Church of the Incarnation, 205 Madison
  at 35th Street (the Tiffany windows here have been newl
  restored); Collegiate Reformed Church, West End at 77th
  Street; Congregation Shearith Israel, Central Park West a
  70th Street (for geometric, abstract, Tiffany windows); Th
  Church of the Holy Cross at 42nd Street between Eighth an
  Ninth avenues; note the Tiffany panels.
- Other windows of artistic interest are to be found at 714 Fift
  Avenue near 56th Street. Here in the landmark Coty Building
  you'll find three René Lalique windows made in 1912.
- Federal Building at 225 Cadman Plaza East (near the Brook
  lyn Bridge): In the large, ceremonial courtroom on the secon
  floor (where new citizens are sworn in) you'll find some re
  stored 1937 W.P.A. murals by Edward Laning, who als

painted the murals in the New York Public Library. Originally intended for the immigrants' dining hall at Ellis Island, these are appropriately entitled "The Role of the Immigrant in the Industrial Development of America"; and, in fact, they depict in dramatic scenes the newcomers of that era working hard in coal mines, on farms, and along railroad tracks.

- The New York Experimental Glass Workshop recently moved to 647 Fulton Street. (corner of Rockwell Street) from Soho. Its blazing kilns and hot liquid glass turning into extraordinary art objects before your eyes make this a not-to-be-missed stop. The workshop has a variety of programs and artists at work, as well as a small exhibition space. When we last visited, a number of artists and students were turning and twisting the molten glass or blowing it into unusual shapes. This form of sculpture dates back to ancient Egypt and reached highpoints in medieval Italy and nineteenth-century France. Today the techniques used produce three-dimensional works that vary from luminous neon glass tubes to sand-blasted objets d'art. The Workshop offers a variety of seminars, classes, exhibitions, and events. Telephone (718) 625-3685.

- Chase Manhattan Bank's new building at 4 Metrotech Center (between Flatbush Avenue and Willoughby Street) has a distinctive high-tech lobby installation by Nam June Paik. There are 429 television sets displaying quickly changing video images. There is also a fluorescent installation stretching forty feet by sculptor Dan Flavin. Also at Metrotech is a sculpture called "Corrugated Rollers" by Ursula von Rydings-vard.

25

A Brooklyn Delight

Botanical Garden Walk

HOW TO GET THERE

Subway: #2 or #3 to Eastern Parkway station or D or Q train to Prospect Park station.

Car: Take the Manhattan Bridge, whose continuation in Brooklyn is Flatbush Avenue; stay on Flatbush all the way to the Grand Army Plaza at Prospect Park, and take the rotary three-fourths of the way around to Eastern Parkway, which borders the park. The Botanic Gardens are immediately after the Central Library building. There is a large parking area (small fee).

SUGGESTED TIMES

Spring is the most spectacular time to visit, although there are blooming periods from late winter to November. Try to go on weekdays when it's less crowded. A Cherry Blossom Festival is held here annually from late April into early May.

The Brooklyn Botanic Garden at 1000 Washington Avenue is one of those surprises you happen upon in New York. In the midst of busy urban sprawl, around the corner from a dreary stretch of Flatbush Avenue (but very near the lovely Prospect Park), you enter the iron gates of the Brooklyn Botanic Garden. There you find yourself in an enchanting, colorful, and completely intriguing world of planned gardens, elegant walkways, weeping cherry trees, and the many sights and smells of the world's most inviting gardens. The area was reclaimed from a waste dump in 1910. It takes up some 50 acres (but seems actually much larger), and you can walk among them quite randomly, from the Japanese paths along a lake to the formal rose gardens, from the Shakespeare Garden to the excellent conservatories. As you will see in the description that follows there are many pleasures in these 50 acres, particularly if you take this outing in the spring.

Every season highlights a different area or style of garden, but surely April, May, and June are the most colorful times to come, when the ornamental trees, luxuriant roses, and many spring flowers are in bloom. But the rock garden is ablaze with flowers during the entire growing season, and the roses bloom with different species through September. A fragrance garden, labeled in Braille for the blind, is another fine section of the gardens; it, too, is open during the spring, summer, and fall.

All of the plants are labeled, and there are more than 12,000 of them. The conservatories and outdoor gardens among them include plants from almost every country in the world. If your taste is for literary references, you can enjoy the Shakespeare Garden, where plantings are related to passages from the Bard's works. If you want to meditate you might choose to sit along the banks of the Japanese Garden's lovely walkways. If you are a horticultural fan, there is a Local Flora section and many interesting displays of temperate, rain forest, and desert plants.

Sometimes described as "many gardens within a garden" (there are fourteen specialty gardens, many linked along a winding stream), the Brooklyn Botanic is one of the nicest places to spend a day in the city. (You can even eat in one of the gardens.) You'll find it a unique blending of intimacy and grandeur that brings to mind the fine gardens of England rather than the wilder acres of the Bronx Botanical Garden or Central Park.

At the two main entrances to the Botanic Garden (on Washington Avenue) you can pick up a very useful map, which will point you in the right direction. A good place to begin your walk is the Herb Garden, near the parking lot. This charming contoured plot contains over three hundred carefully labeled herbs that have been used for medicine and cooking since the Middle Ages. Intricate Elizabethan knots form an intriguing

pattern amid the plantings and add a unique element to thi.
garden. From here you can take a lower or upper walkway. The
upper path will lead you to the Overlook, bordered by gingke
trees and to the grassy terrace known as the Osbourne section
where a promenade of green lawns with stylishly shapec
shrubs and freestanding columns await you. The pleasant, leaf·
lower lane will take you past groupings of peonies, crabappl
trees, and wisterias to the Cherry Esplanade. We recommen(
you see this garden in late April or early May, when the dee}
pink blossoms of the Kwanzan cherry trees are a breathtakin,
dreamlike pastel. The trees are arranged in rows alongside tall
Norwegian maples whose dark red leaves create a wonderfu
contrast in color.

The adjacent Cranford Rose Garden, with its nine hundre·
varieties (over five thousand strong) is the third largest sucl
garden in the country. In this acre of pure enchantment yo·
can identify the roses and study them carefully or simply enjo
the overall quality of their rare beauty.

On the hillside behind a wooden fence is the Local Flor·
section, an unusual and less frequented garden. In these tw

secluded acres the nine ecological zones found within a 100-mile radius of the Botanic Garden have been re-created in dioramalike form. Serpentine rock, dry meadow and stream, kettle pond, bog, pine barrens, wet meadow and stream, deciduous woodland, border mound, and limestone ledge habitats are displayed with their corresponding flora and rock formations. This rare outdoor classroom is meant for serious observers and nature lovers (school groups are not invited) who want to spend time carefully examining the 100 or so plant varieties indigenous to this area, such as the many ferns, phlox, grasses, magnolias, pines, rhododendrons, larches, oaks, heather, persimmon trees, mosses, and dogwoods found here. If you wish to study the plants further, you can pick up a guide called *Local Flora Section*, available at the bookstore, since the plants in this garden are not labeled.

From the Local Flora section walk down the hill, past the hedgewheel, a whimsical composition of eighteen different hedging plants (boxwoods, viburnum, holly, and yew) to the lovely rock garden on your right. Here, rounded glacial boulders define the site that is planted with contour evergreen

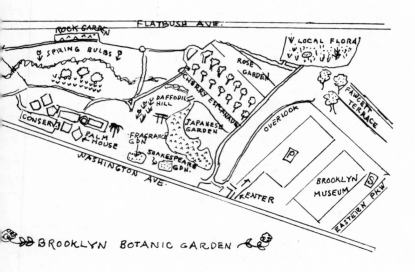

shrubs, different types of ground cover, and flowering plants that provide a vivid palette of color for much of the year. Along the path are clumps of spring bulbs, honeysuckles, and forsythias. You'll walk past a bed of barberries that contains twenty varieties, from exotic bamboolike plants to delicate specimens with dainty red and yellow buds. A stream meanders by, flanked by weeping willows, adding to the effect of a romantic English garden.

Eventually you will come to the conservatory complex (called the Steinhardt Conservatory). Here, three new, beautifully designed greenhouses contain a rich collection of tropical, temperate, and desert plants, including some three thousand pounds of cacti and succulents brought from the Arizona desert. Throughout the year you can enjoy the wonderful flower displays as well as the permanent collection of palms, ferns, and exotic specimens that grace these pavilions. We particularly liked a grotto (in the Tropical Pavilion), carved out of granite, and filled with ferns, and the Aquatic House, containing two pools and various plants according to natural habitat. You can view the deeper pool from two perspectives: at the Aquatic House, where you look down on it, or from windows in the Exhibition Gallery on the lower floor, where these unusual aquatic plants can be examined from an angle people rarely see. One gallery is devoted to bonsai, and you can admire the prized collectors' items (some date from the 1920s) in their many varieties, from the most formal upright to surprisingly naturalistic styles. The curious and intricate art of dwarfing plants is carefully explained and described. The resulting "tray" gardens are real miniature versions—down to the last detail—of regular pines, bamboos, maples, or elms. While you are within the conservatories don't miss the Exhibition Gallery in the central lower level. It features horticultural displays and art exhibits relating to plants in an atriumlike space. On a recent visit we enjoyed seeing a show called "My Garden," a group of alabaster flowers in sensuous configurations by the English sculptor Diana Guest.

Outside the conservatories, next to two reflecting pools, is the elegant Victorian Palm House, once the main conservatory. This lovely old building (now used for special gatherings) adds a dash of turn-of-the century glamour to the complex. Nearby is the Administration Building, the focus of the many educational and research programs conducted by the Botanic Garden. Workshops, lectures, exhibits, concerts, films, and classes on just about anything relating to plants are held here. In addition, there is an Herbarium (which includes some 250,000 dried plant specimens), a plant and bookshop, and a horticultural reference library.

The Magnolia Plaza, just outside, a terrace where over eighty magnolia trees bloom in May, is formally designed with concentric circular and linear paths. The path to your right (as you face the plaza) will take you to the Fragrance Garden, a delightful, intimate spot that is a pleasure to the senses. Here, plants labeled in Braille can also be identified through touching and smelling.

You'll find the Shakespeare Garden off to the east of the pathway. Here the tiny signs not only identify the plants but indicate Shakespeare's references to each flower. This is great fun for those of us who remember our plays and sonnets, and for those who don't—for there is a guide available at the bookshop. It also includes a full map, noting where to find such flowers and apt quotations as "I think the king is but a man, as I am. The violet smells to him as it doth to me," (Henry V), "For though the camomile, the more it is trodden on, the faster it grows, yet youth, the more it is wasted, the sooner it wears," (Henry IV), and "What's in a name? That which we call a rose by any other name would smell as sweet," (Romeo and Juliet). In addition to the many plants of note, the garden itself is laid out in a charming, orderly fashion surrounded by a serpentine wall. An oval brick path, a fountain, and a bench contribute to the impression of an English cottage garden of Shakespeare's times. Be sure to pick up the guide with its many nice illustrations of Elizabethan gardens before you get to this pretty spot, for it will add to your pleasure.

And, finally, you will come to what is arguably the highlight of a visit to the Botanic Garden: the exquisite Japanese Hill and Pond Garden. Designed by Tokeo Shiota in 1914, this prize garden reflects the religious and natural symbolism inherent in Japanese gardens in which various elements are combined to form a harmonious blend of beauty and peace. The Japanese garden is regarded as a holy site, as well as a place for quiet reflection where the visitor can be at one with nature. And, incredibly, in the heart of Brooklyn, one of the city's most populous areas, this garden provides just that. Walk past the massive Komatsu stone lantern (dating from the seventeenth century) and enter the circular viewing pavilion, which welcomes the visitor, as it represents the home of the host. Before you is the breathtaking pond surrounded by a magical tableau of hillside cascades, grottoes, paths through shaded pine groves, and carefully planted shrubberies. A brilliant red torri, a wooden gateway indicating the presence of a nearby temple, stands in the pond, its dramatic image mirrored in the reflecting water. In spring, flowering quince, tree peonies, and weeping Higan cherry trees add even more splashes of color. As you view this rare spot, you will be eager to wander about and explore the garden. Your walk will take you around the pond, through winding paths flanked with junipers, hollies, and yews that are shaped like sculptures, flowering shrubs and trees, past the cavelike grottoes and up the hill to the Shinto shrine found within a quiet grove of evergreens.

Although the garden is relatively small, it is beautifully designed to give the impression of spaciousness as well as intimacy. To leave the Japanese Garden you must retrace your steps to the entrance, which will put you near the Herb Garden from where you began your circular walk.

The Botanic Garden is open Tuesday–Friday (May–August), 8–6, and weekends and holidays, 10–6; from September to April it is open Tuesday–Friday, 8–4:30, and on weekends and holidays; 10–4:30 There is no entrance fee. The Conservatory's hours are Tuesday–Friday, 10–4 and weekends and holidays, 11–4. There is a small entrance fee. For information, call (718) 622-4433.

... And in Addition

- There are too many to list here, but among the Botanic Garden's offerings are classes in everything relating to gardens, from Japanese gardening and painting, to cooking with herbs. There are demonstrations, slide presentations, an event called "Garlic Day," tours (both of the Botanic Gardens them-selves and of American and international garden shows), many programs for children, and some of the most original-sounding events we've seen listed. You can buy plants for your own garden here, learn what to do with them, paint them, photograph them, arrange the blossoms, and watch the birds in them. There are so many events here that a calendar is published every two months. To receive it, call (718) 622-4433 or 622-4544.

- Visit the Brooklyn Museum next door, one of the great muse-ums in the country, with its wonderful collections of Egyp-tian art, as well as Greek, Roman, Coptic, and Nubian art and European and American painting. Notable additions to the museum corridors are five W.P.A. murals rescued from other sites. These large abstract works by pioneer American mod-ernists Ilya Bolotowsky, Balcomb Greene, Paul Kelpe, and Albert Swinden were painted between 1936 and 1937 for a housing project. With the emphasis in W.P.A. art on Social Realism, the choice of abstract art for a public project was a daring one; they are believed to be the first such murals in the United States.

  The museum also sponsors film and dance programs, art classes, craft demonstrations, and lectures. Open Wednes-day–Saturday, 10–5; Sunday and holidays, 1–5. Telephone: (718) 638-5000.

- Don't miss the many sculptured figures that decorate the outside of the Brooklyn Museum. Representing everything from classical ideals to ancient heroes, these giant sculptures were made by leading sculptors of the past, including Daniel Chester French, Charles Keck, Adolph Weinman, Karl Bitter, and Herbert Adams, among others. Of particular interest—in addition to the thirty sculptures around the cornices—are the Daniel Chester French figures on either side of the entrance. Representing Brooklyn and Manhattan, these two colossal, classically robed figures were intended to adorn either end of the Manhattan Bridge.

- Rotunda, The Brooklyn War Memorial, Cadman Plaza West: changing exhibitions in this historic building. Telephone: (718) 875-4031.

- Also in the classical style is the Soldiers and Sailors Memorial Arch in Grand Army Plaza not far from the Brooklyn Museum, at the intersection of Flatbush Aveneu and Eastern Parkway. Here you'll find a great arch modeled after the Arc de Triomphe in Paris and decorated with exuberant sculptures by Frederick MacMonnies. Among its many heroic ornaments are bronze horses "Victory" and "The Army"; the entire construction was dedicated to the defenders of the Union in the Civil War. Of particular interest on the arch is the city's only sculpture by Thomas Eakins, better known as one of the country's leading realist painters and an early proponent of the art of photography. You'll find Eakins' work inside the arch: two bronze reliefs—one of Lincoln and one of Grant—each on horseback.

   There are additional sculptures in and around Grand Army Plaza, including a recent bronze portrait head of John F. Kennedy by a Brooklyn sculptor, Neil Estern.

- Adjacent to the Brooklyn Museum is one of New York's most beautiful open spaces, Prospect Park. Here you'll find a variety of sculptures at the various entrances and within the park itself. At the entrance to the Prospect Park Zoo is a lioness and three cubs by Victor Peter, a French sculptor. Another Daniel Chester French work, a Lafayette memorial, can be seen at the 9th Street entrance to the Park. The 3rd Street entrance is flanked by a pair of heroic panthers by Alexander P. Proctor. Frederick MacMonnies is well represented here by a statue across from Grand Army Plaza (James Stranahan, a founder of Prospect Park); Horse Tamers, which stand on two pedestals designed by Stanford White at the Park Circle entrance to the park; as well as the great arch mentioned earlier. In the center of the park is a group of oddly chosen great composers' busts, including Edvard Grieg, Carl Maria Von Weber, Mozart, and Beethoven by lesser known sculptors. You'll find these sculptures in the Flower Garden, which also contains a bust of Thomas Moore, the Irish poet, by John G. Draddy (who also produced religious works for St. Patrick's Cathedral). Also near the Flower Garden is a World War I memorial, including tablets by Daniel Chester French and realistic bronze figures by Augustus Lukeman.

A major work is the Bailey Fountain, north of the great arch. This elaborate creation includes a variety of nude bronze figures representing Triton, Neptune, Wisdom, and so on. It is by Eugene Savage, and its style has been described by some art historians as "Grotesque."

- The New Waterfront Museum, 81 Front Street: group shows of contemporary works. Telephone: (718) 596-2507.

STATEN ISLAND

26

Snug Harbor

Gardens and Contemporary Art on Staten Island

HOW TO GET THERE

Staten Island is easily reached by public transportation, but you will need a car if you want to see the many additional spots listed here in one day. Snug Harbor is located on the north shore of the island at Richmond Terrace and Snug Harbor Road, conveniently only 2 miles from the Staten Island Ferry Terminal. The Snug Harbor trolley or the S40 bus will get you there. From Manhattan, the best route is by ferry and bus. From Brooklyn, Queens, or Long Island, you should drive via the Verrazano Narrows Bridge (take Bay Street with the harbor on your right, until you find yourself on Richmond Terrace at the ferry terminal. Snug Harbor is on your left, after 2 miles). From New Jersey take the Staten Island Expressway (I-278) to Clove Road/Hyland Boulevard exit. At the traffic light turn left at Clove Road to Richmond Terrace, and right at Snug Harbor. For specific auto routes, telephone (718) 448-2500 from 9 A.M. to 5 P.M. Monday–Friday.

SUGGESTED TIMES

The grounds are open seven days a week (except major holidays), from 8 A.M. to dusk. Open in the evening for occasional special events. Guided tours are offered free, by appointment. We recommend a visit in springtime or early summer, when the fine gardens are at their best.

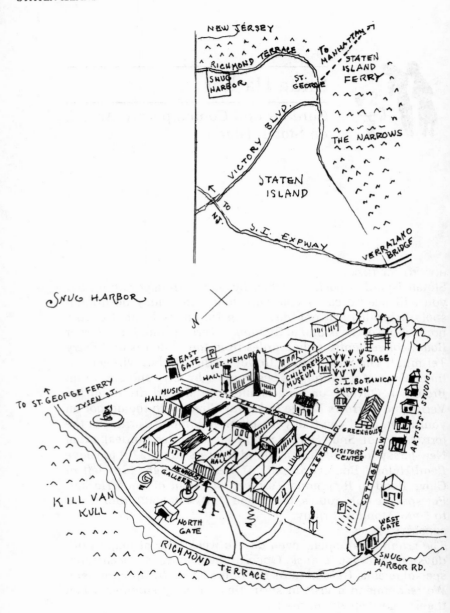

SNUG HARBOR

Snug Harbor on the north shore of Staten Island is a "find" for jaded New Yorkers, art and garden lovers, and anyone else who wants to spend a stretch of time in an unusual and harmonious setting. Originally founded in 1801 as a hospital for retired sailors, its beautiful and expansive grounds and buildings are landmarks. The first of its historic buildings was erected in 1831. There are both large public structures in a variety of architectural styles—ranging from Italianate Revival to Beaux Art—and a row of small Gothic Revival houses once built to accommodate the tradesmen who served the sailors' home. The grounds include the Staten Island Botanical Garden, a conservatory, a concert hall, exhibition space, and much, much more. All these buildings are prettily set on an 80-acre tract of land just across the road from the shoreline and surrounded by outdoor exhibitions of contemporary sculpture. Unlike many such cultural centers, Snug Harbor has an informal air. It is a place that has walkways and byways and open doors; its gardens are invitingly simple and its signs of do's and don'ts minimal. There are no citylike aspects to Snug Harbor; you might be in a place far removed from the bustle and commerce of New York when you wander around here. But Snug Harbor is, indeed, a busy cultural center that includes top attractions (like the Metropolitan Opera and Shakespeare in the Park) in its offerings.

As you enter at the main gate (follow signs on Richmond Road), you will find yourself on a pathway with the parking lot to your left. Walk through the parking lot to the Visitors' Center in one of the main buildings, where you can pick up a map and other material on the Snug Harbor complex of buildings and gardens.

On leaving the visitors' desk, walk (directly before you) to Chapel Road to see the wonderful row of five small Victorian cottages. These once housed the baker, gardener, engineer, and farmer who helped to run Snug Harbor in the nineteenth century. Built between 1885 and 1890, they are undergoing renovation with the commendable aim of providing, within the next year or so, living and studio space for resident artists. Several are already occupied. The pathway (Cottage Row) has a duck pond on the left, near which you will see one or two of the outdoor sculptures mentioned in the walk.

Opposite the cottages are the greenhouse and the particularly charming flower gardens. The landscape of the entire park is Victorian in feeling, and so are the garden areas. Among the highpoints of this landscape are the trees, including wonderful willows and a superb collection of flower gardens. The Botanical Garden, which moved to the site in 1975, has put in a variety of small gardens: a formal English perennial garden, a butterfly garden (whose plants are specifically nourishing to butterflies), a Victorian rose garden, an herb garden featuring medicinal and culinary plantings, a "white" garden, which experiments with vertical plantings, a bog garden, and—inside the conservatory—the Neil Vanderbilt Orchid Collection. Any garden enthusiast will enjoy the way these small treasures of planting are arranged—each (in its own season, of course) is a treat. A variety of tours, lectures, and demonstrations are available, but you can also enjoy wandering on your own.

Of particular charm near the gardens is the Chinese-style pagoda built by Charles Locke Eastlake of England. This little pavilion is a concert site and additional Victorian touch to the landscape. At the end of the garden is a dark-green lattice-worked enclosure, which we found particularly appealing. It is planted with charming flowers, and you can sit on the white wrought-iron benches and enjoy a summer's day.

You are now in an area called South Meadow. We suggest turning toward the old dark-red buildings to the east. These house, among other things, the Staten Island Children's Museum, a cheerful place that features all sorts of hands-on exhibitions for the small fry in the family. There are numerous workshops and events with small admission charges.

Near the museum is an old and charming building known as Veterans' Memorial Hall. This is the site of many concerts—from chamber music to jazz. Built in the style of a nineteenth-century parish chapel, the Hall provides an intimate space for small events. In front of the Hall is Chapel Road, once again, and here are the first of the major Greek Revival buildings of the complex. These pale cream, mostly renovated, buildings house a variety of Snug Harbor's organizations: there is the

Great Hall, the Music Hall, the Art Lab, and, in the next row, the Main Hall. Art Lab, the art school found at Snug Harbor, also has shows of visual art. Among recent exhibits was an all-island high school show and individual exhibitions in its Atelier Gallery. These grand buildings are both architecturally and historically interesting.

The Main Hall's rotunda and ceiling contain 1884 murals that have recently been renovated; these are Victorian-style paintings with Italianate motifs.

In the Main Hall you'll find the Newhouse Gallery, one of Snug Harbor's main attractions. The Newhouse Gallery is Staten Island's principal art space, and as such is an important part of the cultural center. The Gallery also curates the outdoor sculpture shows, which are perhaps Snug Harbor's major contribution to New York's contemporary art scene.

Scattered throughout the lovely grounds of the center are about twenty contemporary sculptures at any one time. Sculptures in stone, metal, and mixed media are widely spaced throughout the green fields. (Pick up a guide to the current show at the visitor's center.) The exhibitions are usually mounted around mid-June and run through the month of October, when most of them are taken down. (A few traditional sculptures remain year-round.) The exhibits of contemporary sculpture are very up to date. The installations (which are most interesting to watch—if you happen to visit just before the show begins) include the works of both New Yorkers and others who have sent in slides or have been invited through such arts organizations as DIA in Soho (see p. 117). A tour of all the sculptures—if you walk at a brisk pace—will take you about one hour. Among the particularly interesting recent additions was an outdoor play sculpture for children designed by Staten Island sculptor Steve Foust, to be constructed and organized by visiting children. Other recent highpoints included *Memorial to Lost Souls at Sea, 1980* by John Chamberlain, and a steel-skinned "sunken house" by Bill Albertini. A few sculptures are also to be seen indoors in the Great Hall. At the Children's Museum you'll find a whimsical wooden carving of a praying mantis by Robert Ressler made from a 100-year-old fallen ash.

. . . And in Addition

● Richmondtown Restoration, 441 Clarke Avenue, (718) 351-1611. This is New York City's only historic village restoration. It sits on the greenbelt area of the island and can be reached by bus or car from Snug Harbor. It consists of twenty-six buildings that have been restored; eleven of them can be visited inside. They represent various historic periods of New York's past, ranging from the seventeenth through the nineteenth centuries. Among the attractions are the oldest standing schoolhouse in America, a general store, exhibitions of crafts and restoration techniques, and a historical museum. While there is little art visible as such, the atmosphere is pleasantly historic, and there are many interiors with genuine artifacts and decorations of the past. This is probably a place best enjoyed by families with children.

● Alice Austen House, "Clear Comfort," 2 Hylan Boulevard, Rosebank, (718) 390-5100. Overlooking the Port of New York in a particularly fine location is the Alice Austen House, a historic site that also houses an exhibition of works by the pioneer documentary photographer, Alice Austen. This Victorian house set in a nice green garden with a view of the Statue of Liberty, is the only museum in the country that commemorates a single photographer's life and pictures.

● The Jacques Marchais Center of Tibetan Art, 338 Lighthouse Avenue, Richmond, (718) 987-3478. In the most unlikely setting imaginable—on a suburban Staten Island street—you'll find this very unusual center devoted to the arts of Tibet. The largest private collection of Tibetan art in the country, the center includes a small garden in Tibetan style, artifacts, and musical instruments, and many, many works of art—all housed in two stone buildings built to resemble a Tibetan monastery. Works from other Asian countries are also exhibited in the chockful, rather small buildings.

● Museum of Archaeology at Staten Island, 631 Howard Avenue (Clove Road), (718) 273-3300. On the third floor of the Main Hall of Staten Island's Wagner College are two attic rooms devoted to a very odd and quite extraordinary collection of ancient and non-Western artifacts. Surprisingly, fifteen hundred objects from disparate cultures ranging from

Sumerian figurines to pre-Columbian terra-cottas are kept here. Because of size limitations, only a small selection can be shown at any one time; recent exhibitions have been devoted to demons from different civilizations, ancient technologies, and winged animals.

- Borough Hall, St. George. Thirteen murals by Frederick Stahr depict Staten Island's history; they were created under the W.P.A. art projects in 1940.
- The College of Staten Island, a branch of the City University, has a new campus which it is endowing with art both indoors and out. Though it is not complete as of this writing, visitors in the near future will be able to enjoy a good-size collection of sculpture in the large grassy areas between buildings and in the "Wooded Park," as well as a number of artworks in various media indoors in the Center for the Arts and other buildings.

Among these works are a wood and granite boulder "Ark" by Daniel Wurtzel on the Great Lawn, a concrete sculpture called "Borromini's Task" by J. Isherwood and a steel wire cone called "Red Inside" by N. Ketchman, both in the Wooded Park. A fiberglass relief by Red Grooms is in the Sports Center. In the Center for the Arts there are silkscreens and lithographs by George Segal, Jean Dubuffet, Robert Rauschenberg, Helen Frankenthaler, and Edouard Manet, among others. (Some artworks are hung in the Mezzanine Lounge, and others in the Gallery itself.) For a complete listing of this growing collection and information on how and when to see it, you can telephone the Public Relations office of the college at 718-982-2332.

. . . AND BEAR IN MIND

The following listings include public collections and exhibition spaces that you will also enjoy visiting. Some of them are seasonal or have changing shows, so be sure to telephone before you go.

The Anchorage: This seasonal exhibition space under the Brooklyn Bridge at the Brooklyn end is a wonderful spot where *Creative Time* installs contemporary shows from July through September. In addition to sculpture there are performances. Located at the base of the Bridge at Cadman Plaza and Old Front Street. Telephone: (718) 619-1955.

Arsenal Gallery, 830 Fifth Avenue at 64th Street. The giant Arsenal building houses a variety of exhibitions, including community arts, antique shows, and other events. New York City Department of Parks administers the gallery. Telephone: (212) 360-8111.

Arts for Transit: A new and welcome program is placing art throughout the city's subway stations. Works by Roy Lichtenstein, Elizabeth Murray, Romare Bearden, Maya Lin, and Andrew Leicester are among those chosen. For information call the Transit Authority at 718-330-1234.

Cooper Union, 7 East 7th Street. Changing exhibitions. Telephone: (212) 353-4158.

Eleanor Roosevelt monument soon to be installed on a corner of Riverside Park and 72nd Street: This memorial statue, by Penelope Jencks, will be one of the few statues of notable women in the city.

Foley Square, Thomas Payne Park between Lafayette and Centre Streets. Regular outdoor sculpture exhibitions.

Henry Street Settlement, 466 Grand Street. This is a multi-arts facility that focuses on emerging artists. There are three exhibition and performance spaces. Telephone: (212) 598-0400.

Herd of sculpted hippos by Bob Cassily is the centerpiece of the children's playground in Riverside Park at 91st Street.

J. F. Kennedy Airport: Among the many major artworks here are a large mobile by Alexander Calder and works by Jean Arp, Ilya Bolotowsky, and Sonia Delaunay, among some forty other contemporary pieces of art. For a full listing, call the Port Authority of New York (art division): Telephone: (212) 466-4211. At the airport also note the International Synagogue, a contemporary building that includes reliefs by Chaim Gross and the adjacent Ferkauf Museum with a fine collection of Jewish art and artifacts.

Ives Memorial, Bear's Community Garden, Brooklyn, southwest corner of Flatbush and Pacific avenues. (two blocks south of the Brooklyn Academy of Music). Wood sculpture of Charles Ives and his father by Scott Pfaffman.

The Kitchen Center, 512 West 19th Street. This is an internationally known showcase for avant-garde art and performance art. It includes gallery space, labs, video, and other facilities. Telephone: (212) 925-3615.

La Guardia Marine Terminal. Here in an art deco ambience you'll also find a W.P.A. mural by James Brooks devoted to the history of flight.

Madison Square Park, Fifth Avenue and 23rd Street. In this urban space are nineteenth century statues by Augustus Saint-Gaudens (Admiral Farragut), John Quincy Adams Ward (Roscoe Conkling), Randolph Rogers (William H. Seward of "folly" fame), and George Edwin Bissell (President Chester A. Arthur). A more contemporary work consists of three tilted slabs of steel called "Skagerrak" by Antoni H. Milkowski.

Marymount Manhattan College, 221 East 71st Street. Changing exhibitions of professional artists' works. Telephone: (212) 517-0400.

Pierpont Morgan Library, 29 East 36th Street. The former library of J. P. Morgan houses a fabulous collection of rare books, manuscripts, drawings, and priceless illuminations. Periodic exhibitions of medieval and Renaissance works are open to the public. Telephone: (212) 685-0008.

"Radicals of the Left" mural, at West Street and Charles Street in the West Village. This outdoor mural on the side of the Pathfinder Press building took eighty artists from twenty countries two and a half years to complete. It includes portraits of numerous political notables of the left from Marx, Trotsky, and Lenin to Sacco and Vanzetti, Bishop Tutu, Nelson Mandela, and Che Guevara.

Roosevelt Island: Amid the new buildings and plazas, you might also find visiting art arranged by A.R.E.A. One artist, Phyllis Mark, designed a giant sculpture on the shore of the island (across from 68th Street at the East River) that is environmental in the true sense of the word, moving with the wind and reflecting changes in the weather. It is one of a number of sculptures set up here, some permanent, some seasonal. For current information on A.R.E.A. installations, call Dorothea Silverman: Telephone: (212) 288-7651.

Sculpture Center, 167 East 69th Street. This gallery features changing exhibits in mixed media.

South Street Seaport Museum, 16 Fulton Street. This museum houses exhibitions relating to New York's past as a shipping center, with old prints, memorabilia, and other items. Telephone: (212) 766-9020.

Space 2B Gas Station, on the corner of Avenue B and Second Street in Manhattan, is a scrap material sculpture. In the area once occupied by a gas station is a massive junk construction by Johnny Swing and Linus Coraggio.

Union Square (between Broadway and Park Avenue and 14th and 16th Streets). A number of notable sculptures dot this urban park. Of particular interest are an evocative statue of Mohandas Gandhi by Kantilal B. Patel, a dramatic Lafayette by Frederic-Auguste Bartholdi, a pensive Abraham Lincoln and a heroic equestrian George Washington, both by Henry Kirke Browne.

Ward's Island. Several contemporary installations are to be found on this island in the East River. These works are sponsored by A.R.E.A. (see Roosevelt Island listing). Among the permanent works on display are Stephen Keltner's *My Two Elizabeths*, Vivienne Thaul Wechter's *Emerging Sun*, and Penny Kaplan's *Silent Columns*.

Three organizations to telephone for information about outdoor art exhibitions and installations are:

A.R.E.A. (Artists Representing Environmental Art), a group that mounts outdoor exhibitions. They are particularly interested in site-specific work, giving the public the opportunity to see contemporary art outside the confines of museum walls. Many of their exhibitions are temporary, although you'll find quite a number of permanent installations in New York. Telephone: (212) 288-7651.

Creative Time, Inc., is an organization that sponsors and locates sites for temporary placement of environmental projects. They will know of the latest in outdoor exhibitions. Telephone: (212) 825-1491.

Food Center Sculpture Park at Hunts Point (Bronx:): This extrordinary new sculpture site has annual exibits of the most avant-garde pieces in and around the giant produce market. Telephone: (212) 931-9500.

New York's Major
Museums of Art

New York's major museums house some of the greatest collections of art in the world. Visit them individually, or combine your artwalk with time at the following museums. (Keep in mind that many museums do not charge admission one day of the week. Call for information.)

American Craft Museum, 40 West 53rd Street, Telephone: (212) 397-0630.

American Museum of the Moving Image, 35th Ave. at 36th Street, Astoria, Queens. Telephone: (718) 784-4777.

American Museum of Natural History, Central Park West at 81st Street. Telephone: (212) 873-8828.

Asia House Gallery of Asia Society, 725 Park Avenue at 70th Street. Telephone: (212) 288-6400.

Bronx Museum of the Arts, 851 Grand Concourse at 161st Street, Bronx. Telephone: (212) 681-6000.

Brooklyn Museum, 200 Eastern Parkway, Brooklyn. Telephone: (718) 638-5000.

The Cloisters, Fort Tryon Park. Telephone: (212) 923-3700.

Cooper-Hewitt Museum, Fifth Avenue at 91st Street. Telephone: (212) 860-6868.

El Museo del Barrio, 1230 Fifth Avenue at 104th Street. Telephone: (212) 831-7272.

The Frick Museum, 1 East 70 Street. Telephone: (212) 288-0700.

The Solomon R. Guggenheim Museum, Fifth Avenue at 89th Street. Telephone (212) 360-3500.

Hispanic Society of America, Broadway at 155th Street. Telephone: (212) 926-2234.

International Center of Photography, 1130 Fifth Avenue. Telephone: (212) 860-1777.

Isamu Noguchi Garden Museum and Sculpture Gallery, 32-37 Vernon Boulevard, Long Island City, Queens. Telephone: (718) 204-7088.

Jacques Marchais Center for Tibetan Art, 338 Lighthouse Avenue, Richmond, Staten Island. Telephone: (718) 987-3478.

Jewish Museum, Fifth Avenue at 92nd Street. Telephone: (212) 860-1888.

Lower East Side Tenement Museum, Gallery 90, 90 Orchard Street at Broome. Telephone: (212) 431-0233.

Metropolitan Museum of Art, Fifth Avenue at 82nd Street. Telephone: (212) 879-5500.

Museum for African Art, 593 Broadway. Telephone: (212) 966-1313.

Museum of American Folk Art, 2 Lincoln Square. Telephone: (212) 595-9533.

Museum of Contemporary Hispanic Art, 584 Broadway. Telephone: (212) 966-6699.

Museum of the City of New York, Fifth Avenue at 103rd Street. Telephone: (212) 534-1672.

Museum of Modern Art, 11 West 53rd Street. Telephone: (212) 708-9400.

National Museum of the American Indian, Broadway at 155th Street, and Bowling Green. Telephone: (212) 283-2420.

New Museum of Contemporary Art, 583 Broadway. Telephone: (212) 219-1222.

New-York Historical Society, Central Park West at 77th Street. Telephone: (212) 873-3400.

Pierpont Morgan Library, 29 East 36th Street. Telephone: (212) 685-0008.

Queens Museum, Flushing Meadow Park, Queens. Telephone: (718) 592-5555.

South Street Seaport Museum, 16 Fulton Street. Telephone: (212) 766-9020.

Studio Museum in Harlem, 144 West 125th Street. Telephone: (212) 864-4500.

Whitney Museum of American Art, Madison Avenue at 75th Street. Telephone: (212) 570-3676. Also Whitney Museum at Philip Morris, 42nd Street at Park Avenue (878-2550).

Yeshiva University Museum, 2520 Amsterdam Avenue at 185th Street, has interesting exhibitions featuring both recent and historic art. Shows include contemporary kinetic glass sculptures, for example, and cultural artifacts of five centuries. Telephone: (212) 960-5390.

Choosing an Outing

If You Prefer a Guided Tour

Lincoln Center	Walk 5
Americana	Walk 8
City Hall area	Walk 9
Columbia University campus	Walk 18
The Cloisters	Walk 19
New York (Bronx) Botanical Garden	Walk 21
Brooklyn Botanic Garden	Walk 25

Crafty Outings

International Art Centers (Manhattan)	Walk 3
Americana	Walk 8
Soho and Tribeca Studios	Walk 13

Waterfronts, Waterfalls, and Waterviews

Tip of Manhattan, Parts I and II	Walks 1 and 2
Midtown Oases, Parts I and II	Walks 14 and 15
Wave Hill	Walk 20
Long Island City	Walk 23
Snug Harbor	Walk 26

Of Special Interest to Children

Audubon Terrace	Walk 4
Museum Mile	Walk 6
Central Park	Walk 17
Children's Sculpture Garden (St. John the Divine)	Walk 18
Long Island City	Walk 23
Snug Harbor	Walk 26

Outdoor Sculpture and Sculpture Gardens

Tip of Manhattan, Parts I and II	Walks 1 and 2
Audubon Terrace	Walk 4
Lincoln Center	Walk 5
City Hall Area	Walk 9
Midtown Oases, Parts I and ii	Walks 14 and 15
Central Park	Walk 17
Columbia University campus	Walk 18
Wave Hill	Walk 20
Flushing Meadows	Walk 22
Long Island City	Walk 23
Snug Harbor	Walk 26

Discovering Ethnic Art
International Art Centers Walk 3
Museum Mile Walk 6
Lower Fifth Avenue Walk 7
Black New York Walk 11

Mostly Contemporary Art
Tip of Manhattan, Parts I and II Walks 1 and 2
Lincoln Center Walk 5
Forty-second Street Walk 12
Soho and Tribeca Studios Walk 13
Midtown Oases, Parts I and II Walks 14 and 15
Wave Hill Walk 20
Long Island City Walk 23
Snug Harbor Walk 26

And Mostly Art of the Past
Audubon Terrace Walk 4
Museum Mile Walk 6
Americana Walk 8
City Hall Area Walk 9
An Auction Outing Walk 16
The Cloisters Walk 19
Brooklyn Heights Walk 24

"Unofficial" Public Art Indoors
Tip of Manhattan, Parts I and II Walks 1 and 2
International Art Centers Walk 3
Lincoln Center Walk 5
Lower Fifth Avenue Walk 7
City Hall area Walk 9
Restaurant Hopping Walk 10
Forty-second Street Walk 12
Soho and Tribeca Studios Walk 13
Midtown Oases, Parts I and II Walks 14 and 15
An Auction Outing Walk 16
Brooklyn Heights Walk 24

Studios and Works in Progress
Lower Fifth Avenue Walk 7
Soho and Tribeca Studios Walk 13
Long Island City Walk 23
Snug Harbor Walk 26

249

INDEX OF ARTISTS AND PLACES TO SEE THEIR WORKS

Also by Marina Harrison and Lucy D. Rosenfeld:

ART ON SITE $16.95

Country Artwalks from Maine to Maryland

A WALKER'S GUIDEBOOK $12.95

Serendipitous Outings Near New York City

To order, please send a check for the listed price to:
Michael Kesend Publishing, Ltd.
1025 Fifth Avenue
New York, NY 10028
Add $4.00 for shipping and handling plus 50¢ for each additional
copy with the same order.
For quantity discounts, contact the special sales department at:
Tel: 212 249-5150
Fax: 212 249-2129